D1068484

Books by EDWARD WEEKS

This Trade of Writing
The Open Heart
In Friendly Candor

Collections edited by Edward Weeks
The Pocket Atlantic

Jubilee: 100 years of The Atlantic
(*with Emily Flint*)

In Friendly Candor

In Friendly Candor

by

EDWARD WEEKS

An Atlantic Monthly Press Book

BOSTON • Little, Brown and Company • TORONTO

COPYRIGHT, 1946, 1947, 1951, ©, 1955, 1956, 1957, 1958, 1959,
BY EDWARD WEEKS

ALL RIGHTS RESERVED. NO PART OF THIS BOOK MAY BE REPRO-
DUCED IN ANY FORM WITHOUT PERMISSION IN WRITING FROM THE
PUBLISHER, EXCEPT BY A REVIEWER WHO MAY QUOTE BRIEF PAS-
SAGES IN A REVIEW TO BE PRINTED IN A MAGAZINE OR NEWSPAPER.

LIBRARY OF CONGRESS CATALOG CARD NO. 59-13734

FIRST EDITION

The author wishes to thank the following for permission to quote from
copyrighted material:
Atlantic Monthly for "The Right to Strike" and "Young Washington: A
   Living Portrait" by Richard E. Danielson; correspondence with Jesse Hill
   Ford; Thomas Wolfe's letter to Mr. Frank Wells; "Brother" and "The
   Goat" by Hans Zinsser.
Henry K. Cushing for lines FROM A SURGEON'S JOURNAL and THE LIFE OF
   SIR WILLIAM OSLER by Harvey Cushing.
Little, Brown & Company and Atlantic Monthly Press for NATURALIST AT
   LARGE by Thomas Barbour; MY ISLAND HOME by James Norman Hall;
   TROUT AND SALMON FISHING by John Hutton; THREE CAME HOME by
   Agnes Newton Keith; RATS, LICE AND HISTORY and AS I REMEMBER
   HIM by Hans Zinsser.
W. W. Norton & Company, Inc. for THE HOUSE ON NAUSET MARSH by
   Wyman Richardson.
Rinehart & Company, Inc. for THE OUTERMOST HOUSE by Henry Beston.

ATLANTIC–LITTLE, BROWN BOOKS
ARE PUBLISHED BY
LITTLE, BROWN AND COMPANY
IN ASSOCIATION WITH
THE ATLANTIC MONTHLY PRESS

*Published simultaneously in Canada
by Little, Brown & Company (Canada) Limited*

PRINTED IN THE UNITED STATES OF AMERICA

For Fritzy
who lived so much of it

Acknowledgments

No editor subject to all the demands of his duties has enough free time in which to write a book and certainly this one could never have been brought to its present shape without the patient assistance and the alert rereading of my associates: Phoebe Lou Adams, Virginia Albee, Dorothy R. Burnham, Peter H. Davison, Louise Desaulniers, Emily P. Flint, Charles W. Morton, Nancy E. Reynolds, Donald B. Snyder, and Beverly Yankee. My heartfelt thanks to each and all of them.

Contents

[xi]

Contents

I
Education of an Editor

Learning from the French

IN THE autumn of 1916 I was slowly drowning as a student of mechanical engineering at Cornell; in my courses in calculus and physics I had the feeling that I was going down for the third time. I had just squeaked through my freshman year, held on perhaps because I weighed 94 pounds and was one of the last crop of coxswains to hear Coach Courtney's high, rasping commands. Now as a sophomore I was on probation, and it was evident that my time as an engineer was limited. I looked for an honorable exit, preferably one that would get me away before the final examinations in the spring of 1917, and I found it as a volunteer ambulance driver in the French Army. We were expected to pay our passage across the Atlantic, and although our luggage was severely limited, it seemed perfectly reasonable to pack in my diminutive trunk a Slazenger tennis racket which I hoped to use on leave.

The S. S. *Espagne* will always float in my mind as the most glamorous ship in the French Line. This was my first trip abroad; Ithaca was the farthest I had ever been from my home in New Jersey, and every impression was as fresh as red paint. I was nineteen, I was shy, and in my gawky, ill-fitting uniform I tried to be as inconspicuous as possible in what was evidently a very gay company.

[3]

There were French officers in their sky-blue and scarlet kepis; a detachment of American nurses, all trim and a few very pretty; pilots returning to the Lafayette Flying Corps, some wearing their decorations; there was a long, emaciated Belgian officer stretched out in his steamer chair, a victim of one of the first gas attacks, now returning from Tucson, white and without hope; there was Cole Porter, with his harmonica on which he played his latest hit, "I've a Shooting Box in Scotland, I've a Castle in Touraine"; there was a bosomy Red Cross worker who seemed to enjoy life after dark in a lifeboat; and, youngest of all, were the several hundred of us volunteers in the American Field Service, on our way to drive ambulances or ammunition *camions* as the French Army would decide.

I was painfully conscious of my uniform. I had always been neat about my clothes, and now here I was decked out as a caricature in khaki. My father's shirtmaker was to blame. Dad had taken me up to be measured for four khaki shirts of the warmest flannel; but the shirtmaker had got drunk, and instead of remembering my small dimensions, he made them to fit Dad, who was a six-footer with a 15½-inch collar. The results were appalling. I had to double the cuffs back, and the folds of extra cloth made my tunic bulge and my neck gape. I knew I could remedy all of this as soon as I got to Paris. Meantime I suffered acutely even when standing in the shadow.

Our ship was unescorted, and when we came within range of the U-boats we all went on the alert. There were lifeboat drills, and at night every porthole and companionway was blacked out. Those of us who patrolled the deck were cautioned against lighting cigarettes, and we were ordered not to wear luminous wrist watches. We strained our eyes to scan the dark, heaving water, and it seemed just a shade theatrical; we all knew of the

[4]

sinking of the *Lusitania* but we were too determined to believe that it could happen to us. We were going to France.

There was something strange and toylike about Bordeaux harbor as we looked down from our high deck, but when we marched ashore, the people who paused to watch us smiled and obviously meant us well in their incomprehensible French. I remember the hard wooden benches of the third-class compartment, and the *chocolat Menier* and the tough, crusty bread which we munched as we jogged along; I slept, and awoke as we entered the vast trainyards of Paris, and then a bus swept us into the full-bloom beauty of the city itself, which we glimpsed on our way to the Parc at Rue Raynouard.

We signed all the essential documents, were addressed by A. Piatt Andrew, our Colonel, and were then given the rest of the day off. I parked my tennis racket at the University Club and made for an English tailor where I ordered a whipcord uniform and light cotton shirts (sitting in my underwear in the shirtmaker's dressing room while the first of them was stitched so as to be free at last of that cursed hot flannel); I had my first dinner and my first champagne at the Hôtel Continental, and afterwards, with Harry Crosby and Tote Fearing, I spent my first evening at the Follies. The uniforms, the fantastic women, the color and vitality of the stage where the argot was quicker than we could follow, the bar during intermission where I had my first drink with an Australian ("Hi, digger, what'll you have?") — this hypnotic experience of sound and sex and laughter was bound together and made real by a sense of exhilaration, by the feeling that we were all in this show together.

We were assigned to the Moroccan Division; 1st and 3rd Zouaves; 1st and 3rd Tirailleurs, and the Spahi cavalry. Here

[5]

the French educated us in many things: to speak French (since they manifestly had no intention of speaking English); to eat horsemeat, which was our main ration at the training camp; to drive our ambulances with a respect for shattered men; to pause and check the shelling before committing ourselves to any crossroads within range of the Germans; and at Verdun, where we served that July and again that November, to do our work by night over roads deep in mud and wrecked beyond belief.

Our real instructors were the *brancardiers,* the stretcher-bearers, men in their gray fifties who had been pulled out of the infantry and assigned to the tender but hazardous task of conveying the wounded in their *pousse-pousses* from the front line to the *poste de secours.* These men were old enough to be our fathers, they had seen more than they wanted of death, and yet they were endlessly patient in their teaching of us raw Americans, to whom a pile of stiffs under a tarpaulin in the shed behind the *poste* was still a curiosity to be stared at. The *brancardiers* taught us their card games and how to enjoy *pinard* at their *popote.* They taught us the humor and irony of the French newspapers; they taught us tenacity and, in their handling of the wounded, the meaning of mercy. And finally, in those perilous days of March 1918, when the Germans had broken through at St. Quentin, they showed us the anguish which is in every Frenchman's eyes when his country seems dreadfully in peril.

Clemenceau and Foch and "Papa" Joffre were the revered leaders then, but the men who imbued us with France, and whose lessons after forty years I still remember, were those weary but tenacious old *bleus.*

My first *permission* occurred after a spell of duty before St. Quentin and a second at Verdun. In September I picked up my

racket in Paris, bought a few books at Brentano's — *Sonia* by
Stephen McKenna, Lockhart's *Napoleon,* and *Le Feu* by Bar-
busse — and with a fellow driver, Dick Salinger, boarded the
night train for Nice. It took us thirty-six hours, for we were side-
tracked all the way down to let through the French troop trains
which were coming to the rescue of the Italians on the Piave.
We had been offered the most exquisite villa overlooking the
harbor of Villefranche, a sanctuary into which French destroyers
escorted their convoys at dusk, with much signaling and tin-
kling of bells. The house — General Pershing was to occupy it
a month later — was luxurious, with long French windows
looking out over the terraces to the Mediterranean. A marvelous chef, delicious wines, and no one at home but ourselves. As
a contrast to Houdainville and Carrière-Sud, our mucky and
most unpleasant *poste de secours,* it was almost unbelievable.
We lay abed until nine, had our breakfast — I remember the
great fistfuls of heavy purple grapes — in the sunlight before
the open French windows, and at half-past ten I took the tram
for Nice. The secretary of the Nice Lawn Tennis Club was Mon-
sieur Lenglen, father of the famous Suzanne. He it was who
provided me with white flannels, tennis shirts, and a guest card.
And for five mornings in a row I rallied and played a set or two
with Suzanne. My service began to come back, and in time I
was able to take a couple of games a set from her. Suzanne was a
brunette, no beauty but *soignée.* She played in white, pleated
skirts above the knee, and over her dark hair she wore a white
bandeau. Her footwork was sure as a ballet dancer's, and her
ground strokes, forehand and backhand, were hit with superb
length and accuracy. On Sundays at Monte Carlo she took part
in exhibition matches for the Red Cross with the best three men
available, and she passed them at the net far more often than

they could pass her. Only her serve was vulnerable by our standards. The pity was that she had not come to America in 1913 when Dick Williams — R. Norris Williams, her hero and a member of the Davis Cup Team — urged her to. No woman in the country could have beaten her then, I feel sure. When she did come after the war it was too late, for she had passed her peak.

On my last day of leave, I played with her until an hour before train time and in one set won three games (tenderness?). Later, as I was rushing to change, I managed to leave my wallet behind in the borrowed flannels. But we had exchanged addresses — I had to if I were ever going to convince the Section that I had met her — and Suzanne's scrawl on that bit of white paper was as valuable to me as the wallet itself which contained fourteen francs and which came back in a package of her wrapping.

There were five Harvard men in my Section: Richmond Fearing, Philip Shepley, Stuart Kaiser, Dick Salinger, and Harry Crosby. I was amused by their flat "a" and impressed by their quiet confidence. Tote Fearing and Stu Kaiser spoke French fluently. Dick Salinger had already made his first attempts at playwriting under Professor George Pierce Baker, and twice in that summer of 1917 it surprised me to find him writing sonnets for the *American Field Service Bulletin.* Among the six of us were four books which we circulated in the Section and gnawed at when we were *en repos.* Harry contributed the *Oxford Book of English Verse,* and Stuart *Pickwick Papers;* I can't remember who owned *Apollo: The History of Art,* and my offering was Lockhart's *Napoleon.*

Of the five, Harry Crosby was the most impulsive as he was

the most generous. We had made friends on the *Espagne* coming over, and when the ambulances were assigned to us, two men to a Fiat, Harry and I became driving partners. It was a lucky partnership for me in many ways: Harry was a fast and confident driver — fast perhaps is not the word for those heavy lumbering Fiat ambulances — and as co-pilot I began to observe his competence. Harry also set me a pace in his writing, for he was the swiftest and most spontaneous letter writer I have ever known. I can see us now, sitting side by side in the tail of the ambulance, half in sunlight, half in shadow, while he sprinted through note after note to Sister, Ella, Kitza, Beanie, his friends back home on the North Shore, Harry now talking to them, now talking to me, as I slowly and conscientiously composed a letter to my family. He wrote as he talked, and his infectious, staccato letters brought him five times the correspondence the rest of us had.

On my return from leave I found Harry in a highly nervous state. His ambulance had received a direct hit at the very instant he had arrived, empty, at a forward *poste*. He was still at the wheel and the fountain of the explosion which enveloped him, and totally destroyed the car, had carved his silhouette on the backboard but had nicked him only in the little finger. I have never known a closer shave and the shock of it was plain to see.

Our Christmas was celebrated in the Vosges. The ambulances were parked two feet deep in snow on the grounds of a château at Darney. Our Moroccans lived hermetically sealed in Moslem warmth in barns and barracks, and we twenty Americans were concentrated in a brick toolshed, lit by one window, heated by one potbellied stove; here we waited for the Christmas letters and packages that never came. How could the French postal service know where we were, how could they care? But they came on January 14; a French *camion* crunched up the driveway and when the tail was lowered out poured bag upon bag upon bag of mail, parcels, love in familiar handwriting. This was the day. The lieutenant secured permission for us to dine in the conservatory of the château, the native Vouvray was brought up from the village and a detail helped Leonard, our cook, prepare the steaks and *pommes frites.* Meantime in the candle-lit toolshed, seated on our stretchers, we were deep in paper, opening, ejaculating and comparing. Johnny Mungan said how would it be if we all chipped in twenty francs each, ten to go to the guy who got the goofiest gift, ten for the goofiest letter — and the pot was collected. After the dinner, after the toasts, after the singing and during the cognac, the judging began. Now I had five aunts and as I was their only nephew overseas they had all been knitting for me. From their gifts I selected three entries: a khaki knitted helmet with no face, a pair of giant woolen bootees to be worn *over* one's rubber boots, and a narrow knitted band of camel's-hair wool with cord ends. "This, my dear Ted," wrote Aunt Liz, "is what they call a Cootie String. We are told that if you tie it around your waist the little rodents are attracted by the body's warmth and when they have gathered sufficiently in the wool, you go off by yourself, detach it, and hang it on a tree." I was awarded the first prize for gifts, but there were those who said I should have had both.

The French war rations agreed with me and, as a late-starter, I was to grow six inches and put on thirty pounds during my two years overseas. The fact that my war letters drew the favorable comment of a New York editor also left its seed of hope. Gradually, I was acquiring a feeling of self-possession.

When men are hard-driven, as in war, they will sleep anywhere: in an *abri* or foxhole or sitting upright in a bucking plane or jeep. Napoleon's officers, those who still had horses, must have slept in the saddle on the long bitter retreat from Moscow, and so too Jeb Stuart's cavalry walking their horses once they were inside the Virginia lines after a raid. I fell asleep twice while driving my ambulance, once at Verdun and again at the time of the German breakthrough in March 1918. In each case the ambulance was empty, and I was returning to the front after a long, torturing drive with seriously wounded men who cried out and beat with their fists against the side of the ambulance. When at last they were unloaded at the field hospital, one dead, two living, I was given a shot of *la gniole,* French white mule, and a mug of scalding coffee, and then with my sheepskin collar up about my ears I started back to the lines in the pre-dawn cold. No lights, and the little Model T Ford, so much more limber and maneuverable than the Fiat, clicking off the kilometers. We had no windshields, and the wind was so penetrating that I stopped to bunch a *blessé* blanket around my shoulders. I could feel the doze coming, and to fight it off I kept banging my head with my tin hat. For a split instant I was back with the family in the library at "1279," with Mother singing, and then I was flung awake as the Ford rocked over tree roots, plowed through the roadside ditch, and hung itself halfway up on the muddy bank. From which as the sun rose we were extricated by the crew of a French 75; the radiator had boiled over and the rubber connection jerked loose, otherwise no damage to the Model T.

But what remained in the back room of the mind, stored away like an unhung painting, was not the comedy of that smoky dawn, with the artillery putting me back on the road, nor the fact that in swerving off the road I had missed colliding with a tree by the narrowest margin. What remained and is still there is the inescapable anguish of the drive in: leaving the *poste de secours* at midnight with the living load, edging into low gear through the slithering mud of the sunken road, lurching in and out of the water-filled shell holes while the voices behind me cried *"Doucement! doucement!"* — past our batteries which made the whole car shudder when they fired, past the crossroads, past the ghostly Indo-Chinese who were silently filling in the worst of the craters, and then the long grind up the hill which was in clear sight of the Germans by day. Not until we had topped that rise with its walls of tattered camouflage could I ease the pressure on the left pedal and let the Ford into high. It was probably not more than forty minutes from the forward *poste* to that point, but in terms of vicarious suffering it felt like infinity.

On one run, in the summer of 1918, I carried a French colonel who had been dreadfully wounded and was bleeding internally. He was clearheaded, very pale, and calm, and he smiled at me as they were loading his stretcher into the holders. All through the early torture I could hear the priest who was riding with him talking in a low voice. We came to the long hill, and as we neared the top I suppose I let up on the low pedal too soon. The Ford bucked and stopped; and at that instant, so the priest told me afterwards, the colonel died. Had I driven better, could I have got him back alive? The question kept recurring in my mind long after the Armistice, when I was in college and suffering from insomnia. Again in my dream I would be lurching through the mud, grinding up the hill incapable of averting what was to happen. Insomnia is a form of self-examination, and perhaps it is just as well that those who have been to war should be left with such reminders of guilt and compassion.

30 Mt. Auburn Street

IN THE summer of 1919 I applied for my admission to Harvard with the cocky assurance common to all discharged veterans. I was twenty-one, I had been decorated with a Croix de Guerre, I had plenty to write about, and I saw no reason why I couldn't qualify for a major in English within a year, or perhaps a year and a half. The Dean of Admissions thought otherwise. He pointed out that my grades in mechanical engineering at Cornell were either just passing or flat failure. He said that Harvard rarely granted anyone a degree in less than two years, and since I was transferring to a new field, I should be admitted as an unclassified student and advance as rapidly as I was able.

Cooled off but still cocky, I arrived in Cambridge the day college opened and after registration I went out to search for a room. As the hours lengthened, the prospects seemed less and less encouraging: each involved three or four flights of stairs ending in a small room under the eaves. I worked my way along Mt. Auburn Street (known as the "Gold Coast," though I didn't know it) and eventually came to a pie-shaped brick building with an odd but discernible face on its rounded front. This, as I was to learn later, was the home of the Harvard *Lampoon*. At the moment its janitor, a tough little number in a dusty derby, sat picking his teeth on the steps.

"Know of any good rooms around here?" I asked. He looked

me over for the fish-out-of-water that I was. "Well," he said, indicating a handsome stone façade halfway up a side street, "why don't you try up there? They might have something for you."

So over I went and rang the bell, and when a white-coated steward opened the door, I inquired if they had any rooms to rent.

"This is the Delphic Club," he said, and shut the door firmly in my face.

When I turned back, my helpful guide had disappeared. Somewhat chastened, I continued on into the less collegiate part of Mt. Auburn Street.

Opposite the new Catholic church was a humble frame building and in the window the beckoning sign ROOM FOR RENT. Miss Phelan, the landlady, as Irish as she was genial, showed me what she had: a bedroom and study on the ground floor. The price was more than I thought I could afford, and while I was hesitating, she led me upstairs. "Here is the bathroom," she said, "and these are our prize rooms" — indicating the suite directly above mine. "They belong to Mr. Hillyer, the poet. He teaches in the English Department."

Prize rooms they certainly were, with waxed hardwood floors, a fireplace with birch logs, chintz curtains at the windows, old prints (two of them, I noticed, of Queen Elizabeth), bookshelves to the ceiling, and in the corner a tea table with what looked to be old china.

Robert Hillyer's room was the luckiest thing that happened to me that year. It was so attractive, after the bare, grim cubicles I had been inspecting, that it made me want to stay; and my acquaintance with Bob, which grew into friendship, added an extra dimension to my education. He was enough older to be my mentor, and his knowledge and love of English were contagious.

This was in the age of Prohibition when cocktails were deviously concocted. My father occasionally supplied me with New Jersey applejack, and this I shared with Bob and his friends. They were a remarkable group: Foster Damon, who was working on his book on Blake; Stewart Mitchell, the managing editor of *The Dial;* Charles Brackett, who had just sold two stories to the *Saturday Evening Post* and was about ready to quit the Law School; Malcolm Cowley, in his last year as an undergraduate; John Dos Passos, who was working on his *Three Soldiers;* and good-natured Ronald Levinson, the classicist, who kept the peace when temperaments clashed. Foster and Charlie Brackett had a natural antipathy for each other. They were both fencers, and lacking foils they would lunge at each other using their right arms as weapons and with enough thrust to imperil Bob's old teacups.

I am gregarious by nature, and what saved me from going too social was the talk and intentness of this group. They lived for writing and they were nourished on books. Secretly I was appalled by how much more they had read than I; now I was trying to catch up, and I remember how surprised I was when Bob remarked casually that his book learning was behind him. He had done it in his years at Kent and Harvard before he went into the service. He had done it; it was in his mind and stored away.

Naturally what Bob did was to share his familiars with me, freshening my understanding of Spenser's *Faerie Queene* and Hakluyt's *Voyages,* and strange books like Arthur Machen's *The Hill of Dreams* and W. H. Hudson's *Green Mansions* and always the Elizabethan poets.

In English A, where I did a good deal of writing about the war, my instructor was Allen French, the Concord historian. He marked my papers with enough A's so that in November I was promoted out of the class. He also invited me to his home in Concord, and on our walks though that village and to Walden he gave me a picture of the Alcotts and Hawthorne, of Emerson and Thoreau I have never forgotten.

The panoramic course in English literature was a larger arch. Here we were lectured to by the big men in the Department, the most remarkable galaxy of English scholars in any faculty here or abroad. F. N. Robinson with his mellifluous voice introduced us to Chaucer; George Lyman Kittredge, the most picturesque professor in the Yard — white beard, immaculate gray suit and sparkling eyes — made us respect the rigorous discipline with which he examined each line of Shakespeare. George Pierce Baker, who had been developing young playwrights like Eugene O'Neill in his 47 Workshop, lectured to us on the Elizabethan stage and on Restoration comedy. John Livingston Lowes, a tiny man to hold such a sepulchral voice and such vast scholarship, spoke to us on Milton; Charles Townsend Copeland on Johnson and his circle; and Bliss Perry, with his charming smile, and in phrases still with the dew fresh on them, deepened our appreciation of the Romantic poets. The terse and brilliant insight they gave us of their chosen fields removed my blinders and left me with the humiliating realization that I knew so little.

I returned home Christmas vacation grimly aware that it would be years before I made up for lost time, and asking myself whether the degree was worth the long pull or whether I would be happier going straight to work. Mother said to hang on and that I would know the answer by June.

A Harvest Hand

By June of 1920, the end of my first year at Harvard, several things had become undeniably clear to me. My love for English, for reading, and for writing was no mere whim: this was something to which I could devote myself, though I did not know exactly in what way, for the rest of my life. Secondly, I was appallingly ill-read. It humiliated me to realize what vast stretches there were in English literature about which I knew little or nothing. To begin to fill in these lacunae would require at least two more years of college, and since my father was having a very rough time in the textile business and since I was the oldest of six, five of whom were of school age, I should have to find some way of earning my keep if I was to continue at Harvard. In this, as in so many other ways, Dean L. B. R. Briggs helped to steer me. He nominated me for the William Meeker Scholarship, a scholarship for an undergraduate showing aptitude in English, which had just been established in memory of Bill Meeker who had been killed in the war. This took care of my tuition; and a war veteran, who was still being treated for his wounds and who felt unequal to the struggle in Cambridge, turned over to me a job which was to pay for my room and board for the next two years, the assignment of covering Harvard for the *Boston Evening Transcript*.

With these two assets in hand, I knew that I could re-enter in

September, but the pressing question was where could I earn the most in the three months of summer vacation. The newspapers that spring had been publishing stories about the bumper wheat crop, larger even than the war crop of 1918, and placards had been posted in Cambridge reading HARVEST HANDS WANTED! SEVEN DOLLARS A DAY AND KEEP. FOLLOW THE THRESHER FROM OKLAHOMA TO CANADA! Well, why not? I thought. Ninety days' labor multiplied by $7 would pay my round trip and leave a tidy surplus. The placard said that applicants should present themselves at the Boston Chamber of Commerce, which I did, and there was given a small voucher reading that "to the best of our knowledge the undersigned is entitled to serve as a harvest hand . . ." I was told to present this at the Kansas City office of the Chamber of Commerce, where I should find my assignment. The voucher had been multigraphed on carbon paper just about as flimsy as my qualifications, I thought, for up till now I had kept at a respectful distance from farming of any kind. The only implement I knew how to use was a snow shovel.

The cash left over from Harvard was enough to buy my ticket to Kansas City and leave me a $20 margin. With this and my precious voucher and an overnight bag I made the trip. At Kansas City I found an army surplus store where I bought overalls, three pairs of socks, blue denims, heavy shoes, and a wide-brim straw hat. I then repaired to the men's room in the basement of the Muehlebach Hotel. There I changed my identity and emerged in the regalia of a harvest hand. At least it was what a lot of other people in Kansas City were wearing. But the clerk behind the wicket to whom I presented my slip at the Chamber of Commerce seemed less than excited by the prospect I offered. "Let's see," he said as he consulted a large map on cardboard, "they're harvesting right now in the vicinity of Colby. If you'll present that slip of yours to Mr. Lauterbach — he's head of the bank there — he'll tell you what to do." "Colby!" I said. "I thought the wheatfields were here."

"Brother," he said kindly, "you've got to go a hundred and sixty-five miles farther west before that bit of paper is worth a nickel."

The following morning at 6 A.M. I stepped down off the train at Colby, then the center of the migrating labor for the wheatfields. I had no breakfast, only a plate of soup the night before, and I was down to 23 cents; hungrily I inquired the way to Mr. Lauterbach's house, a neat, white-frame dwelling not far from Main Street. It was Mrs. Lauterbach who came to meet me, smiling and German. She must have seen that I was famished, for soon I was seated on the porch step gorging myself on a plate of ham and eggs and chips. Then her husband appeared and to him I surrendered at last my priceless voucher. He read it without quivering an eyelid. "Go back to Main Street," he said, "and sit down there on a curb with the others. That's where they'll sign you on. Good luck!" And we shook hands.

They had been digging up the pavement on Colby's one thoroughfare, and on the facing curb with their feet in the dust sat two long rows of tanned, big-fisted men. I joined the end and listened. Most of them, it seems, had been harvesting for the past fortnight on the sections 20 to 25 miles to the south. Now, as in a big checker game, they were passing through — leaping over, as it were, the men who were presently employed in order to get the next jobs to the north. The man beside me, who had been sizing me up as an Easterner, said kindly, "When you get paid off, Slim, don't carry your money. Buy an express check. There're too many guys who'll work you over when you're asleep." Even as we were talking, Fords in clouds of dust came rattling in at either end of the street, and from them stepped a farm owner or foreman who walked down the line in quiet scrutiny. The rugged and competent guys were signed up before 10 o'clock, and by noon the choice had gotten down to the smaller apples, and to me.

I was employed by a Mr. Carpenter, one of three brothers who had married sisters and whose farms adjoined each other ten miles from town. Mr. Carpenter was harvesting two sections and a half, and for that purpose he needed four harvest hands, two for each header-box, a "stacker" whom he found in old Pops, a 71-year-old pioneer neighbor, and the threshing machine which he rented and operated.

I have never lived as long on any single day as I did on that header-box. My partner, a high school student five years my junior, was born to the pitchfork, and he played it as rhythmically as if he were playing a violin. I played mine as if it were a snow shovel, digging, jerking and heaving at the in-pouring wheat in a series of convulsions that raised blisters on my hands and thirst in my throat. We had a stone crock full of water at the head of the wagon, and during the twenty minutes it took us to empty the box I could hardly wait until the jug was uncovered. I had neither the rhythm nor the accuracy of the native; had I been able to ease the tension of the work, stretching it out for an hour longer each day, I think that by the end of a week I should have been able to carry my share — but this was harvest labor at harvest wages. We slept in the haymow, awoke at 5 and caught the horses in the corral. We had our breakfast and were in the fields by 7, worked straight through until noon, ate a huge lunch with grease gravy and sour pork, lolled in the shade until 1:30, and then went at it again until after 5 o'clock. Full of hope at sunrise, I was burnt to a crisp by 11 and literally limp as a wet rag when the evening wind began to cool us off. After supper, which came out of cans and was just as heavy as lunch, the local boys took turns wrestling the stranger in our midst, a cowboy from Wyoming, while I lay on the ground, propping my head up, watching but too weary to cheer.

The cowboy was a stranger, but of course I was a freak. They called me Slim — Fats, Heavy, Slim are the obvious labels if no more familiar nickname is available — and almost everything I did had for them its amusing side, which they accepted, for the most part, with solemn and kindly attention. The boss invited me one morning to hitch the team on my header-box. The horses were patient and I did exactly as I thought I had been told, except that somehow when the last trace was in place, the entire contraption — wagon tongue, leather traces and all — had sunk to the level of the horses' hocks, a bare six inches above the earth. I was puzzling over this, wondering what I'd left out, when the explosion of laughter poured in from every crack and crevice where the other members of the crew had been watching the performance. On Saturday after work my partner and I followed old Pops across the fields and through the bed of a dried-up creek (where for one brief instant I almost stepped on a sunning rattler) to see the sod house in which Pops, a little bald eagle who might have been painted by Grant Wood, and his sweet-faced, gentle wife had lived during their first decade in Kansas. That meager little hut, half underground, with its floor of hard-packed earth, gave me a clearer understanding of pioneer homesteading than ever I had had from a book, just as the wind rustling the corn and the wheatfields under the full moon with the sound almost of running water gave me the sense of the space and beauty of these endless plains.

Threshing, as anyone knows, requires perfect teamwork. The field is divided in half, and each of the two teams must fill and empty its header-box of wheat in the same space of time, in order that the threshing machine need never halt in its pendulum progress. It soon became evident that my inefficiency was putting too much work on my partner and was slowing down our team and thus the action of the entire crew. By midafternoon, the threshing machine would be waiting for us to unload. The evening of the seventh day in friendly agreement the boss paid me off, and next morning I trudged back to town, the bills in my socks lest I be stuck up by one of the other jobless hands.

Back in Colby, for the first time in life I faced the acute question of self-support. Up one side of Main Street and down the other I went looking for work. There were three jobs open. The painter needed an assistant, but to qualify I had first to join the union, which would require both time and money. Road-building was going on, and the foreman offered me a job with the "other Mexicans," provided I could stand the sun — in the heat of the day it was well over 100 degrees — and the digging. My blistered hands and the memory of the fields disqualified me. But in the window of the Athens Cafe was a sign, DISH-WASHERS WANTED. I applied and was accepted. Terms: bed (shared with another man, the cook); board (such as I had the stomach for); and two dollars and a half a day. The pillow was so grimy that I used to spread my one clean handkerchief over the square of it I expected to sleep on. The cook, not much given to baths, got drunk on Saturday nights on Ed Pinard's hair tonic which did not improve either his odor or his *esprit de corps*. Saturday night was a time to endure, and since I was on too familiar terms with the food we were serving, I used to blow myself to a dinner at the other restaurant in town with which we were competing but about whose food I still had some illusions. We did our biggest business over the weekend, and I remember coming down one Saturday morning at 6 just as the cook opened the door of the big old-fashioned icebox. He drew his head back in dismay. "Boy! Smell those sausages. They sure won't last till Monday." And without a change in his voice he said, "Slim, chalk up on the board 'Special Today — Wheat Cakes and Sausage.'"

The work was dirtier than any KP I was ever sentenced to in the army, while the temperature in the kitchen was enough to blister even a Harvard veneer. My hours were from 6 to 6. Breakfast started briskly at 6:30; it was served table d'hote and called for five (granite) plates and one cup to the order. The staple was buckwheat cakes, and when cold they served me admirably as swabs for syrup or gravy. Midmorning and afternoon I drew my day's supply of hot water from the bakery next door. Other times I used a tin scraper, bent from a can, and bread crusts to enforce my cold rinse. It was not a finicky business. During my time eight men and one woman worked and talked beside me at the sink. The men, going north to new jobs, would put in for a day for the sake of three square meals. The woman, with her husband, a Swedish carpenter, was working her way East. She could engineer the job far better than I, and while she was there I surrendered the lead to her. So I washed dishes for two weeks — and never broke one! (It would have taken a hammer.) Then I headed East, poorer and wiser. But the experience, something over a month in all, was as valuable to me as the money I made in succeeding summers as a tutor.

I came back to Harvard with more to write about, and write I did, three times a week for the *Transcript* and every weekend for my course in composition under Dean Briggs. I wrote a dozen short stories for him and a bundle of essays, and the A he gave me in English 5 at the year's end was the grade that meant most to me in college. One of my stories, a love affair in the Blue Ridge Mountains entitled "Ink," won a contest sponsored by the *Harvard Advocate*. A prize of $25 in cash had been announced, but the *Advocate* was hard up those days and instead of paying me they elected me to the staff, no money changed hands, and everyone was satisfied.

As the assistant editor of the *Advocate,* I soon discovered that our circulation was limited to members of the freshman class and to the parents, aunts, and uncles of the editors. Indeed we were so short of cash and advertising that under the prodding of our business manager, Roy Larsen, we decided to produce a special issue, an issue which would satirize some well-known New England institution. The *Lampoon* had sold out several editions in Boston and New York of its parody issue of the *Transcript,* and as we looked over the field it was clear that the *Atlantic Monthly* was our nearest and most available target. There were five editors of the *Advocate:* we familiarized ourselves with the twelve issues of the *Atlantic* for the previous year, 1920, and then divided up the contents by five.

In that year Ellery Sedgwick, the *Atlantic*'s editor, had published at length a sentimental, somewhat questionable diary by Opal Whiteley. So for our leader Stedman Buttrick contributed

A Harvest Hand

"The Journal of a Bleeding Heart" by Isette Likely. Mr. Sedgwick seemed to have a fondness for articles written by inmates of American prisons who had different reasons for objecting to their board and lodgings; so in second place we ran an article entitled "Prison Cruelty in the Harvard Yard." The *Atlantic* of 1920 was concerned about the morals of the Younger Generation, and to ridicule this alarm I wrote a paper on babies, "Babes I Have Known." From the twelve issues we picked out four poems, which we reprinted with slightly lubricous alterations, giving them in each case what seemed to us a more appropriate title. Roy Larsen had no trouble soliciting advertisements for *this* issue of the *Advocate,* and on the cover we superimposed a replica of the *Atlantic*'s buff-brown table of contents so that at a distance we looked like a somewhat thinner brother of the famous sheet.

When the advance copies came off the press, William Whitman, the president of the *Advocate,* and I went in to see Mr. Sedgwick. I remember with what trepidation we entered his big high-ceilinged office on Arlington Street (the room I have occupied since 1938), and how I screened our presentation copy behind my back as we approached his desk and shook hands. When we were seated and he asked us what he could do for us, I solemnly laid the copy before him. His face was expressionless as he skimmed the table of contents; then with a snort he began reading in and out of the opening pages. When his snort turned into laughter, our case was won. We left with an order for 1000 copies which he intended to distribute to the colleges using the *Atlantic* in their English courses.

As a senior editor with a paying job in journalism, I had come to know the abler writers then in college. There were two freshmen whose work we were publishing in the *Advocate:*

Walter D. Edmonds, who came from upstate New York and
had already begun to write about the Canal country, and
Oliver LaFarge, who with his high cheekbones and jet-black
hair looked like one of the Indians he was later to dramatize,
and whose nickname "Inky" could have come either from his
hair or from the ink on his fingers. These two, together with
Berry Fleming, who lived across the hall from me in Hollis
Hall, were our three best in fiction. Bill Whitman, my room-
mate, and David McCord of the *Lampoon* were the best of our
poets; John Finley, Jr., then as now was the leading classicist; and in my class with Dean Briggs was a short, fastidious
man from Kansas City who rather shocked the Dean with his
allusions to sex and who gave evidence of being a good critic.
His name was Virgil Thomson.

Fair, with a Scopas profile, John Mason Brown was the
best talker of us all; he had an outrageous wit and he empha-
sized his points with his chin, lifted when he was in earnest,
lowered when in doubt or in mirthful acknowledgment that
he had been scored on. He had come to Harvard to study English
literature and, more particularly, the theater. With Donald
Oenslager to design the sets, he became the leading spirit in
the Dramatic Club, and with Philip Barry he became one of
the shining lights in Professor Baker's famous 47 Workshop
(of which President Lowell did not approve). Since he hailed
from Kentucky and was master of every variation of the Southern accent from Lady Baltimore cake to the sugar cane of
Louisiana, he was constantly being cast for Colonel-Massa parts
and as constantly walking out of them into something better
in G. B. Shaw, Sheridan, or Galsworthy. The Signet Club table
was never happier than when he was at the center of it, and
the mischief he made with Louis Allard, Wheeler Williams,

and Dave McCord I grin to remember. When he graduated *summa cum laude* in 1923 and went abroad to study theatrical production in Scandinavia and the Continent, John was at the point of his career when he could have been actor, author, or dramatic critic. But not for him "the road not taken." He has lived to be all three.

I have a memory for details, and there are certain scenes at Harvard which I like to sort through. I remember Professor Kirsopp Lake lecturing to us in his Oxford accent about the Old Testament, and how the big lecture hall would hush as with tears in his eyes he talked about Moses and the Promised Land; square-cut Charles Homer Haskins, the historian, called the "Iron Duke," and what a different, vital world he opened for us in his discussion of the medieval mind; and little John Livingston Lowes reading to us from manuscript the chapters of his new book, *The Road to Xanadu*. In my first seminar with him I came to discuss the subject of my long thesis. "I thought, sir," I began confidently, "that I would like to write about the love influence on the poetry of Byron and Keats." (All this in three months!) Lowes never cracked a smile. "Isn't that rather a large assignment, Mr. Weeks? Wouldn't it be better to concentrate on one?" he queried. "Which would you suggest?" I asked. "Keats," he said gravely, and the matter was settled.

Professors were more accessible then than they are now. Dean and Mrs. Briggs used to have open house every Thursday, and a wide circle of graduates and undergraduates would form about her rocking chair where she sat knitting as Jonathan, the cat, played in and out of her skirts; it was a pleasure and lesson to hear the Dean direct the talk so that everyone got his word in and no one monopolized. And I remember Copey's beautiful candle-lit rooms in the south entry of Hollis, with books from floor to ceiling, and on the floor undergraduates packed as close as their hunkers would permit, listening to Copey read aloud, or meeting for the first time a great editor like Max Perkins or hearing Dr. Morton Prince expatiate on automatic writing — a subject, as he told us, on which Gertrude Stein had written a thesis for William James when she was at Radcliffe.

Dean Briggs was my mentor, and I worked for him as for no other. Once a month I climbed the three flights to his office under the eaves of University Hall, and as we went over my compositions I received his friendly guidance, and those bits of wisdom and stimulus which so endeared him to students. Always I meant to ask him whether he thought I was justified in pursuing a literary career, but somehow the question was never put into words. He never let it be; instead he would ask how I was sleeping — made curious, no doubt, by the dark circles under my eyes, for I lived with a good deal of insomnia those days; and hearing my candid reply, he prescribed a glass of milk and a few pages of Thomson's *Seasons* which he said was the most quieting poem in the English language. He urged me to try for the Boylston Prize in Public Speaking, and when I won it with my recitation of Kipling's short story, "Wee Willie Winkie," he was pleased, and said that with my memory and lack of nervousness I should continue to speak when I had the chance.

With Cattle to Cambridge

THERE are advantages in crossing the Atlantic on a cattle boat out of Montreal, the most obvious being the free ride for a scholarship student, outward bound for graduate work at Cambridge University. I can think of two others: the musical Scottish dialect you hear on the Clydesider and the down-to-the-heels hunger which will assail you when nine days later you arrive in Glasgow, as I did. I had not been a success with a pitchfork in Kansas, but I had come to Montreal on the advice of a Canadian friend who was quite positive that I could do what was expected of me on the cattle boat. At the station I checked my luggage and then went down to the dockside to sign on. I wore an old gray suit and a brown felt Harvard hat with a hole in the crown. At the office on the docks I introduced myself to a hefty Irishman in his fifties, who smelt strongly of rum. He was the foreman of the cattle hands, and he stipulated the form of our contract: to get my berth it was understood that I would turn over my pay of $36 to him. I wrote this off on a small slip of paper and now all I had to do was work my way across the Atlantic.

In the office I met the other cattle hands: a big rawboned Australian veteran who had been harvesting in Canada, and who, as it turned out later, had served in the same sector with me before Amiens in 1918; a Cockney waiter who had been fired from the Canadian Pacific hotels, and a wizened English sheepherder from Calgary. Our Irish boss, an ex-prizefighter, pointed out the ship and told us to be aboard by 1 o'clock; we'd be sailing on the outgoing tide that afternoon.

I went back to the station and collected my luggage which a taxi driver deposited on the pier as close to the gangplank as he could — steamer trunk, suitcase, and portable typewriter. There lay the ship, fresh painted, 9000 tons and riding high. A railroad spur ran out on the pier and leading from it like a high-arched bridge was a wooden ramp which would pour the steers from their freight cars into the waist of the vessel. The cattle train from the West had not yet arrived, and for the moment all was serene. Looking down at me from the rail were a half dozen of the crew, dark-haired, red-cheeked Scots, smoking and spitting into the crevasse between the ship and the dock. They considered me without comment.

The trunk was too much for me to handle by myself, so I went up the gangplank as casually as possible and attached myself to the end of the group at the rail. Silence settled on us all. At last the Scot nearest me turned my way.

"We'el," he said, in a brogue too rich to reproduce, "an' I suppose ye write for the papers?" I nodded.

"Aye. An' you'll be looking for local color?" Again it seemed easier to agree.

"We'el," he said, "you'll find it and it'll all be brown." With that priming he condescended to give me a hand.

We cattle hands were not treated as part of the crew: we had no rights in the forecastle, and were never allowed in the mess. We slept and ate, the four of us, in a tiny, hot deckhouse right over the propeller. The foreman kept aloof. Our food, the salt fish or stew, with bread thrown in on top and a pannikin of tea, we had to fetch from the galley and carry staggering back to our cubby across the pitching deck. It was all much too close.

The cattle train was late, so late that the captain had begun to show his impatience on the bridge. The delay gave our Irishman an opportunity to go ashore with the result that his rum content was higher now than it had been in the morning. When at last the cattle cars were shunted into view, it was plain that the steers would have to be poured aboard in short order if we were to sail on the tide. Each steer, some of them seeming to me of formidable heft, carried a headrope around his neck. Customarily the cattlemen from the train were responsible for tying them up. But there wasn't time for that, and when the last protesting animal had clumped down the runway we cast off with our entire herd, 280 steers and 11 bulls, milling about in the closed-in runway which encircled the ship like a racetrack.

Luckily, our passage down the St. Lawrence to the Straits of Belle Isle was smooth, for hour after hour our four-man squad and the foreman struggled to tie up the beasts. This was our technique: the Australian would isolate a steer with his pitchfork and start him down the runway by twisting his tail. Inside the runway — and I thought at considerable peril — stood our rummy foreman waving his arms. He was supposed to stop the express train, and when the steer swung toward the stanchion, I, on my knees, reached up, jerked free the knot in the headrope, quickly passed the end of it through the hole in the stanchion, and made it fast. This worked all right for the first three, but the fourth steer didn't stop. He plowed right by, stepping hard on the foreman's right foot. The Irishman was hurt, and he retired, cursing, to his bunk. That left four of us, and it was another two and a half days before we had the last of the herd lashed down. There was one little black bull, wily as the devil, who kept slipping out of his headrope and who roamed free longer than any other.

By this time we were in high seas. The October gales were making up and we were all seasick in varying degrees in our stuffy little cabin which rose and fell like an elevator. The Cockney swore that he was too weak to work, and since the foreman was still nursing his wounds, we pallid three had to tend the steers by day. We shouted at the Cockney that it was his responsibility to keep night watch, and showed him how to jerk the headrope free for any steer who might be thrown to his knees. Until I had got my sea legs, food had lost all charm (there wasn't much in what came to us from the galley), and I did without it. Then one evening while off duty I gave the cook a dollar for a slice of mutton as thick as a leather sole. This I gnawed away at for the next forty-eight hours. It was like swallowing fiber, but it started some juice flowing and it stayed down.

The steers did not enjoy the motion any more than I, but they had too many stomachs to be spectacular in their sickness; they simply became mad with thirst. Twice a day Digger, the Australian, and I would heave our wooden buckets out of the high wooden tuns, which held the water, six buckets to a beast — and the one we hadn't got to would always knock over at least one bucket in his eagerness.

On this long voyage I had two consolations. One was H. M. Tomlinson's superb collection of sea essays, *Old Junk,* which I read in the sunny afternoons, lying on bales of hay. The other came on the ninth day: a green and golden moment of dawn as we passed the bell buoy at the mouth of the Clyde and

With Cattle to Cambridge

I, standing in the bow, half shivering in the cold, saw the sheep on the distant uplands, the shipyards in the distance, and realized that we were close to Glasgow.

I landed in Scotland hungrier than I had ever been in my life. The purge of that nine-day voyage during which I had subsisted upon that slab of mutton, bread, and strong tea had left me ravenous. I took a room at the Queen's Hotel, and for the next two days did little else but eat. After a hearty lunch I would take a bus to the art museum or go for a ramble through the busy streets, but after an hour or two the feeling of repletion would be gone and the sight of a Scottish tearoom with its scones, fruitcake, and cherry tarts would bring me to a stop. I couldn't pass that window. In I would go to relish that fourth meal — the thin-sliced bread and butter, the hot scones, the strawberry jam with berries as big as your thumb, then the pastries and the tea, cup after cup. I had so much and so often that when at last I stopped at Cook's to purchase my train ticket for London, I discovered that I did not have enough English money left to pay for it.

I showed the clerk my letter of credit on Baring Brothers. "But, sir," he explained patiently, "this is only good when you deposit it in person in London."

"But how am I to get to London without a ticket?" I asked.

"You should have thought of that before, sir," he said reprovingly. But after a rather searching look he added, "Even though it is against regulations, I'm afraid I shall have to lend you the funds out of my own pocket."

I took down his name and address while he made out the ticket.

It was a long run from Scotland, and when at midnight we

arrived in the black cavern of the King's Cross Station in London I found that my Scot had figured my allowance with a nicety, for I had exactly a shilling left — this and my letter of credit.

I appealed to the bobby who was directing traffic outside the station.

"Officer," I said, "is there a house nearby where I could find a room for the night?" And I told him of my plight.

"Why, certainly," he said. "Come along." And he led me down a side street to a brick house that still showed a light. " 'Ere's an American, Mrs. Hopkins," he said to the landlady. "Can you take him in for the night?" And she did.

She had a boiled egg and sausage ready for me the next morning; then, leaving my suitcase and portable with her as hostage, I went down to Baring's to deposit my letter of credit. Now with cash in my pocket I could breathe easier.

My next call was at the London bureau of the Associated Press. I asked to see Robert Collins. "Mr. Collins," I said after we had shaken hands, "do you plan to have a correspondent at Cambridge University for this year?"

"Cambridge? Why, I don't think we've had a correspondent there since, let me see, since 1914. Have you had any experience?"

"Yes," I said, "some. I covered Harvard for the *Boston Evening Transcript* these last two years."

"Well," he said, "there is no reason why we shouldn't try you on space. You keep in touch with the Americans who are there, mail us your copy, and anything we wire home will be paid for at the rate of a shilling a line." With that verbal agreement as an incentive, I took the next train to Cambridge.

Cambridge is a medieval little town, set in the midst of the

Fens country, and although much of the fens (or marshes as we would call them) have been filled in, the Lady of the Fens, a dank mist with a cutting edge, infiltrates the towers and courts at nightfall, and during the winter months is seldom penetrated by the sun before 10:30 in the morning.

My first impression, even in October, was of being unbearably cold. I was cold when I shaved (in my unheated room in the morning), and I stayed cold, and when I went to bed at night it was like sliding in between panes of glass. The English students never thought of wearing overcoats. The cap and gown worn carelessly over their tweeds seemed their only protection. They obviously had a warmer insulation than any I had brought with me from America, and on the second day I bought some for myself — woolen underwear half an inch thick, and a heather-colored tweed cut with the nap so long that the hair seemed to grow on it overnight.

The cap and gown is a college uniform to be worn at all times — to classrooms, at meals, in the library, and when calling on your tutor. I had not realized this when I paid my first call on my tutor at Trinity College, Gaillard Lapsley, an authority on English constitutional history, an American who had lived so long in England that he had acquired the manner and accent of an Etonian. We shook hands and then with that diffident cough of his he reminded me that he really could not receive me until I was *in statu pupillari,* that is to say in a Trinity cap and gown. So I went to the nearest haberdasher on Trinity Lane, purchased the dark blue knee-length gown and the mortarboard, and then went back for our talk.

Harvard had granted me the Fiske Fellowship and there were no strings to it. Mr. Lapsley asked me what I wanted to study, and I told him that I really hadn't made up my mind. I knew that I had to do a certain amount of journalism for my keep, and for the rest I wanted to fill in the gaps in my reading, and not be worried too much about examinations. "My dear Weeks," he said, "I want you to read as much as you please; you will find the long vacations very happy for that, but while you are here in term I suggest that you attend lectures on subjects you couldn't conceivably have worked out for yourself. I mean, for instance, the lectures on English constitutional history, which will show you the long struggle men had to gain their legal liberty here before the States came into being. I won't expect you to write papers, or to take the examinations, but I do think you will be rewarded if you attend the lectures and follow some of the required reading on this subject."

He was right, and so I did: I attended his lectures on English constitutional history and those by Kenneth Pickthorn and I plowed through the required reading in Bishop Stubbs. I followed other leads too. Arthur Quiller-Couch, the University Professor in English, was to deliver some ornamental talks on Dickens and Thackeray, and I enjoyed them. I also put down for a course with him on Aristotle's *Poetics,* a discussion group which met in his library at nine in the evening. I went to hear Dr. Shepherd, later the Provost of Kings College, talk on the Greek dramatists, and watched spellbound as in the enthusiasm of his words he would thrust his hands down into the pockets of his gown and then, forgetting he had them there, suddenly bring his arms up shoulder high, giving him the momentary appearance of an umbrella inside out. I listened to Clapham on economics, and to Walter de la Mare, who gave the Clark lectures on literature, and who was melodious and poetic.

The English colleges at this time were an incomparable

bachelordom. The undergraduate lived alone, in beautiful quarters, well served and well fed; the "bedders" built your morning fire in the study and did not rap on your bedroom door until the kidneys and fried eggs under the pewter covers had been brought in and placed before the coals. Trinity had a famous kitchen, and the dinners served in our rooms by a private waiter were famous for their mutton with its thin edge of crisp fat and the *crème brûlée,* a delectable dessert.

Life in Cambridge was a series of concentric circles to which the stranger was admitted on friendly if temporary terms. Francis Hopkinson, whose door was opposite mine on Great Court, was Whip of the Trinity Beagles, a "blood," gay and exquisitely dressed, a collector of ancient spurs and a giver of hilarious dinners, above whose din one heard the bleating of the beagles' horn. George Kitson-Clark, Patrick Duff and Stephen Runciman were scholars marked for high place with whom it was stimulating to have tea after Hall. ("Have you brought your shooting irons with you?" asked Runciman, only half facetiously, one evening.) The rugger and rowing Blues were marked men with their Hawk's Club ties, and George Tregoning, a fine oar from Harrow, and Arthur Young, the scrum half, went out of their way to be hospitable. As a wiser man has said before me, the ideal society is one in which the dividing line between the exclusive and the excluded is painless.

It was my livelihood, and in a way my privilege, to keep track of fifty-two Americans who were rather widely distributed among the five thousand British and colonial students at the university, and to file with the A.P. such stories of their activities as might interest the home-town papers. Arthur Goodhart, a don of Corpus, helped me with this. Harry Atkinson, a class ahead of me at Harvard, had won his Trial Cap and was one of the two leading contenders for the bow oar in the varsity. Reddy Key, who later made a distinguished record in the State Department, and Everett Case, the present President of Colgate, were on the university tennis squad which was captained by Jimmy Van Allen of Newport. So, incidentally, was I, though only good enough for a Fenner's blazer. Ted Hilles, now a professor of English at Yale, was the best miler in Trinity and might win his Blue against Oxford. Ed Pulling, headmaster and founder of Millbrook, and Arthur Gardiner, who is in our Embassy in Saigon as I write this, were playing varsity golf, and what Bernard Darwin wrote about them in the *Times,* I relayed home. I kept track of them all, even Anson Phelps Stokes, now the Episcopal Bishop of Eastern Massachusetts, but then our youngest, who had come over fresh from boarding school to get a head start on his studies at Yale.

Morley Dobson, poet and scholar of Corpus Christi College, formerly of Poughkeepsie and Harvard, was my companion on many a bicycle trip, and together we rode more than 2500 miles through the English lanes with their hawthorn banks or on old Roman roads. We cycled with the intent of finding and of reading the English authors in their own environment. Thus we followed Chaucer's pilgrims from Southwark southeast to Canterbury to the shrine of Thomas à Becket; we traced Pickwick through London and to his adventures in Kent; we spent a heavenly Easter vacation climbing and reading with Wordsworth, Leigh Hunt and Coleridge through the Lake Country. And now in May I was thinking of Thackeray as on spring evenings he gambled away the patrimony he had not yet inherited, in the room catty-cornered from mine in Great Court; of Byron as he vaunted his swimming; and of Rupert

Brooke who had defined so attractively the loves of this university town only a decade before I was tasting them.

My fellowship could have been renewed for another year, but I was twenty-five and ambitious and in love. It was time I began to dig in, and I knew it. Entertaining my American cousins Alice Duer Miller and her son Denning, my classmate who was then studying at Christ's College, passing them fruitcake in our huge study above the Queen Anne's Gate, with the windows opening onto the beauty of Great Court, I caught myself thinking, "When the money's gone — what do you think you'll be doing just four months from now?"

It was by the happiest chance that I shared the beautiful tower rooms with an Englishman, H. R. Creswick. Our study occupied the whole square of the tower and measured twenty-nine by thirty-two feet, the black walnut paneling went back to Charles II, the fireplace had seats on either side of it, and in one corner where we kept our tea things was the circular staircase which still led up to the parapet. Dick Creswick, who like myself had not come straight from school, was even then a connoisseur of rare books. He showed me where to find the bargains at David's bookstall in the Market Place, and many of the leather backs now in my library were procured on his advice. Dick's natural proclivity was to lead him on into library work, and he is one of the few men in library history to have served successively as Deputy Librarian of the Bodleian at Oxford and then as University Librarian at Cambridge.

Dick is and always has been my closest link with England, and when I flew over in July 1943, it was he who conducted me through the treasure rooms and fireproof vaults of the Bodleian, of which he was then in charge. That same weekend we took tea with Mr. and Mrs. John Masefield in Abingdon, and Dick modestly mentioned the Friends of the Bodleian and their hope that the library might be entrusted with one of the poet's manuscripts. Masefield flushed with pleasure and, after consulting with his wife, suggested *Reynard the Fox*. A long pause, and then the poet shyly cleared his throat. "My good friend Thomas Hardy and I corresponded regularly for twenty-five years," he said, "and after his death Mrs. Hardy returned my letters. I wonder if you would care to have that correspondence too?" Dick smiled and nodded, and I had a momentary vision of the keepers of treasure rooms back home who would envy such luck.

Greenwich Village

In THE autumn of 1923 three of us set up bachelor quarters in Greenwich Village: Eliot Cabot, who had a good part in *White Cargo,* Berry Fleming, who was contributing to *Life* and *Punch* and writing his first novel, and I, who was working as a book salesman for Boni & Liveright. The Village was convenient and inexpensive; it had an assortment of gaily decorated basement restaurants with thumb-worn menus in French and Italian; a French bakery where one could get *croissants* and large square rolls crusted and split, with poppy seeds on top, two for five cents; one-man bookstores run on a very personal basis where you just might bump into Sherwood Anderson or Maxwell Bodenheim; Webster Hall, where the costume party on New Year's Eve was the nearest thing to the Beaux Arts ball; Washington Square, where you could loaf in the sunlight of a Sunday morning; the Provincetown Players on MacDougal Street, where I was to see *Desire Under the Elms;* and it had walk-up apartments in old brownstone fronts such as a thirty-five-dollar-a-week man could afford. The cheapest were those whose windows gave on the Sixth Avenue El.

I did the housekeeping, and it was a Box and Cox arrangement, for Eliot seldom returned from Broadway until long after we were asleep, and he was never up by the time that I had to leave for the office. I only saw him Sundays when we breakfasted late. Breakfast was my dish and it never varied. On my way home I would pick up the big square rolls at the French bakery. Next morning after I put the coffee on, I'd heat them in the oven with a chunk of butter melting in the center. On top of this I would introduce a three-and-a-half-minute egg, with paprika to taste. All on one plate and very good.

We came to gradually on Sundays, and in bathrobes ate a lazy breakfast, shared our gossip, and afterwards Berry, if urged, would show us the sketches he was preparing to submit to Oliver Herford, one of the *Life* staff, on Monday.

Our apartment was the top floor of an old brownstone which trembled each time the Elevated roared by. Our landlord, a mysterious Greek doctor, conducted an enormous, silent practice on the first floor. The second floor was occupied by a fading Italian countess and her professorial husband who had been reduced to serving as a translator at the nearby municipal court. Their rooms were heavy with ancient velvet portieres, massive gilded furniture, books on shelves and on the floor, and dust everywhere. She cooked their meals on a gas ring on the windowsill. The third floor was ours and, as we had an extra cot, we were a last resort for friends looking for a free bed.

I took the Sixth Avenue El uptown to reach Liveright's office on West 48th Street, where I was beginning to know — at least by sight — some of our more famous clientele. I recognized dour Theodore Dreiser with his ponderous manner, and Ludwig Lewisohn, bright-eyed and animated, whose *Upstream* had been a sweeping success and who was now about to publish his novel *Don Juan.* I must have been out selling books when Eugene O'Neill called; we were publishing his one-act plays that autumn, but if he had any business to transact, it was probably down at the Algonquin where the more desirable authors were entertained. I did see Sherwood Anderson, who was Mr. Liveright's latest acquisition and a legend in the Village. Anderson had soared into our thinking with his *Winesburg, Ohio,* and his short stories were acclaimed even in London, where they were published by J. C. Squire in *The London Mercury.* Mr. Liveright coveted his future books, and he got an option on them by the simple expedient of tracing Anderson to his lair in the Village. All we knew at the time was that Horace had returned with a signed contract and a smile on the face of the tiger. The other side of the story was told to me by Mr. Anderson years later, when he was a guest on my radio program. The furnished room on the third floor back where he received the publisher was threadbare, and Mr. Liveright, a born gambler when it came to advances, lost no time.

"Mr. Anderson," he began, "I'm a great admirer of your work, and I want to make it easier for you. What I propose is to send you a check for one hundred dollars every Monday, and regard this as an advance against the royalties on your next novel."

"Every Monday?" said Sherwood, thoughtfully. "One hundred dollars?"

"Every Monday," said Horace, and the deal was made.

"That next Monday," continued Sherwood, as he reminisced, "I couldn't wait for the postman. I was down there in my bathrobe when the letters came through the slot. Sure enough, there it was. The check. I certainly ate well that week, took some friends out and we had steak. The checks kept right on coming. But somehow it would get around towards Friday, and I wouldn't have done even as much as half a new chapter of *Dark Laughter*. By the end of the month I knew this couldn't go on, so I went up to see Horace at 48th Street.

" 'Mr. Liveright,' I said, handing him back the contract, 'I don't want this any more.'

" 'Who's offering you more?' he asked.

" 'No, it's not that,' I said. 'I just can't work that way. You'll get the book, but give me back my poverty.' "

I was confronted by my own more modest decision in the Christmas season of 1923: should I accept Ellery Sedgwick's handwritten offer to join the editorial staff of the *Atlantic* at the princely sum of forty-five dollars a week, or should I continue as I was going in Manhattan? Mr. Liveright when I told him did more than match the Boston offer, and I knew that I was working in keen and friendly competition. Julian Messner, under whom I had been selling the Liveright line, was a man of integrity whose judgment was respected throughout the trade. Dick Simon, who had given me my early instruction in salesmanship and who was now leaving to form a firm of his own with his friend Max Schuster, would continue to help me, although I think he had already concluded that I might be better at editing than on the business side. Bennett Cerf had just moved uptown from Wall Street and had the desk next to mine on the third floor of Liveright's. These were friends and, with Manuel Komroff, who was in charge of the manufacturing department and Beatrice Kaufman, the wife of the playwright, who was our head proofreader, they were taking a personal interest in my development. Beatrice had evidently been talking about me one day at lunch, and as I came within earshot I overheard her say — "and he'll be making his twenty thousand a year before long." To a forty-five-dollar-a-week salesman that confidence of hers was something breath-taking. Would I be jeopardizing all this if I went to work for the *Atlantic?* My father thought I would, and he spoke plainly. "The salaries in Boston are low," he said, "and Mr. Sedgwick has a reputation for changing his assistants every three years. Why take the gamble?"

Is there something in the Anglo-Saxon blood which is aroused by the odds-against bet and was there something in my New England experience which now compelled me to come back? The pay I knew would be less, and it might be decades before I reached that figure which B. quoted so blithely, but this I knew: that I would be bound to grow in Boston, and that the chance of working on *Atlantic* manuscripts under Mr. Sedgwick would give me more latitude and a harder test than anything I could expect under Liveright's editor, C. R. Smith. So I decided to take the long shot.

Over and Under Editing

ELLERY SEDGWICK, to whom I presented myself the Monday after New Year's in 1924, was in his prime, and one of the ablest magazine editors in the country. His office, which I remembered from my previous visit, was flooded with light from the windows overlooking the Public Garden and from those to the west on Marlborough Street. The open fireplace, the marble bust of Charles Eliot Norton, and the portrait of James Russell Lowell, the *Atlantic's* first editor, hanging above the mantel, gave the place a traditional aspect very different from the exotic flamingo panels in Mr. Liveright's sanctum, one of which concealed a bar and the other a shower bath. I was attracted at once by Mr. Sedgwick's engaging black eyes and by the charm of his voice. His hooked nose and the muscles in his jaw spelt decision, and with his crisp dark hair, graying at the temples, his heavy lower lip and ruddy complexion, he had a Spanish buccaneering look not without distinction.

He put me at my ease and we talked for a little about Thomas Wells and Fred Allen of *Harper's* and my work in New York; it was clear that he had no recollection of our earlier meeting at the time of the *Advocate* parody. He explained my duties as a "first reader" and he then introduced me to his second in command and my immediate superior, Miss Florence Converse, with whom I was to share an office. Miss Converse was a short trim little woman in tweeds behind whose steel-rimmed spectacles dwelt a critic who was also a poet. A Wellesley graduate and a protégée of Miss Vida Scudder, Wellesley's famous scholar-teacher, Miss Converse had done her first professional reading under Bliss Perry. She handled manuscripts with sensitivity and with dispatch, and when she was operating on a book manuscript, cutting out and tying together the excerpts for a two- or three-part serial, or when she was removing the superfluous and purple passages from an overwritten descriptive essay, no surgeon with a scalpel was ever more swift or sure. Our desks were adjoining and at a V angle to each other with the light at our backs; at such close range I came to appreciate the checking, the sandpapering, and the rewriting that went into every issue; I learned to respect "F.C.'s" judgment and I tried to emulate the firmness and the consideration with which she dictated her letters of rejection. Mr. Sedgwick trusted her absolutely, and when he was away from the office on his annual trip to England or on longer voyages to South America and to Japan, she made up the issues and her decision was final.

The office we shared was a large high-studded room with windows giving on a fire escape where the Common's pigeons nested and cooed. In the center of the room on a large circular mahogany table stood three tin breadboxes. They held the daily inflow of manuscripts and were labeled respectively Today, Yesterday, and The Abyss of Time. When Miss Converse was with me we polished off an average of a hundred and sixty manuscripts a day, and by 5 P.M. there would be only a few left in one box. When she was away, and I was on my own, I lived in the Abyss. We two did all the reading.

Every place has its scuttlebutt which tells the juniors what they need to know about the high command, and I soon got my bearings. Mr. Sedgwick, whose family had long been the squires of Stockbridge, Massachusetts, had entered publishing in New York after his graduation from Harvard in 1894, and after teaching for a year at Groton. He had worked for D. Appleton, one of the old-line book publishers; he had served briefly as an assistant to S. S. McClure before that meteoric editor burned himself out; and most notably he had revitalized *Leslie's Monthly Magazine,* running it on initiative and bank loans at a time when the magazine had been given up as dead. He actually made money out of *Leslie's,* and a reputation that extended as far as Boston.

In 1908 the circulation of the *Atlantic Monthly* had declined to something less than ten thousand readers. I cannot find the true figure and it doesn't matter. What does matter is that the proprietors, Houghton Mifflin and Company, had lost confidence and were trying to decide whether to sell the periodical or to convert it into a limited circulation, limited to ten thousand readers who would pay ten thousand dollars a year for their exclusive privilege. It was at this point that Mr. Sedgwick stepped in and made an offer. His bid was accepted; what he paid I have never known, but it is fun to guess, and I should put the figure at approximately $50,000. Rumor has it that Mr. Mifflin authorized the sale feeling confident that Mr. Sedgwick would go broke in two years and that the property could then be picked up by its former owners and a trial made at that limited subscription.

But when Ellery Sedgwick brought his powerful personal magnetism to bear, the magazine began to respond as it had under Walter Hines Page in the late 1890's. The two men had much in common: each believed in our expanding destiny as a world power; each was a profound admirer of England and drew as much as forty per cent of an issue from English writers; each fought strenuously for higher standards in American education, and each, incidentally, was a Democrat. Instead of failing, the circulation doubled in two years. The *Atlantic* had thirty thousand subscribers by August of 1914, and under Sedgwick's truly brilliant editing it nearly trebled its growth during the First World War.

I had never been a fast reader in college, indeed I could seldom travel at faster than thirty-five pages an hour with those solid volumes we were required to read in the Widener Library. But now I had to step up the pace. By narrowing my gaze to the center of the page and reading straight down, I found I could get a glancing comprehension at double the speed. What was equally important, I arranged the day's reading as if it were a diet. I would begin with the hardheaded articles, the papers on economics, foreign policy, the scholastic theses, in the morning when I was fresh. At eleven I would switch to short stories. After lunch I would make penciled notes for those rejections which merited more than the printed slip. Sometimes I wrote just a single line of hope in pencil at the bottom of the rejection slip; sometimes I went into constructive detail in a separate letter, with the result that the manuscript would almost certainly be revised and returned to us in ten days.

No day's reading is ever the same. A cool perceptive essay by Agnes Repplier or Willa Cather could give a brightness to the morning very different from the feeling which overcame me if by bad luck I chanced on a succession of papers by cranks. Over a six-month period I kept a tally of the "nut" manuscripts and found that they divided fairly evenly between

California and New York City. Theosophists, the writers who talked familiarly to God, and those who took themselves seriously as the New Messiah, gravitated naturally to the land of Aimee Semple McPherson. There they found supporters, founded their temples and held forth. Lower Manhattan, on the other hand, was at this period the homeland of free verse, much of it splintered prose which, as it was subdivided in short staccato lines, looked like what the Chinese student called "goggerel." Poems would begin like this:

COSMOS
out of the womb of Time
came forth the azoic globe
earth,
a spark in space

and run on for two more pages, single-spaced. I have always suspected that H. G. Wells's *Outline of History* was a formative influence here. Among the traditional versifiers were a surprisingly large number of women who belonged to "The Samarkand School"; these were possessed with the desire to wander off with "gypsy lads" and "open hearts" along roads which always led to Samarkand for the closing rhyme.

A first reader becomes hypersensitive to those words which are being overworked in the popular vernacular, and some which used to make me wince were "opalescent," "plashing," "realistic," "sensed," "convincing," "reaction," "intriguing" — there were times when it took forceful restraint not to check them. But we did not leave our marks on manuscripts that were going back.

As a veteran I felt no lack of confidence in judging the articles, personal documents, and stories that had to do with the war. For short stories I had an insatiable appetite, and on my own I wrote to those whose work I most admired. It was too late to try for Katherine Mansfield, but we did secure one of the last by Rudyard Kipling, and I was much excited by Rudolph Fisher, a Negro X-ray technician who wrote powerfully and most knowingly about the Harlem and West Indian Negroes and who would have done some fine books for us had he lived. F. Scott Fitzgerald's generation was mine, and I laughed at and partly resented the fussy, overly nice criticism which the *Atlantic* used to publish about our Flaming Youth (read, as a sample, "Cornelia Discusses an Eligible Young Man" by Stuart P. Sherman, in the *Atlantic* for September 1924). I noticed that there were three areas of controversy which kept appearing and reappearing: Prohibition, anti-Semitism, and the influence of Roman Catholicism in a democratic society. As a Wilsonian Democrat I welcomed material about the League of Nations. I read with respect what Dean Inge, Samuel McChord Crothers, and Rufus Jones had to say about the spirit. And I wondered about our poets, so many of whom were genteel and so few of whom were young. While I was at Liveright's we had published a long poem, *The Waste Land*, by an American in London named T. S. Eliot, but for reasons I have never fathomed he was neither invited nor published by the *Atlantic* of the 1920s.

There were certain unwritten laws in the *Atlantic* office which were conveyed to me either by Miss Converse or by our head proofreader, Miss Caroline Church. The word "nigger" was not to be used if it could be avoided nor were the four-letter words, and as for "bitch" or "bastard," they were suggested either by "b ——" or by "S.O.B." Our fastidious readers, so the saying went, were "our permanent and valuable core";

they were swift to voice their displeasure, and they always had been. In 1869, when the magazine published Mrs. Harriet Beecher Stowe's spectacular article protesting the indignities endured by Lady Byron ("The True Story of Lady Byron's Life," September 1869), fifteen thousand of our most fastidious canceled their subscriptions within a period of twelve months, an example not lost on later editors.

I remember in the spring of my first year we received from Miss Amy Lowell a poem entitled "Fool o' the Moon," a poem which, as she explained to Mr. Sedgwick in the accompanying note, had been most warmly received when she read it aloud. In details somewhat explicit for a spinster it described the love affair between the poet and Lady Moon, ending with the curtain line, "I have lain with Lady Moon." Mr. Sedgwick accepted the challenge and the poem, but I noticed that it was held in the icebox for some months, in fact was not actually published until July, when the schools and colleges which used the *Atlantic* in their English classes were dispersed and there was small likelihood of protest from their professors.

We were the first magazine of national circulation to publish a story by Ernest Hemingway. "Fifty Grand" told of a professional boxer, the welterweight champion, who was training for a title fight. He is past his prime, and so sure he is to be beaten that he bets $50,000 with the professional gamblers that he will lose. The climax of the fight, when the professional gamblers try to double-cross him, is as rugged and punishing a piece of prose as we have ever published, and I was proud that we took it without question or change. None of us had any way of knowing that "Fifty Grand" had already been declined by Ray Long, the editor of *Cosmopolitan,* by the *Saturday Evening Post* and *Collier's,* and that Max Perkins had tried to cut it for

Scribner's and had given up. No one would think of objecting to it today, and because the writing had such force and authority behind it, few did then. We accepted it in midwinter and printed it in July of 1927.

I knew when Mr. Sedgwick had the manuscript of "Fifty Grand" in his hands, seated as I was in my room with both doors between us closed, for he let out a crescendo of short explosions, "oh-oh-Oh-Oh . . ." — and whenever he did this it was a sure indication that he had found something exciting. But when some long-promised beauty turned out to be a lemon, he could be heard moaning, beginning on a low note and swelling in volume, "Ohoooo *Oh,*" which told F.C. and myself what we had already suspected — that he had a dud.

Like every young editor I was keen to bring into our columns the work of my friends and of writers I admired, and within limitations I was encouraged to do so. The poems of Robert Hillyer, John Crowe Ransom, Theodore Morrison, Morley Dobson, and William Whitman; a paper on hunting, "The Ibex and the Elephant," by Douglas Burden, and another fine pair, "Tiger, Tiger" and "Elephant," by his white hunter in Indo-China, a Frenchman, J. M. DeFosse; stories by Manuel Komroff, and essays from three Englishmen who impressed me at Cambridge, J. B. S. Haldane, H. M. Tomlinson, and Walter de la Mare.

As a book salesman in New York I had the chance to skim through some of the new volumes by our competitors, and one day at The Sunrise Turn, a personal bookshop uptown, I stood absorbed for forty minutes with a new book entitled *The Cabala* by an unknown named Thornton Wilder. Now I wrote to Mr. Wilder on *Atlantic* stationery telling him of my admiration for his first book and suggesting that if he had a new one in progress we might like to consider it for serialization. He replied that he was working on a novel about South America, was three-quarters finished, and that he would send me the carbon copy. So we were presented with a preview of *The Bridge of San Luis Rey*. It was beautifully episodic, and even without the ending — the bridge had not yet collapsed — it seemed to me clear that this would be a great attraction for new readers. My two superiors, however, thought otherwise and I was left to write a very difficult letter of rejection.

A first reader is no good unless he is outspoken, and I was not always tactful. The treasurer of the *Atlantic* was MacGregor Jenkins, a genial, loquacious gentleman with a streak of sentimentality a yard wide. His anecdotes ran on forever, and I found myself keeping away from his open office on the third floor, for once entrapped you had to listen. I had very little liking for his short bucolic essays, sometimes about Amherst, where he had spent his boyhood and seen Emily Dickinson over the back fence, sometimes about his barn and its inmates in Dover. It seemed to me that his cows and chickens had no place in the *Atlantic,* and I was too young to respect the generosity in the acceptance. Each time they presented themselves I denounced his manuscripts and two months later there they were in the new issue.

I chafed under such restraints but not for long; I was learning fast and I did not miss New York. To be a junior on the *Atlantic's* staff in those days was to be borne along on a powerful current. Sedgwick had a flair for social criticism, and he found those who could probe for him with authority, and deep. He found William Z. Ripley, the Harvard economist, who in three devastating articles, "Main Street to Wall Street," "Stop, Look and Listen," and "More Light and Power Too" (January,

September, and November 1926), laid bare the malpractices of high finance, the fabricated reports to the stockholders, the interlocking directorates, the scandal in public utilities which were lazily winked at in the boom. In this case Ripley's probing laid the groundwork for the S.E.C. Sedgwick persuaded a New York lawyer, Charles Marshall, to write an Open Letter to Governor Alfred E. Smith questioning whether the Governor's faith as a Roman Catholic disqualified him for the Presidency. The issue was hot and sensitive, especially in the South, and it is greatly to Sedgwick's credit that the Governor took the challenge seriously and published his historic reply in the *Atlantic's* columns. Again, it was Sedgwick who diverted away from the *New Republic* and into the *Atlantic* the 16,000-word investigation of the Sacco-Vanzetti trial in which Felix Frankfurter, then a professor at the Harvard Law School, proclaimed the innocence of the accused. These were just a few of his ten-strikes, and they explained why, after twenty years, the magazine was solidly in the black and no longer a "kept" journal as it had been at Houghton Mifflin. We were a small team who assisted a great editor, and there were three in particular who contributed mightily to this transformation: Donald B. Snyder, the assistant publisher who came aboard the year after I did; Teresa S. Fitzpatrick, who under the signature of "Christine Lowell" invited the subscribers; and Daisy Zanck, who was our entire manufacturing department and who handled the costly details of printing and paper and advertising make-up with incredible economy.

"Don't overedit," Mr. Sedgwick once wrote. "By so doing you will estrange your writers and rob the magazine of its indispensable variety." But the temptation to overedit is insidious.

One of our elderly proofreaders simply could not cope with profanity; left to herself she would have removed every word of it, and after one or two angry run-ins with young contributors we wisely shifted her to our textbooks. The genteel tradition of the *Atlantic* was what Henry L. Mencken had in mind when in the early edition of *The American Language* he wrote: "All the more pretentious American authors try to write chastely and elegantly; the typical literary product of the country is still a refined essay in the *Atlantic Monthly,* perhaps gently jocose but never rough — by Emerson, so to speak, out of Charles Lamb."

When Mencken took upon himself the editing of the *American Mercury,* I was surprised to learn that he was overediting in his way just as much as we were in ours. As a first step we always corrected the spelling and punctuation in accordance with "Atlantic usage," and our cutting and rewriting was the second step, depending on how much we thought the manuscript needed. In general our tendency was to lean down the material whereas Mencken fattened it. He had his pet glossary of adjectives and epithets, and these he imposed upon the text of his contributors: a professor was referred to as a "bunkum professor"; ministers were "high priests" and political commentators were "soothsayers"; for politicians "the Honorable" became a term of contempt; these and similar endearments were bestowed upon the other members of Mencken's "booboisie" even though it may never have occurred to the author to do so when he wrote his piece. I remember how surprised I was when I first saw a manuscript which had been accepted by the *Mercury* and then returned for the author's approval with such additions written in. If the *Atlantic* by its overediting achieved a genteel sameness, Mencken by his achieved a rowdy sameness. With his magnificent prejudices he himself was never at a loss for fresh satire — Billy Sunday, the revivalist, was "America's celebrated pulpit-clown." But when his habitual glossary was imposed upon his contributors they came to sound as if they were Mencken's younger brothers, and the magazine lost its difference.

For four years I read in that back office, and if my father's warning was accurate, my time in Boston was nearly at an end. Yet when the summons came I was not ready for it. I sat across from Mr. Sedgwick on that rectangular Italian chair on which so many contributors had squirmed with discomfort before me; I looked out at the Public Garden thinking "Here falls the ax" — but that was not exactly what he was saying. He was saying something about making a permanent place for myself in the organization, editing the *Atlantic* books which grew out of the magazine. He was saying that a contract had been drawn with Little, Brown & Company, who would manufacture and distribute our books, and that as the Director of the Press I should deal directly with Alfred McIntyre, their President, and Roger Scaife, who handled their manufacturing. I was to be on my own . . . I said I wanted to think it over.

I had seen Dick Simon regularly ever since that day in 1925 when he came to Boston to sell the first Simon & Schuster list. He used to dine with us in our apartment, and I remember his taking out of his suitcase the dummy copies of the first crossword puzzle book, and of a larger volume by a writer called Will Durant. "You remember him," said Dick. "He used to write the introductions for the Haldeman-Julius ten-cent books. He's cut down all their philosophers for them. Quite a man!" That, of course, was the beginning of *The Story of Philosophy*. With Dick I had talked over the possibilities of coming back to

New York, but on the other hand, if I stayed on here in Boston, I would be my own boss, with my own list of authors to build up, and a staff consisting of one secretary, the loyal Frances Bates. Sure to be fun and it might pay off. I decided to stay.

It was a hurtful shock to me that we lost our most profitable author, James Truslow Adams, within months of my taking over the Atlantic Monthly Press. It could not have come at a crueler moment, for Mr. Adams's most popular book, *The Epic of America,* was at the top of the best-seller list when without a word of warning he decided to transfer his future writing to Scribner's. The reasons were human enough — and none of us had anticipated them. As an undergraduate at Yale, Mr. Adams had majored in history, and on his graduation he had confided to his favorite professor that he wanted to write, and as a first step should he take his Ph.D.? No, said the professor, not if you want to write history; go down to Wall Street, save just as much money as you can for fifteen years, and then if you still want to write get out on your own. Adams did just that, and fifteen years later he retired from the market with a competence which enabled him — as a bachelor — to research and to write about colonial America. The *Atlantic* published his essays in the magazine and it also published the early books, *The Founding of New England* and *Revolutionary New England,* which established his reputation as a historian. Mr. Sedgwick had given him the idea for his *The Epic of America,* and it seemed to me rank injustice that he should quit us in the high tide of his success. What had made the difference was his marriage. When Adams married in midlife, he wanted to be assured of steady royalties — his savings were no longer enough; and when Scribner's approached him with an editing and writing contract which offered him and his wife security for years, he took it without question. I felt he should have divided his books between the two houses, but I knew that we had been remiss in not gauging his concern for the future. I did not recognize it as such at the time, but this was my first lesson in underediting.

A second instance of underediting occurred in the following year and this had to do with a dear friend of mine, Walter D. Edmonds, of whose work I was intensely proud. Walt Edmonds in college was one of the most clearly developed young writers I have ever known. He spent the summers at Boonville, close to the Erie Canal country; he had sold his first short story about the Canal to Scribner's shortly after graduation, and the plans for his first novel, *Rome Haul,* were already in part on paper. Mr. Sedgwick had persuaded him to send his work to us, and in time we were to print all of his historical novels: *Rome Haul, Erie Water, Drums Along the Mohawk, The Big Barn, Young Ames,* and last but not least that superb collection of his short stories, *Mostly Canallers.* It had never occurred to us that these short stories which had been written for an adult audience could with a very few adjustments be converted into delightful illustrated books for children. When Dodd, Mead and Company invited Walt to turn one of his stories into a juvenile he politely declined and referred the suggestion to us. Alfred and I showed no enthusiasm — we felt it would distract him from his novels.

A year later Dodd, Mead renewed the offer and this time Walter accepted with the result that today they have nine of his books under their imprint, and young readers the country over have relished them. This again was a costly instance of under-editing.

These two errors of omission coming so early in my experience as an editor of books made me realize, dimly at first but with increasing clarity, that the editor's relations with his author can never be the same year in year out. They must be resilient and subject to the swiftest change. At the outset the editor, the publisher, has the authority and the young author coming to him is eager for every bit of advice, every bit of editing, every bit of support that can be given. But the moment that author has become established this relationship is altered. Now it is the author who has the authority and in many cases he no longer needs or wants the advice which had earlier meant so much. Thomas Wolfe, who accepted so eagerly all the editing which Maxwell Perkins devoted to *Look Homeward, Angel,* no longer had need for such close attention when he was writing *Of Time and the River.* Now it was Thomas Wolfe who had the authority, and this I suspect was something which Max Perkins overlooked.

Sinclair Lewis, who revered Alfred Harcourt as a publisher and loved him as a friend, wrote his best novels for Harcourt Brace and was eager to invest his small savings in that firm at its inception. But after *Elmer Gantry* and *Dodsworth,* somehow the old familiarity induced a complacency toward the new book that Lewis resented. The advertising wasn't enough, so the letters say, and by inference neither was the solicitude. Alfred Harcourt had been guilty of underestimating the perpetually new needs of a writer. He had been guilty of underediting.

In the years of editing that lay ahead of me I was to realize that whether I was editing books or the magazine, my relationships with every writer who was dear to us had constantly to be redefined. What is true of friendship is true of editing: the understanding must be continually refreshed. Over the years I have edited 317 different volumes for the *Atlantic,* and

I hope there are more to come. Each has presented its individual problem, as these next chapters will show, and in each I have tried to remember that it was my job to help when the author needed it, to reassure him, to call out of him his best, but always to bear in mind that the final decision was his.

11
Friends and Authors

Charles Nordhoff and
James Norman Hall

I WAS nineteen when I went to Paris on my first leave in the autumn of 1917, and to me the French aviators with their Croix de Guerres with palms, one palm for each German plane destroyed, were much more glamorous than any cocotte. I had been in the army long enough to realize that those bronze palms meant an Army Citation, the highest. Lieutenant George Guynemer, the French ace who had shot down fifty-three Germans, I had seen face to face at the front that August, just a month before his death, his extraordinary pallor — for he was tubercular — accentuated by his jet-black uniform with its breast of decorations; now in Paris, lunching on the Boulevard des Italiens, I found myself seated at the table next to Nungesser, France's second ace, in his sky-blue tunic and swank trousers of the same hue, with the bright scarlet stripe. The French had tolerance in such things: any pursuit pilot good enough to be an ace could choose his own uniform.

We who were in the ambulance service knew that we were in a minor league, and after six months at the front the natural impulse was to try for a transfer to the Lafayette Flying Corps, which was originally a single French squadron of American aviators who had scored against Baron von Richthofen's Circus and whose Indian-head insignia, painted on the planes, was made famous by the exploits of Raoul Lufbery, Norman Prince, Bill Thaw, James McConnell, Conrad Chapman, and Harold Willis. It was Willis who, after he had been shot down and captured by the Germans, made repeated attempts to escape from prison camp; on his third try he was one of thirteen who broke clear. Ten were recaptured, two of them wounded, but Willis was one of the survivors who reached the border; he swam the Rhine and knocked at a Swiss farmhouse at 3 A.M., stark naked but for the bacon grease which protected him from the chill of the water.

Such men were our heroes, and in these post-Hiroshima days their idealism and their air duels seem as far distant as if they had been members of Jeb Stuart's cavalry.

My application for a transfer was turned down, but in the years after the war I was to know two of these pilots with intimacy and affection: Charles Nordhoff and James Norman Hall. Nordhoff, from Lower California, Harvard Class of 1910, was an erect six-footer, blond with blue eyes, very diffident and a lone wolf until he met Jim Hall. Hall, a farmer's boy from Colfax, Iowa, and a graduate of Grinnell, was slender and dark with a homespun simplicity, altogether one of the most modest and gentle men I shall ever know. His hair was black and close-cropped; his nose, a long aquiline beak, had a noticeable break to it, the result of being smashed against the control board when his Spad made a forced landing into some trees behind the German lines. The two men came to know each other in Paris after the Armistice. Their initial meeting was not a success, but the ice thawed when they were assigned to write the official history of the Lafayette Flying Corps. So began their inseparable friendship and what is surely the most remarkable collaboration in American literature.

Charles Nordhoff and James Norman Hall

Those days in Paris in the spring of 1919 were to set the pattern. Nordhoff was the gourmet and he introduced Jim to grilled kidneys and escalloped brains, steamed snails and frogs' legs. Over the wine they planned their future: neither was content at the thought of returning to his former activities — Nordhoff to the lonely ranch in Lower California, Hall to the blend of settlement work and free-lancing which had barely supported him in Boston. Nordhoff came of adventurous blood: his grandfather for whom he had been named was a contemporary of Herman Melville's and had served on warships and whalers in the Pacific. The old man had written books, so had his father, and that was what they, too, proposed to do. Where could they live on next to nothing and write as they pleased? Bermuda was a possibility, for both of them hankered for island life, but Bermuda was dismissed when their thoughts turned to the South Seas.

"Why shouldn't we go as soon as we are demobilized?" Nordhoff said. "We'll both be at loose ends. We're not married and have no jobs to return to." This was their dream as they brought to completion their two-volume history in Paris.

Hall from the outset was the more experienced writer and the more poetic. He had been on a bicycle trip in the British Isles the summer of 1914 when war was declared, and romanticist that he was he promptly enlisted in the British army, faking his credentials as a Canadian. He was trained as a machine gunner, came unscathed through the hard fighting of 1915, and when the British, who finally discovered his origin, sent him home with an honorable discharge a year later, Jim wrote his first war book, *Kitchener's Mob,* which appeared chapter by chapter in the *Atlantic;* so did his second, the chronicle of his later experiences as a volunteer in the Lafayette

Escadrille, which was published under the title *High Adventure*. It was on the strength of these two books that the young veterans were given the modest advance of $1000 by Harper and Brothers which paid their way to Tahiti in February 1920.

At the Aina Paré or "Paré's Retreat," an old, ramshackle hotel overlooking the lagoon, they rented two rooms opening on the upstairs veranda with brass bedsteads, china crockery, mosquito nets, and a tin bucket for slops. This was their living quarters, and their workroom for years. The place was riddled with termites, but it was the view that claimed them, the view from the veranda giving out to the open sea with the mountains of Moorea in the distance. Stevenson said that one's first tropical landfall touches a virginity of sense. "There is a magic about these islands," wrote Hall, "that is time-defying; that loses nothing of its power however long-contained one's association with them may be. Landfalls or departures, by day or by night, each one seems to be the first and most memorable." This magic, which informed every book they wrote about Tahiti, made its fresh impress in their first, *Faery Lands of the South Seas;* they finished the book for Harper's in ten months and it was as agreeable to write as it is to read. The essay form was always congenial to Hall though less so to Nordhoff, who preferred narration; the chapters grew unpretentiously out of their experience and assimilation as they came to understand the language and character of the place.

Nordhoff's blondness and austerity endowed him with an almost godlike attraction for the daughters of Papeete and it was in the cards that he would be the first to marry. He fell in love with a very beautiful Polynesian, the daughter of a chief, and their marriage in 1921, which was opposed by his family and about which he was at once proud and sensitive, temporarily broke up the teamwork. When Nordy established his new home some distance from Papeete, Jim was left for a time on his own.

Hall as a bachelor, and up until his marriage to Sarah Winchester in 1925, was subject to occasional bouts of self-doubt and loneliness. His tether to Iowa was so much stronger than he had anticipated; his loyalty to Grinnell and particularly to Professor Payne, his mentor on the faculty, called him back; so did his memory of the New Hampshire hills in the autumn and Walden Pond, where, when he was working in the Boston slums for the Society for the Prevention of Cruelty to Children, he would go for solitary refreshment. Nor did Jim's short stories and verse bring him the wider readership he needed. He had always yearned to be a poet and from boyhood he had written reams of verse; at its best it held a nineteenth-century charm and sincerity but rarely that fine edge of distinction which he brought to his short stories like "The Forgotten One" and his essays — and of the latter he sold only enough to pay the more pressing of his debts. Hall's love of people saved him from depression and on the island these were his dependables: Chin Foo, the Chinese moneylender who helped him when he was "stony"; Harrison W. Smith, a graduate of the Massachusetts Institute of Technology, long resident in Tahiti, with whom he talked books endlessly, particularly those of his great models, Conrad, Lafcadio Hearn, and Wordsworth; Robert Dean Frisbie, a young American beachcomber whom Jim bailed out of trouble and encouraged to write; and Captain Viggo Rasmussen, on whose trading schooner Hall could always find a berth. These, his letters from home, and always Nordy, gave him buoyancy.

A voyage to Iceland — the opposite end of the earth — did

not pull him out of his rut or provide the source material for the book he hoped would defray the cost of the trip, and after his marriage Hall was really hard-pressed. He must have been very grateful when in 1927 Nordhoff proposed that they join forces again, this time to write a novel about the Lafayette Escadrille. Nordy had already tested his wings in two books for boys, *The Pearl Lagoon,* based on his own early life in Lower California, and *The Derelict,* both of which had sold quite well under the Atlantic imprint; his hero, Charles Selden, had grown old enough for the war, and what was more natural than that he should be a pursuit pilot in their old squadron, embodying the adventures — Hall's combats and nearly fatal crash in the trees, Hal Willis's famous escape — which they knew to the last detail?

This was their first venture in fiction; the chapters were evenly divided between them and were written apart — I can still see the typing, Nordy's a rusty brown, Hall's a newer ribbon and black — and then tested and revised in the Aina Paré workroom. They adopted a style which had many points in common; they were equally fluent in the war idiom and dialogue; Hall did the better description, Nordhoff the faster action. Editorially my most constant problem was in the opening paragraphs of each chapter; since they were writing apart they invariably spent too much time reidentifying the characters before they embarked on the new episode. This was best cured by cutting and by tying the transitions together, which I did in Boston. When *Falcons of France* was submitted, they asked that their chapters be separately initialed in the table of contents, and this I overruled since it broke apart the very unity they were after. In this book for the first time they succeeded in fusing their creative abilities and I did not want any reviewer drawing invidious comparisons as he might have done had the chapters been initialed. They were coming to realize how much each supplemented the other: Hall's self-distrust evaporated in the face of Nordy's confidence, his tough realism and his forward drive, and when Nordhoff was tempted to push the narrative too fast, Hall would intervene to give something of the horizon view, the elevation of the spirit which is also part of the pilot's experience.

Falcons of France was serialized in *Liberty,* for which each of the team received $5000. Hall's share was gone in six months. He had been troubled about the health of their only son, Conrad Lafcadio Teheiuri Hall, and when in 1930 he and Sarah brought the ten-year-old boy to the Mayo Clinic it was to discover that he had contracted amebic dysentery; the cure would be long-drawn-out and there was the strong likelihood that the boy after his recovery would not be able to resume year-round residence in Tahiti.

With this sadness in his heart and knowing that Sarah's second child was on the way, Jim went East to New York to see if he could sell the play, *The Empty Chair,* which he and Nordhoff had devised about the Falcon's aviators. The play-readers liked it, but the producers were unwilling to gamble on any more war material. Then a friend, James Curtis, said he would back it. Hall's decision, expressed in a letter to Mr. Sedgwick, is characteristic:

The public appetite for war plays seemed to me jaded, and much as I should like to see our play put on, I could not bring myself to accept Jim Curtis's generous offer to back it. I felt that he would not have an even break for his money, so I talked him out of the business. I had a hard time persuading him to withdraw. It was really an amusing situation: there was he more than willing to go ahead, and actually urging me to let him do it; and there was I talking against my own interests! The worst of it was that I was by no means persuaded that the play would not succeed. Perhaps it would have made a real "hit." But my reasoned judgment said "No," and I am glad that I remained firm in my decision. If the play had been put on and had failed, Curtis would have stood to lose $15,000 or $20,000, and although he assured me that he could easily afford to lose that amount, I would have felt very badly had he done so, and so, I am sure, would Nordy.

This prompting to resist the gamble of Broadway at a time when he was broke, and when I was shopping out his short sketches to the *Boston Globe* and the *Christian Science Monitor* at $12.50 apiece, is Jim to the bone.

Falcons as a book, in its gay French jacket painted by Julian Peabody, was slowly attracting attention. A second printing, then a third, were sold out, and on Jim's return to the islands we urged that the collaboration be continued. Not a boys' book this time but a mature novel — and surely the theme was to be found out there in the Pacific. The answer came from Hall's library. In 1916 when he was an aviation cadet at Buc, he had picked up in a Paris bookstall Sir John Barrow's factual account, published in 1831, of the *Bounty* mutiny, the most famous rebellion in the British navy. Barrow had written it down as the Secretary of the Admiralty and when one day Hall quoted from him, Nordhoff caught fire. The scene is described in Hall's autobiography, *My Island Home:*

I saw in my friend's eyes a Nordhoffian glow and sparkle which meant that his interest was being aroused. "By the Lord, Hall!" he said. "Maybe we've got something there! I wish we could get hold of a copy of Barrow's book."

"I have it," I replied. "I bought it in Paris during the war."

The result was that Nordhoff took the book home to read and the next day he was back, and he was in what I can only call a "dither" of excitement. "Hall, what a story! What a story!" he said, as he walked up and down my veranda.

"It's three stories," I replied. "First, the tale of the mutiny; then Bligh's open-boat voyage, and the third, the adventures of Fletcher Christian and the mutineers who went with him to Pitcairn Island, together with the Tahitian men and women who accompanied them. It's a natural for historical fiction. Who could, possibly, invent a better story? And it has the merit of being true."

"You're right, it *is* a natural," said Nordhoff, "but . . ." he shook his head, glumly. "It must have been written long since. It's incredible that such a tale should have been waiting a century and a half for someone to see its possibilities."

Jim was right: not Melville nor Stevenson nor Conrad had ever applied himself to this long-vibrant theme.

Their first task was to project themselves into the British Navy at the time of Nelson, and this they did with the help of Mr. Sedgwick and by assimilating the mass of eighteenth-century literature which at his direction was shipped out to them from London. Charts and the deck plan of the *Bounty* were tacked on the wall of their workroom; Lieutenant-Commander J. A. B. Percy, R.N., who had been helping with the detective work, went on to build an exquisite and accurate model of the *Bounty* which we purchased for them. The *Bounty* was an armed transport of 200 tons, which had been fitted out for the purpose of transporting a cargo of young breadfruit trees from the South Seas to the West Indies; the stern quarters were converted into a greenhouse, the living quarters for officers and men were more than usually cramped, a circumstance doubtless contributing to the tension aboard ship. Nordhoff and

Hall read all the contemporary accounts of Captain Bligh, and they studied the log of his 3600-mile voyage in the open cutter in which he and the men loyal to him were set adrift; they read of the court-martial and of the confessions of the recaptured mutineers which were sent to them in photostats from the Admiralty; they read and were shocked — Hall in particular — by the brutal discipline, enforced by the lash, which then prevailed in the Royal Navy. Imperceptibly this absorption of the lucid, ordered prose of eighteenth-century England, falling on the inner ear, formed their style for the new book.

Nordhoff began; he was to carry the tale through the outward voyage; he would draw the portraits of Captain Bligh with his harsh temper and of Fletcher Christian, the second in command who repeatedly tried to intercede for the men. All this would be told through the eyes of young Midshipman Byam. Nordhoff would give the impressions of the seamen as they entered upon the almost untouched beauty of Polynesia, and of the love affairs which bound both Christian and Byam to the island. This, of course, he was perfectly qualified to do, for through his wife and his father-in-law Nordy had come to acquire a word-of-mouth knowledge of Polynesia before the white occupation.

Hall took up the story at the outbreak of the mutiny, early on the homeward voyage. He was responsible for the mutineers' return to Tahiti and the secession when they began to quarrel among themselves under Christian's leadership; he would describe the arrival of the *Pandora,* the ship which was sent from London to capture the mutineers; he would tell of its shipwreck and of the eventual court-martial of the survivors, the execution and the ending.

But as the book came to be written these boundaries tended

to disappear. In the Aina Paré, they read aloud the chapters to each other, and there were frequent interruptions. Jim kept pausing to describe and to wonder; Nordhoff would grow impatient to keep the narrative moving, and it was inevitable that they should work in and out of each other's pages as their spirits prompted.

Thus in the chapter where Byam surprises Tehani at the pool, it was Nordy who went too fast, and Hall interposed. It was not enough that Byam should see her in her loveliness; they must swim together, and there must be provocation before the surrender. The scene could not be taken swiftly, and in the end it was Hall who wrote it in three times the space of Nordy's original scene.

This process of interruption and expansion reveals the complete confidence they had in each other, and it also explains why it was so difficult for either of them to initial — even for my personal copy — those chapters for which Hall was finally responsible in the *Bounty Trilogy*. It is enough to say that their contributions to these three books and to *The Hurricane*, the novel which followed, were in equal strength.

When the manuscript of *Mutiny on the Bounty* reached Boston in the early spring of 1932, it did not take us long to realize that we had a book of exceptional beauty and one which drew a striking contrast between the golden age of Polynesia and the tough brutality of man to man which existed aboard Bligh's ship. It was a big novel, and perhaps its length was responsible for Horace Lorimer's decision not to serialize it in the *Saturday Evening Post*. But our confidence in the book was sustained by the judges of the Book-of-the-Month Club who chose it for their October selection, and when this was announced, the bidding began in Hollywood. Paramount seemed keenly interested but backed away when they estimated the production costs if the shooting was to be done in the South Seas as the authors insisted. Fox Films continued to bid, and as I reread today the messages which passed between Brandt & Brandt, who were acting as the authors' agents, and our office, I am amazed at the figures even though this was at the very bottom of the depression. Fox bought the book with a down payment of $1000 against a final selling price of $12,500. What a figure for a film in which Charles Laughton as Captain Bligh was to play the finest part in his career, and in which Clark Gable as Mr. Christian and Joan Crawford as Tehani made new reputations! These negotiations which I relayed to Papeete by cable left the boys, as Hall said, "dazed," but they recovered promptly enough to ask that we wire some of their new royalties to put their good Chinese friend and banker back on his feet again.

Insecurity was not new to them; the depression did not deflect their interest in the eighteenth-century mutineers. With hardly a day's pause they went to work on the sequel of what happened to the mutineers *after* they had set Captain Bligh, and the eighteen men who remained loyal to him, adrift in the open boat. The mutineers were still in possession of the *Bounty* and still under the nominal command of Fletcher Christian, the acting lieutenant who had led the uprising. The rebels soon began quarreling among themselves. The more indolent remained in Tahiti, where, in time, they were tracked down by H.M.S. *Pandora* and taken back to London to be tried for their lives. But the more audacious Mr. Christian, with eight of the crew and eighteen Polynesians (twelve women and six men) sailed away in the *Bounty* in September of 1789 for an unknown destination. The *Pandora* could not find them and no word came; for eighteen years they were given up for lost. Then in February 1808 an American sealing vessel, *Topaz,* in need of water sent the longboat ashore to an uncharted, supposedly uninhabited rocky-tooth, and there on the plateau of Pitcairn Island they discovered the remnants of Christian's colony, a colony of many women and English-speaking children presided over by the last living survivor of the mutiny, Alexander Smith. So much for history.

What had happened on Pitcairn was a bloody race riot, and the team had a hard time in bringing it into focus. When the mutineers had deposited their stores, their livestock, guns and ammunition on the uplands of Pitcairn, they destroyed the *Bounty* and locked themselves in. But there was a natural antagonism between the whites and those they called "Indians" and even more between the men who had wives and those who wanted them, and when this was exacerbated by a virulent homebrew made from ti roots, there could be only one result. In the ensuing riot every man fought for his life, and only one, who had been wounded and hidden by the women, survived. Nordhoff and Hall had planned to tell the story in the third person by omniscience, but as murder followed murder the narrative became too sanguinary and repetitive. When they had finished 65,000 words Nordhoff threw up the sponge.

"You will receive the first thirteen chapters of Pitcairn Island, by this mail," he wrote on May 22nd. "Hall and I agree that it is no good, though we differ strongly as to why. If you could tell us precisely what is wrong with the story, and why, one or the other of our opinions would be confirmed and we should be able to go on with it immediately having agreed to abide by your word. Please go into all the detail you have time for, as this is damned important to us."

When I read the fragment I had to agree. It was much too full of bloodshed for either interest or sympathy. Walking to the office one morning soon after, I had a clue. I had been thinking of the American ship *Topaz,* and of what a surprise it must have been to the boatswain when with his crew he toiled up the path to the plateau, there to be greeted by that incredible colony. There must have been a feast, and while they were eating and afterward the white-bearded patriarch, Alex Smith, would surely have told the American sailors how they got there and of the fighting which almost wiped them out. He would have told only as much of the final tragedy as he could have seen before he was wounded, rolled up in the matting, and hidden by the women, and his telling of it would have been softened by time and by loyalty. If the boys related the story through his eyes it would hold warmth and a certain pathos.

I outlined all this in my next letter to Tahiti, and the suggestion broke the log jam and they began to rewrite; but that Nordhoff still had his misgivings he expressed to me in his letter of September 10, 1933:

. . . The 65,000 words we have done will have to be scrapped — not a sentence or a paragraph can be used. Yet even now, I am far from convinced, as is Hall, that Smith can tell the story as it should be told. I believe old Shakespeare himself would have had to reflect for a moment or two before sitting down to dash it off. It *should* be told, I think, in a robust, bloody, and slightly pornographic Elizabethan fashion, but the meat would be too strong for the women who seem to buy about 80% of all novels. To romanticize it and tone it down as we tried to do, goes against the grain — mine anyhow. It is not a story of ladies and gentlemen, but of waterfront wenches and coarse red-blooded seafaring men, who loved carnally,

Charles Nordhoff and James Norman Hall

hated lustily, and murdered one another in the cheerful manner of the renaissance. Infidelities, poisoning and raw severed heads were humdrum to them. Well, all we can do is our best.

Meantime, in the two months while they were waiting in despair over Pitcairn, they had been impelled to write a short book, a clear, cool little gem, the story of the hazardous trip in the open boat which brought out the best of Bligh's leadership as the cruise of the *Bounty* had brought out the worst. He had piloted the outcasts 3600 miles to safety, a feat of hardihood and navigation for which, like Lindbergh, he was proclaimed throughout Europe. Here the boys had only his log to work with — supplemented, of course, by their knowledge of the islands through which he had threaded his way; and it was a work of imagination to describe the enormous fortitude and the near-death which was endured in that frail boat, twenty-three feet long, with a beam of six feet nine inches and its human cargo of nineteen thirsting men. They wisely told the story through the eyes and apprehension of the acting surgeon of the *Bounty,* Thomas Ledward, who by training would be best calculated to notice every change in the behavior and psychology of the suffering seamen.

For Pitcairn, as I had done earlier with each of the other books, I sent out to the authors seven or eight pages of typewritten reading notes and suggested corrections which they would annotate, accepting or rejecting as they saw fit. My notes ran like this — and I am picking at random:

CHAPTER 3
Page 3   Christian's remarks to Ned should be low-voiced and for his ears alone. Insert "quietly" after "he said."

Friends and Authors

CHAPTER 6

Page 4   I am reminded that McCoy's speech in Chapter 3 was not marked by such a heavy brogue as is here present. I like his accent but it should be consistent throughout.

CHAPTER 10

Page 11   I doubt if Prudence would actually load the musket until she was sure Williams was asleep.

CHAPTER 11

I question whether the résumé which begins this chapter affords the proper sequence to the poisoning just witnessed. The time element seems to deprive the crime of the immediacy it should have.

CHAPTER 12

Page 16   Wouldn't Martin shout and wouldn't his shouts be overheard? Why this long walk before dispatching him?

CHAPTER 15

Page 9   "Neatly and modestly clad" sounds a little like a missionary report. I prefer something more vivid.

CHAPTER 19

Page 3   You forgot that Smith is actually *telling* what happened. He'd be much more terse. And his own actions *must* not be so disgraceful. Condense and rewrite if necessary.

Page 6   How much of this drinking is based on fact, how much on fiction?

There was no air mail to Tahiti in those days, so I had to wait two months for their corrections which came back in bulk, and in one envelope from Hall was this note which I cannot quote with any attempt at modesty:

Charles Nordhoff and James Norman Hall

. . . I believe that you were born to be a publisher. You must,
somehow, have sucked in printer's ink before you had a tooth in
your head. What amazes me, in a man who has such an appalling
number of typewritten pages to read, is your gift — your genius I
had better say — for taking such pains in reading. No smallest slip
on the part of an author escapes you. In considering the larger
aspects, you are able to keep details in clear focus behind them, and
busy as your mind, and hands, must be, you find time to put an unerring finger on weak or shoddy spots in a manuscript however beautifully glossed over they may be. I doubt whether many publishers
have this dual gift, so valuable to the writers whose work passes
through your hands.

The *Bounty Trilogy* is as alive today as when they wrote it.
I put it in the very front rank of American historical fiction,
and so I think will readers to come. The financial returns were
solid but not spectacular. Hall's half, as much as he could
spare, went into a Boston trust fund; Nordhoff used his to acquire real estate in Tahiti, but it speaks for the longevity of the
books that the *Trilogy,* with illustrations by N. C. Wyeth, has
earned as much for the authors' families since their deaths as
it did while they were alive.

The team next devoted themselves to *The Hurricane,* a book
for which I have a particular fondness since it was dedicated
to me. Here again the writing was equally divided between
them, and here again there was a magnificent film for which
they were fairly paid. This was the last book they were to do on
their high plateau. Teamwork as sensitive and as difficult as
this cannot be sustained indefinitely, and I think Nordy would
wish me to say that in their collaboration after *The Hurricane*
he deferred more and more of the work to Hall. Jim never
mentioned this to me, but I could tell from our correspondence

that it was so. Nordy's marriage was going on the rocks. He was harassed with grief and at this point the drive had to be Hall's.

Young Conrad Hall was in school in California, and his presence there was an incentive which brought Jim back more frequently. He would turn up in that wide-brim, cream-colored Texas hat which some friend had given him and a small overnight suitcase holding the barest necessities, and yet always among them gifts for his friends in Boston. Guava jelly which Sarah had made for my wife and pink pearls for my daughter Sara. He constantly made plans for one last plane trip around the world, and he once got as far as Boston on the outward leg, but his tether worked both ways, for a long-distance telephone call to Sarah and his daughter Nancy reduced him to tears and he canceled the flight.

No Pulitzer Prize was ever awarded to Nordhoff and Hall, and for twelve of their twenty years of writing together they were unrecognized and in debt. Jim carried the load almost alone at the end, and he was doing his own books too: his book of seafaring fantasies, *Doctor Dogbody's Leg;* his novel *Lost Island,* which had its origin in Nordy's long siege of sea blindness incurred when he was fishing with his father-in-law at sunrise; and the *Tale of Mowie,* the legendary romance of how the islands were settled by adventurers from the mainland of Asia.

Nordhoff died in Santa Barbara in 1947 and Jim wrote:

"Now that Nordy is dead, I write in a vacuum, so to speak. There is, actually, no one here to whom I can appeal for criticism and advice, and as I read over my stuff I often get deeply discouraged and disheartened. I wish that you might have time to give me some criticism in detail." And he urged me again to visit him in Papeete as they both had with such tempting invitations in 1934.

In 1950 he came home for his Fortieth reunion at Grinnell, and the college delighted and embarrassed him by making him a Doctor of Letters. He had been troubled by a rather painful numbness in his left leg during the long flight, and when he came on to Boston he had a foreboding checkup at the Massachusetts General Hospital. He was warned that it was arteriosclerosis and that trouble was ahead and his one thought was to get back to Sarah. He said little about it to any of us at the time, and the bright spot of that visit — for me — was a luncheon for him at the Tavern Club attended by some of his old friends in aviation: Harold Willis, Charlie Codman, Paul Rockwell, and myself. The talk went back to the Lafayette Escadrille and to those gay spirits who had made it the unique squadron that it was. And I remember Hal Willis at a pause in the conversation leaning across the table and saying with that shy bark of his, "Jim, there was one thing about you which we all felt at the time, though I doubt if anyone bothered to say it. You were the greatest Christian of us all."

Mazo de la Roche

PRIZE contests were a novelty when in 1926 we made our plans for a semiannual competition in fiction. The Atlantic Award was set at $10,000, which was big money for those days (with a purchasing power of twice what it is today), and we made it a condition of the award that the prize-winning novel should also lend itself for serialization in the *Atlantic*. February 1, 1927, was the closing date, and it was our guess that upwards of 500 book-length manuscripts would be submitted, a guess which seemed confirmed in the early stages by the inauspicious number of thumb-worn travelers, Westerns, honeysuckle romances of the Confederacy, stories of rumrunners, and battle scenes of the First World War which straggled into the office bearing every evidence of having been repeatedly rejected. But shortly after New Year's Day the heavens opened, and we were suddenly swamped by a deluge of fresh manuscripts. They came in all sizes, some of more than 1500 pages, some handsomely bound and insured, and some — the most difficult to cope with — came in installments, the author struggling desperately to get at least four-fifths of the narrative into our door before the deadline. The total count was 1117 (one contestant, I remember, submitted six), and when unwrapped, recorded and stacked on trestle tables in our largest storeroom, they looked like reading for a lifetime.

Theodore Morrison, now himself a novelist and a member

of the English Department at Harvard, and I were the first readers, and it was obvious that we should have to have outside help. We recruited our wives, both of Bryn Mawr; they were known as "the Harem"; were paid, if I remember rightly, a dollar an hour, and they did their reading right there in the storage room. I also asked the head of the Boston Public Library to designate one of their reliable readers to whom we might send 200 to 300. At the outset our objective was to weed out the incompetent and we aimed to return 80 a day. The manuscripts to be declined were marked with a big "D" on the yellow report sheet and beside it, briefly, the reasons for the rejection. Manuscripts about which the reader had doubts with a minimum of hope were marked "D reread," with a fuller report, and those which recommended themselves as semifinalists for the award were reported on at length and placed on a separate table where eventually they would be read by all of us.

Of the first hundred manuscripts which we shipped to the librarian, not one, in her opinion, rated better than a plain "D." This seemed to me either bad luck or poor judgment, and I decided to check her reading. The first eight which I picked out at random were certainly duds; the ninth I noticed, as I picked it up, had at least been typed by a professional. The reader's comment said: "This is the story of a large love-making family in Canada, dominated by the old grandmother. The brothers have unseemly affairs with their sisters-in-law, and there is quite a lot about the stable, including the odor. Not recommended." I glanced at the title page, which was certainly uncommon:

JALNA
by
Mazo de la Roche

And I began to read. Three hours later I was still reading.

Now that I have served as a judge in more than a score of prize contests, I know that when a winner emerges it is rather like a quarter-miler breaking clear in the home stretch. Such was the case with *Jalna*. (The librarian, incidentally, we paid for her unimaginative thoroughness, but discouraged from further endeavor.) *Jalna* was the book to beat, the contestant against which all others were measured.

Jalna was indeed the saga of a passionate Canadian clan, dwelling and feuding on the shore of Lake Ontario, a family protective in their loyalty and downright in what they disliked. The grandmother, old Adeline, who ruled over them and who was ninety-nine when the book began, was indomitable and seemingly indestructible. She seized the imagination the moment she appeared on the page, and it was her gusto, her will and her pride which gave the book so much of its animation. Morrison and I were captivated by the story, as were our associates, and we passed it on with enthusiastic reports to the other judges, Mr. Sedgwick, and Alfred McIntyre and Herbert Jenkins of Little, Brown. In the course of the next two months the field was narrowed down to twelve manuscripts, and then to the six finalists, every one of which we were to publish. *Jalna* was the unanimous choice for the prize, and *Red Rust* by Cornelia J. Cannon was the runner-up.

In May I went to Toronto to represent the *Atlantic* at the banquet in honor of Miss de la Roche. The check had already been deposited to her account, but I carried with me a blank check in a sealed envelope for theatrical effect and the congratulatory speech which I had prepared in Boston. Miss de la Roche had invited me to tea, and I remember thinking that the apartment was rather small, perhaps because of the few large heirlooms which gave luster to the room, chief of them the oil painting of her great-grandmother which had been brought from Ireland in a sailing ship. Mazo's Scottie regarded me dourly (she was later to be the heroine of a most endearing dog book) and I was given a warmer welcome by Mazo's cousin Caroline Clement, a delicate little blonde with Watteau coloring. Mazo de la Roche herself was tall and slender, aquiline, with dark eyes and soft auburn hair. I had the impression that here was a person of remarkable, wiry strength.

This, the first of my many friendly visits to Toronto, was a leisurely one, and I am everlastingly thankful to the late Hugh Eayrs, then the head of Macmillan in Canada, for drawing me so agreeably into the circle of Mazo's friends. Hugh was her publisher and literary adviser. She trusted him absolutely, and it was he who counseled her to submit the book in the *Atlantic* contest when the American branch of Macmillan failed to show the enthusiasm which he felt the novel deserved. Hugh told me of the relationship between Caroline and Mazo, of how they were cousins who had been brought up as sisters — living inseparably in the same household and, for much of the time, in a world of imagination created by Mazo. In the family drawing room the young girls would often act out the plays which Mazo had written. Their kinship, which has been vividly described by Miss de la Roche in her autobiography, *Against the Wind,* had its roots in the Ontario lake shore, in their love for horses and dogs and for their spicy, sometimes eccentric family circle of aunts and uncles. Mazo's father was of French and Irish descent, generous, impulsive but not successful, and when he died, the fruit farm, the last of his ventures, had to be sold, and the two girls with Mazo's mother returned to Toronto, where Caroline entered the civil service.

Then later as our friendship deepened, I came to understand how indispensable was the partnership of these two. Actually it took twelve years for Mazo to establish herself; during that period of trial and disappointment she published a volume of short stories, another of one-act plays and her two early novels, *Possession* in which we see her father, and *Delight.* In the evening Caroline read aloud what Mazo had written that day, talked it over with her, and made constructive remarks. She was a perceptive reader and her appraisal has sustained every book in its progress.

Before I left Boston I had inquired of our head proofreader, Caroline Church, who had been copy-editing the manuscript for the magazine, whether there were any points about *Jalna* which she wished me to discuss with the author. Churchie had a nice regard for the decencies of life. She thought for a moment and then she said, "Mr. Weeks, you know I've been troubled about the size of that house, Jalna. For the life of me I don't see how they could all fit into it, especially when Eden, the married son, brings his wife there to live. There just aren't enough bedrooms. Why don't you see if she has really worked it out." Good. This was in the days when the Watch and Ward Society had gone to extremes in banning books in Boston, and naturally I had some fun at Mazo's expense after the *politesse* in my speech. As I turned toward the guest of honor to make my point I saw that she was blushing, and later when we were standing together in the receiving line she said, "It was wicked of you to say what you did about those bedrooms, because your proofreader is right — there aren't enough. We shall have to make some changes in the proofs." Ten days later when I returned to Boston I received the following note shepherding back to us the first batch of corrected galleys:

Mazo de la Roche

Dear Ted:

In thinking over the sleeping space in the house, I find that there should have been six bedrooms instead of five. I have, therefore, made this change in the proofs. I have also added a few words to the effect that the attic was divided into two bedrooms which in my own mind was clear.

Of the six bedrooms, Renny and Wakefield occupy one, Piers and Finch another, and the remainder are occupied by Nicholas, Ernest, Meg and Eden. When Piers marries, Finch goes to one of the attic rooms, and when Alayne finds that Eden has been unfaithful to her, she takes the other attic room. Grandmother's bedroom is on the ground floor, and the servants, Wragge and Mrs. Wragge, have their quarters in the basement. This, I think you will agree, is very *snug* . . .

Well, there they were, all decently settled in their own beds, the original and irrepressible Whiteoaks whose doings have come to fill fourteen volumes. In the course of the serial, *Atlantic* readers began to claim their favorites. No one could resist old Adeline, so sudden in her rage, so eager for affection, munching her food with such relish or petting her irascible parrot, Old Boney, with his Hindu oaths. She ruled the reader as she ruled the clan despite her ninety-nine years. Of the men it was Renny, her eldest grandson, who most resembled her — Renny with his red-fox head and his lean strength, who could make any horse — or woman — do his bidding. And in contrast to Renny were the two artistic members of the family: Eden, the poet, romantic and clever; and Finch, the moody, vulnerable adolescent, the musician to be. These were people you could see: Uncle Nicholas with his gout which made him so grumpy; Wakefield, the youngest, precocious and theatrical, whom everyone spoiled; Piers, the stolid farmer of

[89]

the family; and Rags, servant to all and doing his raddled best to keep the rambling, crowded house in order. They were charged with life. I once heard a Canadian remark that the Whiteoaks were not typical of Canada. No indeed, they are not "typical" of any region, but their family loyalty, their bickering and their zest are qualities which bind together any big family anywhere.

Mazo had no intention of writing a sequel to *Jalna*. While the sale of the book was climbing to 100,000 copies, she and Caroline were making plans for their first trip abroad, to Sicily, thence to the Continent, and on to England. At Taormina they met and were much attracted by a young English couple; the husband was an artist whose career had been interrupted by a serious attack of tuberculosis, his wife was caring for him and their baby daughter, and was expecting their second child that summer. They cheered the invalid with talk of a reunion in London when it was hoped that his convalescence would be at an end.

But when several months later the travelers reached England, it was their grief to learn that the artist had died of a hemorrhage in Sicily and that the wife, borne down by sorrow, had lost her life in giving birth to their son. Two infants under two years of age — with the nearest of kin an aged great-aunt. With boldness and generosity that are characteristic Mazo de la Roche applied for the legal adoption of the children. It was a brave undertaking on the strength of her first successful book and, speaking as an editor and godfather, I can testify that the buoyancy and perennial refreshment which Esme and René have brought into Mazo's life are equaled by the love she has brought into theirs.

While they were abroad we forwarded many scores of letters from the *Atlantic* office, and in them readers demanded to know more about the Whiteoaks. "To whom will Adeline leave her money?" they asked. "May we know the outcome of Renny's affair?" queried a reader in Australia. ". . . Alayne, poor Alayne, pitchforked into the Vesuvius of Jalna." "I am an old lady," wrote J.H.B. from Maryland, "but I hope I shall live long enough for you to give us another Jalna book. Of course I am in love with Renny, who is a splendid man, but not without faults."

There was one technical difficulty which might prove to be embarrassing in a sequel. Never thinking that she was at the outset of an extended family chronicle, Mazo de la Roche had fixed an actual date for Gran's birthday. In *Jalna* she has Mrs. Wragge bake a three-tiered birthday cake with, on the side, in silver comfits, the date of Gran's birthday, "1825." Gran was in her 101st year at the close of the story which would bring us into 1926, and the book itself was published in 1927. Thus when in 1928 she began to write the sequel, Miss de la Roche found that she was limited by the calendar: the ages of all the family in *Jalna* were fixed and could not be altered. Most novelists like to space their incidents through one or more decades, but she never enjoyed this latitude; because of that inescapable date on the birthday cake, she has had to confine the adventures of each new book to two years at most. This has meant that except for the death of old Adeline, there could be no great climax of finality in the Whiteoak novels. Instead, we have the various members of a family going about their many private concerns, sometimes jealous, sometimes furious with each other, but always maturing; each book resolves a personal crisis — Renny's inarticulate effort to regain Alayne's love, Finch's struggle to become a pianist and to have Sarah,

Wake's passion for the stage — with such naturalness that we almost forget the author's skill.

To write of death is the test of every novelist. In *The White-oaks of Jalna* the impending death of old Adeline supplies the mounting suspense; and as we detect the signs of her failing, we begin to worry as if she were one of our own. That final scene in which Gran has her gallant backgammon game with Mr. Fennel, the rector, is one of the most stirring that Mazo de la Roche has ever written. After Gran's death the writer said to herself, "There, this is the end." But the novelist did not know her own mind. She did not realize how completely the fierce, affectionate old tyrant had come to possess her imagination. Old Adeline's death did not settle the score. For one thing she had left her money to the most talented of her grandsons, Finch, the nineteen-year-old musician, and what was he going to do with it? Had he the strength to break away from home and develop himself as a concert pianist? And if he took Gran's money with him, would the house go to rack and ruin? Finch was turning out to be the most talented as well as the most reliable of the younger generation. With editorial curiosity, I tried to probe the future. "Finch," I wrote to Mazo, "will need to get away for study and travel abroad. Sensitive as he is he'll have a hell of a time when he falls in love. Wake will be coming to man's estate. Furthermore, I think there is something owing to Piers and Pheasant — especially the former, who for all his stolidity has certainly shown himself a man of strength and capacity. Of course, there will be deep tragedy if for some physical or economic reason Jalna had to be given up and the family dispersed to the city. This is the tragedy that occurs so relentlessly in the States where the comfortable home in which one is born is too often turned into a filling station or apartment house before one's life is half spent." Insistent questions like these poured in from readers now as numerous in Britain as in America, and they compelled the writing of the third novel, *Finch's Fortune.*

It is unusual for an author to devote the most creative years of her life to writing about the activities of a single family. Mazo did her best to escape from her predicament. In the 1930s, when she was living in England, she repeatedly locked the Whiteoaks out of her imagination and went to work on new themes. I don't know how much this effort cost her; what I do know is that the Whiteoaks went right on living in the back room of her mind.

"You ought to be forced by law," J. B. Priestley said to her when first they met at a party in London, "to write a new novel about those Whiteoaks every year for the next twelve years. But," he added with emphasis, "no more about that fellow called Renny. I hate thin horsy men."

"Don't listen to Jack," put in his wife, "he's just jealous of Renny."

The compulsion to go on with the Whiteoaks came from within, and once Mazo de la Roche realized that it was unavoidable she was as happy in her writing as Galsworthy was in his devotion to the Forsytes. A dramatization was made of the first two novels, and the play which resulted, *Whiteoaks,* was produced in London in 1935, and played for more than 800 performances. Then it was brought to New York, where it scored a solid success with Ethel Barrymore in the part of old Adeline and Stephen Haggard, Finch to the life.

It was because of old Adeline that Mazo de la Roche decided to turn the clock back, a decision which her publishers for a time considered rather risky. How, we wondered, would readers respond to a book which showed us Gran in her early seventies and Renny a wild youngster of seventeen? Would it be plausible to go back that far, or even further to the 1850s, when Adeline was a bride and when Captain Philip Whiteoak, late of the Hussars, was superintending the building of Jalna? Turning the clock back meant that the family tree had to be projected backwards as well as forwards, every date had to be checked with slide-rule accuracy. And could Mazo de la Roche write as vividly of the past as she had of the present?

My very efficient secretary, Jeannette Cloud, became the custodian of the family tree. On huge sheets of graph paper she worked out the genealogy; she nailed down the birthdays of all the legitimate — and illegitimate — offspring of the Whiteoaks (one or two of them had gotten out of line); she computed the ages of the servants, the neighbors and of all the visitors the boys brought home, and as far as necessary she clarified the family relationships in Ireland and London. This became the Jalna *Who's Who* against which each new manuscript was checked, sometimes to the author's exasperation, mostly to her relief.

Mazo overcame our misgivings, first in *Young Renny,* and then even more triumphantly in *The Building of Jalna,* in which she showed us the young couple who had come so confidently from an army garrison in India to the wilds of Ontario to stake out their 300 acres and rear their family. Here was the living history and the heritage from which the contemporary stories derived, and if she strayed from the straight and narrow path of authenticity, there were readers — as well as proofreaders — to help her with the corrections. When she was writing *The Building of Jalna,* she chose a certain hymn to be sung by the passengers of the sailing ship. She took pains to

verify the date on which the hymn was written and found it to
be a year or more later than the year in which Philip and Adeline had crossed the Atlantic. "Still it is near enough," she
thought, "no one will notice." But she was wrong. A few weeks
after the publication of the book she received two letters, one
from England, the other from Massachusetts, both giving her
the correct date of the hymn.

A gentleman wrote in from China saying that she had inac-
curately described the characteristics of the Dutch face. A well-
known English musician set her right on several points in connection with Finch's music. This is not to imply that Miss de la
Roche is a careless craftsman. It is simply to say that it is no
light assignment to be responsible for the many diverse activities of a family now in its fourth generation. Each book widens
the circle and it is sheer virtuosity that keeps the episodes
in verisimilitude and away from the melodramatic. Here I could
sometimes help.

There is nothing soft about the Whiteoaks. They blaze with
anger when aroused; they live with a high emotional voltage:
when Finch decides to drown himself, or Renny is tempted to
choke the life out of Mr. Clapperton (who has proposed to sub-
divide the neighborhood into bungalow lots), the crime is but
a step away. It is a real thing that could take place any minute.
In their rage and in their drama, in their comedy and devotion,
Mazo de la Roche's novels are, as Sterling North well says, "a
blend of two great traditions, the English tradition of smooth,
well-rounded narrative with good characterization and the
lusty American tradition with its humor of exaggeration and its
moments of irrepressible animal spirits. Probably the finest
extensive work on an American family which the continent has
yet produced.

"Scarcely less important than the family itself," continued Mr. North, "is the estate, Jalna, with its wide acres, rambling stables, great oak trees, lawns, gardens, and orchards. One feels certain he has explored every room of the big house from Finch's narrow corner under the sloping eaves to the disordered kitchen and pantry in the basement where Rags and his temperamental spouse prepare the marvelous dinners. Certainly one could describe to the very pictures on the walls the bedrooms of Ernest, Nicholas, and Augusta, Alayne's cool and tidy bedroom, the careless but comfortable quarters where Renny, even after his marriage to Alayne, continues to sleep with pampered young Wakefield. Downstairs is the great living room with its fireplace, the dining room with its Chippendale and Sheraton pieces, and Adeline's bedroom with its imposing and unusual bed. A cacophony of the ugly and the beautiful . . ."

It is quite impossible for me to speak objectively about an author who for more than three decades has been my very dear friend. I have had the fun of editing each one of the Jalna novels, and the pride — and sometimes amazement — of seeing what this sturdy, loyal family has meant to other families the world over. I have said that Mazo de la Roche's achievement makes me think of Galsworthy — as it does of Trollope. I am too close to her to attempt a comparison in quality, but I do know that neither of them ever created more living people.

Miss de la Roche's novels about the Whiteoaks of Jalna have been translated into fifteen languages. A million and a half copies of them have been sold in the United States and considerably more than that number in Britain and throughout Europe. It is significant that their period of greatest currency was during and immediately after the Second World War when Mazo's writing carried a very special message to those who were living in exile or under domination, to those whose homes were broken or destroyed. The petitions sent to her in thankfulness by Polish prisoners now liberated, the pathetic little hand-carved chest conveying the blessing of the Balt D.P.'s, the letters from families in the Dutch underground and French resistance, the letters of inquiry from Norway and Czechoslovakia attest the hope and vitality which her books held out to others. For family fealty there is one tongue and universal sympathy.

Harvey Cushing

JAMES NORMAN HALL was the most humble author I have ever worked with, and Dr. Harvey Cushing was the most exacting. I made my first bow to him in the spring of 1928 when he was Surgeon-in-Chief of the Peter Bent Brigham Hospital in Boston and the greatest brain specialist in the world. He had acquired a reputation for performing miracles, and a fearsome reputation among those who worked under him; young nurses went in to his operations trembling, and there were interns who never forgot what he taught them but who hated his guts. Because of the professional demands upon him, he wrote only occasionally, but what he wrote had the fine edge of distinction and the driving force of his personality. His two-volume biography of Sir William Osler, who had been his teacher, was regarded as the definitive study of that great Canadian physician and of the famous associates at Johns Hopkins who had worked with him. Now we had accepted for publication a collection of Dr. Cushing's papers; the book was to be called *Consecratio Medici,* and it was my responsibility to see the manuscript through the press, to check the Doctor's corrections, learn his preferences for the binding and jacket and to make sure that there was nothing to offend him in the blurb. He took the proof-reading very seriously, had an eye like a hawk for printers' errors or a loose line, and made meticulous corrections, first in the galleys, and then in the page proofs. Nothing escaped him. I had heard that he was a perfectionist and, in his taut, decisive way, intimidating; now I knew it.

When the last page of his book had been corrected, I went up to his office in the hospital to collect the proofs and to say good-by. Dr. Cushing's reception room in the hospital was really a library: here was his famous collection of medical books, bound in vellum and calf, many of age and rarity, locked in behind the Victorian glass-fronted shelves. On top of the shelves at the height of my eyes was an assortment of his war souvenirs, tin hats of the soldiers whose skulls he had operated on, punctured by shell fragments coming up or going down; photographs of field hospitals in the quaggy mud; a medical team solemnly seated before a tent, and beside the picture a dud which had thudded close but never exploded.

As he escorted me to the door, he paused for a moment before one of the bookcases and lifted down a delicate object on a stiff piece of cardboard. It was a pair of field glasses — or rather it was half a pair of field glasses — which a French officer had been looking through when he had suffered a direct hit from a German sharpshooter. The bullet had smashed the glass and metal into the man's right eye and dangerously close to the brain.

This took place during the First Battle of the Marne in the autumn of 1914. The officer lived, but no surgeon dared operate until months later — in April 1915 — when Dr. Cushing, in an operation which took hours, and which is still one of the most notable in the record of the Neuilly Hospital, extracted the bits of the metal from the Frenchman's head. The patient survived, and here were the field glasses and the scraps of metal to show what one brain could do to save another. It was a sight to shudder over, starkly impressive to one who had seen too many wounded and dying men in France. But now it was time for me to depart; Dr. Cushing had replaced the relic, and as we started to shake hands he gave me an impulsive grin. "Weeks," he said, "here's the makings of a good book. But one that can't be published till I'm dead."

"Where?" I asked. He was pointing to a row of eight large leather-bound volumes in the bookcase beside us.

"My war journals," he said. "More than a million words, and full of indiscretion. Well, thanks for your help. Good-by."

That is not something an editor can forget. Six months later I rang up Dr. Cushing's office and told his secretary, Miss Madeline Stanton, that I would like to speak to the Doctor if he wasn't too busy. When I heard his voice at the other end, I said, "Hello, Dr. Cushing. This is Edward Weeks. How are you feeling?"

"Who is it?" he asked. "Weeks? Why, I'm feeling all right. How are you?"

"Fine," I said. "Well, good-by." And I hung up.

Another six months later I did the same thing, rang him up, and this time he was operating so it wasn't until late in the afternoon that he came to the telephone. I went through the same routine: "Dr. Cushing, this is Edward Weeks. How's your health?"

"Say, what is this?" he asked. "You've done this before. Why are you so concerned about my health?"

"Well," I replied, "you said I couldn't print those war journals until you were dead, and I want to know whether my chances are improving." I could hear the bark of his laugh at the other end of the line.

"Oh, you go to hell!" he said.

That was in 1929. When the stock market crashed that autumn, much of Dr. Cushing's savings were lost in the wiping out of Kreuger & Toll. So, although he was now in his sixties, he continued to operate on a full-time schedule and to carry on his teaching at the Harvard Medical School with undiminished vigor. For he had to recoup. In the autumn of 1932 he knew that he was entering on his last year before mandatory retirement, and he had already installed Dr. Elliott Cutler as his successor at the Peter Bent Brigham. He had hoped that the Harvard Corporation might prolong his usefulness at the Medical School, but when no special treatment was forthcoming he accepted the Sterling Chair of Neurology at Yale which President Angell had proffered to him without publicity. In effect this transferred his genius (and his library) to his alma mater before President Lowell woke up to what was happening.

If I was ever to have access to those war journals, it would have to be this summer before Dr. Cushing cleared out for good. The books, I understood, had been transported from his office to his home in Brookline, and there in June I went to pay him a call.

The Doctor greeted me in his shirt sleeves and relaxed. "We've been uprooting," he said, and the house showed it, for the rooms had already been half dismantled. "The family has gone up to Boar's Head for the summer," he said, "but I think I'll stay on here. I've got twenty years of records to sort out."

"Let me get a man to help you," I said. "Listen, I'll get a Ph.D. from Yale. You can stow him in one of the empty rooms upstairs, and together he and I will go through those journals of yours, marking the passages which we think are of general interest and which ought to be published. We'll pay for him; it won't commit you to a thing if you don't like the final result.

Besides, his companionship may compensate a little for your not being at Old Bores' Head."

"Boar's Head," he said, correcting me, and then he saw I was teasing. "Well, if you want to take the risk, it's all right with me."

Yale willingly supplied me with the Ph.D., Ralph E. Collins, a quiet-spoken, agreeable individual who could type like the wind, and together we took our way slowly through those eight huge volumes, marking with white slips the passages to be copied. Dr. Cushing had served as an operating surgeon with the French in the first winter of the war, and in the spring of 1915 he visited the Royal Medical Corps in Flanders. In 1916, sure that we would be involved, he was intent on organizing a medical unit in America. With Base Hospital No. 5 he went back to the front early in 1917 and was attached to the British Army through the campaigns of Messines Ridge and during the dreadful slaughter on the Somme and at Passchendaele that autumn. In 1918 he was attached to the A.E.F. and with his operating teams he took care of most of the head wounds resulting from the fighting at Château Thierry, the Argonne and St.-Mihiel.

The diary was graphic and sparky, forthright, crackling with anger or humor, full of denunciation of all that was unsanitary and incompetent, charged with compassion for those who bore the brunt of the fighting. He began operating at 8:30 A.M., and on record days he would be called on for as many as *twelve major cases*. No operation was of less than an hour's duration; some took twice that amount of time. There he would stand hour after hour on the little stool which gave him the elevation he needed as he worked over the unconscious soldier.

By midnight or after he would be too excited, his nerves too taut for sleep, and so, on old temperature charts, scraps of yellow paper, anything that was handy, he would write down the details, the humor and exasperation of that exhausting day; thus the piano wires of his mind were relaxed. Day after day the entries are made at "2:00 A.M." and here's how they read:

Operating from 8:30 A.M. one day till 2:00 A.M. the next; standing in a pair of rubber boots, and periodically full of tea as a stimulant . . . It's an awful business, probably the worst possible training in surgery for a young man, and ruinous for the carefully acquired technique of an oldster. Something over 2000 wounded have passed, so far, through this one Casualty Clearing Station.

Some of the journal was indeed too personal and some of it too technical; but the great passages were a spirited, magnificent chronicle of a doctor at war, and often we read and reread aloud before we could bring ourselves to move on:

Neuilly, April 29, 1915

Several unsuccessful trials this morning to extract the shell fragment by the aid of the magnet from the brain of poor Lafourcode. I was afraid to use the huge probe which they have and so determined to make, or have made, another — of which later. We had tried every possible thing in our own cabinet and in those of the lower floors without success. Finally, while I was at lunch, Boothby hit upon precisely what was needed in the shape of a large wire nail about six inches long, the point of which he had carefully rounded off.

Well, there was the usual crowd in the X-ray room and approaching corridor, and much excitement when we let the nail slide by gravity into the central mechanism of smiling Lafourcode; for at no time did he have any pressure symptoms, and all of these procedures were of course without an anesthetic. While the X-ray plate was being developed to see whether the nail and missile were in contact, who should drop in but Albert Kocher with a friend from Berne; and then shortly a card was sent in by Tom Perry's friend, Salomon Reinach, Membre de l'Institut, author of the "History of Religions," and much else.

So all together we finally traipsed into the first-floor operating room, where Cutler mightily brings up the magnet and slowly we extract the nail — and — there was nothing on it! Suppressed sighs and groans. I tried again, very carefully — with the same result. More sighs and people began to go out. A third time — nothing. By this time I began to grumble: "Never saw anything of this kind pulled off with such a crowd. Hoodooed ourselves from the start. Should have had an X-ray made when the man first entered the hospital." The usual thing, as when one begins to scold his golf ball.

I had taken off my gloves and put the nail down; but then — Let's try just once more! So I slipped the brutal thing again down the track, 3½ inches to the base of the brain, and again Cutler gingerly swung the big magnet down and made contact. The current was switched on and as before we slowly drew out the nail — and there it was, the little fragment of rough steel hanging on to its tip! Much emotion on all sides — especially on the part of A. Kocher and Salomon Reinach, both of whom could hardly bear it.

Or this, written when the Battle of the Somme was in progress and the wounded were swamping the Clearing Station:

This sergeant of the Machine Gunners had almost the whole of his right frontal lobe blown out, with a lodged piece of shell almost an inch square, and extensive radiating fractures, which meant taking off most of his frontal bone, including the frontal sinuses — an enormous operation done under local anaesthesia. We crawled home for some eggs in the mess and to bed at 2:30 A.M. — six hours for these two cases.

This man "Chave" — queer name — when roused from his semiconsciousness made it known that he had some precious false teeth. They were removed, somewhat more easily than was his broken frontal bone. They must have been on his mind, for I remember when rongeuring out fragments of his skull he kept muttering that I was breaking his teeth . . . He seems to be all right today, and is wearing his teeth.

There was a fierce driving dedication in Dr. Cushing which showed in his features, the long dominating nose, the blue eyes that could turn so swiftly cold or angry, the tight lips with the lines of sorrow that deepened in his cheeks after the death of his reckless and beloved son Bill — this was the face of a driver. But beneath this exterior was a tenderness which went deep and which shows itself repeatedly in the journals. Harvey could steel himself against death on the operating table, but the death of friends was a different matter, as witness this account of Jack McCrae, the Canadian poet and physician:

January 28th, 1918. Boulogne

I saw poor Jack McCrae with Elder at No. 14 General last night — the last time. A bright flame rapidly burning out. He died early this morning. Just made Consulting Physician to the 1st Army — the only Canadian so far to be thus honored. Never strong, he gave his all with the Canadian Artillery during the prolonged second battle of Ypres and after, at which time he wrote his imperishable verses. Since those frightful days he has never been his old gay and companionable self, but has rather sought solitude. A soldier from top to toe — how he would have hated to die in a bed. A three days' illness — an atypical pneumonia with extensive pneumococcus meningitis, as we learned this afternoon — for Rhea came for me and we went out with Sir Bertrand Dawson. They will bury him tomorrow. Some of the older members of the McGill Unit who still remain here were scouring the fields this afternoon to try and find some chance winter poppies to put on his grave — to remind him of Flanders, where he would have preferred to lie. Was anyone ever more respected and loved than he? Someone has said that "children and animals followed him as shadows follow other men."

We saw him buried this afternoon at the cemetery on the hillside at Wimereux with military honors — a tribute to Canada as well as to him. A large gathering of friends — all who could get there, even from a distance: the Canadian Corps Commander with his divisional generals; General Dodds, Jack's former Artillery Commander; General Sloggett and the D.D.M.S. of our district; the Base Commandant; we Americans, with some Portuguese M.O.'s from No. 3 Canadian; all the C.O.'s and Consultants of the neighborhood.

We met at No. 14 General — a brilliant sunny afternoon — and walked the mile or so to the cemetery. A company of North Staffords and many R.A.M.C. orderlies and Canadian sisters headed the procession — then "Bonfire," led by two grooms and carrying the regulation white ribbon, with his master's boots reversed over the saddle — then the rest of us. Six sergeants bore the coffin from the gates, and as he was being lowered into his grave there was a distant sound of guns — as though called into voice by the occasion. An admirable prayer by one of the three Padres who officiated. The Staffords, from their reversed arms, fix bayonets, and instead of firing over the grave, as in time of peace, stand at salute during the Last Post with its final wailing note which brings a lump to our throats — and so we leave him.

At the summer's end, and before the family had returned from Boar's Head, Collins had typed about 45,000 words, enough for four full-length *Atlantic* articles. The master copy was the Doctor's, I kept the carbon. We shook hands all around and then went our separate ways. But I had left a number of slips in the big books just in case I might be asked back.

That autumn Dr. Cushing was intensely busy settling the library and himself into the new quarters at New Haven and adapting himself to the fresh regime; he must have pushed himself hard, for he was ill for a considerable period in the midwinter and early spring of 1934. I wrote to say that there was to be a German edition of *Consecratio Medici* and added: "There are times when I would give a good deal to be able to dip into those war journals of yours. They have the fervor and intensity which bring back the old days and make one feel twenty years younger." Perhaps this gave him the nudge he needed in his convalescence, for in July back came the manuscripts we had prepared in Brookline, carefully checked and ready for the *Atlantic.* He was still uneasy lest he be violating medical confidence, and he sought the reassurance of Boston medicos to whom he showed the proofs. They had no misgivings, and he got his final answer when the first of the four articles appeared in October.

Letters poured in on him from all over the world, one of the first a moving note from a veteran in Texas whose life he had saved. Friends in Baltimore, friends in England urged him to continue. Meantime, we had grown apprehensive on another score, for we knew that rival publishing houses were interested, and in the emergency Mr. Sedgwick pressed our claims:

2 January, 1935

Dear Harvey:

I really hope very much you will see Weeks. His confidence in the proposed book is complete, and he is not by profession a chaser of rainbows. To me, there is interest in the fact that during a period of five weeks, while your articles have been running, a count was made of the new subscriptions received from physicians and surgeons. They amounted to almost 1900. But even if I had no statistics at my disposal, I should be sure in a realistic meaning of the word that your war diaries would not only sell widely, but that they would take a permanent place.

Please don't let this chance go, but whatever is your final decision, this letter is simply to ask you to give an hour to Weeks.

On January 20 I made my initial visit to the big house on Whitney Avenue where I was installed with the journal in a little sun porch off the living room. Fourteen months later, after eleven visits and the exchange of 113 letters, *From a Surgeon's Journal* came off the press. The manuscript had grown from 45,000 to 190,000 words. Not a sentence was rewritten; my editorial touch was needed only in the preparation of an Introduction and Afterword — and here Harvey edited me. Caring for Cushing as an author was a full-time occupation: the enormous correspondence, the give and take which engrossed us and our secretaries, was concerned, fastidiously and impatiently, with questions of propriety, typography, punctuation ("In the manuscript, Miss Stanton was apt to put a line of dashes whereas I think they had better be two or three inches of dots"), illustrations, capitalization ("In the matter of *Cap, Capt., Captain* and so forth it does not seem to me that consistency is necessary"), maps and libel. As the book grew, the royalty terms which he demanded rose; the contract was renegotiated three times; he never would accept the libel clause; and midway in the manufacture he obliged us to discard all galleys in the original type face and reset the entire text in a format more closely resembling a diary — which we did at the cost of $2100.

The record of this intercourse is probably of interest only to other publishers, but I wish to set down a few of the hot points to record an aspect of editing not generally appreciated.

Harvey Cushing

The Type Page. We had twice shown him sample pages and we thought we had won his approval when in came this blast:

23 September 1935

Dear Ted:

After your telephone message yesterday, I looked over the galley proofs and found so many things to criticize that I wired you last night suggesting that you hold up the printing of any further galleys until you heard from me about them. Herewith my criticisms for your information and discussion.

The book which we counted on as being 350 pages I understand has expanded to 450 pages, which is a little larger book than we had banked on. You will recall my criticism about the earlier sample sheets, that they were too open; and I think that that is even more pronounced than before on these galleys. I believe it is possible to make a far better looking page and save a great deal of space. I have an idea that we have rushed into this without sufficient consideration of trial samples; and even though it may cost something to set the thing up differently, I believe that we should do so . . .

27 September 1935

Dear Ted:

My grouse about the business is that we flew into this galley before actually coming to any agreement as to format. I disliked intensely the original page in the dummy first provided and didn't think that the second that was sent on was much of an improvement. After that, you got busy with a tennis tournament [I was in it for exactly two days. E.W.], or something of that sort and that's the last I heard of it until we saw the galley which I think is worse than second-class.

This grouse is not going to be cured by taking soda . . .

Telegrams were exchanged and four days later I wrote to say that I should come down the following day and that we should then "go to the mat." Who came out on top will be seen from the following memorandum from Alfred McIntyre to the head of the manufacturing department.

October 4, 1935

Mr. Scaife:

I have seen Mr. Weeks this morning with regard to Cushing's book. He had a very satisfactory interview with Dr. Cushing except that it is obvious that the book must be entirely reset. The type used for the diary date lines is unsatisfactory and these date lines must be on the right-hand side of the page. The insertion of leads in abbreviations of names, such as A. E. F., is unsatisfactory. These have to be closed up. Cushing's manuscript has so many em dashes that it becomes necessary, in order to have the book look right from his standpoint, to use en dashes instead. One or two other difficulties have presented themselves.

I have therefore agreed that we shall set new sample pages which must take care of all these difficulties, and that when we receive the O.K.'d page in writing from Dr. Cushing, we will reset the book completely and the expense of typesetting already done will be divided equally between the Atlantic Monthly Press and ourselves. We shall set from corrected galley proofs carefully marked for style in respect to the points mentioned above, thus putting the entire responsibility of having things right on the printer. The price of the book will have to be $5.00, and we shall have to make new estimates in the hope that we can afford to include 32 pages of half-tones, at least 12 maps and an end-paper map in one or two colors, since this is what Cushing wants.

When this is all settled, he will sign the contract on the basis of a 15% royalty.

Mr. Weeks learned yesterday that his Life of Osler had to be entirely reset.

I hope that the sales of the book will justify all this expense and effort.

A. R. M.

The Afterword, on the writing of which, incidentally, I had taken pains.

H.C. to E.W., 7 February 1936.

. . . Now for your epilogue. I can't truthfully say that it makes me want to sit up and cheer and sing Fair Harvard. It possibly was just a flier and that you wanted us to work it up.

E.W. to H.C., February 12, 1936.

. . . I hold no brief for the Epilogue. In the words of John Keats, "I am always awkward in making a bow." It was simply my wish to indicate that after the Armistice you began to show the effects of the steady pressure under which you had been working. You were dead tired; you were fretful with red tape (as was everyone else) and very eager to get home. Having made a calculation of the expense of the war in terms of flesh, and having seen at Rheims a rather typical flash of French militarism, home you went. Correct the script any way you see fit, or omit it entirely. It's all one to Hippocrates.

H.C. to E.W., February 20, 1936.

Dear Ted:

I am sending on the *Afterword* for your perusal; and also a suggestion which might help balance the book since I have left in the Afterword some quotations from Walt Whitman's "Memoranda" of the Civil War which he jotted down when he was a Red Cross worker visiting hospitals in Washington. If you have never seen the book, I recommend it to you. If you approve of leaving in these two quotations, to which Osler called my attention else I should never

have heard of the book, I suggest that we put in somewhere in one
of the preliminary leaves, possibly, for example, on the verso of the
dedication to K. C., what I have put on the following sheet.

You may not think it is necessary to put in the "Afterword" all
those entries from the "Canopic," but I rather want to get in somewhere the idea of the accumulating demoralization of the breakdown
that followed the Armistice and the absolutely unnecessary humiliation in the way of physical examinations and things of that kind to
which most of us, officers as well as men, were put before they were
allowed to land. The Base Hospital No. 5 people had a most awful
time at Camp Devens, which I shall tell you about some day. If
they hadn't been so effectively cowed, they certainly would have had
a mutiny . . .

Libel. H.C. to E.W., November 5, 1935.
". . . I am leery about all this business in article three
about matters 'libellous or otherwise injurious.' "

He had his way and in the end *we* assumed the risk for libel
for which the author is usually held responsible. All went well
on this side, but on the day when Constable published the English edition, there was an immediate explosion in London. In
his journal Harvey had remarked inadvertently that it had
been raining pitchforks and his Burberry had leaked like a
sieve. We had spelled it with a lower case "b," but even so the
manufacturers of the famous British waterproof were not to be
mollified. A "burberry" was a Burberry and no Burberry ever
leaked. They sued for damages, demanded an apology, that
books be recalled and that the offending page be corrected
and recast — all of which was done at our expense.

Our work together was not as fractious as it must sound. The
visits to New Haven were often gay. Barbara, the youngest of
the Doctor's daughters, was a debutante and a perfectly lovely

one, and girl friends of hers from Brookline and Dedham were usually in attendance with Yale undergraduates swarming in and out; doctors from England dropped by occasionally to take tea and Harvey would question them about the threat of socialized medicine, and when the weather was fair Thornton Wilder and John F. Fulton might spend the afternoon with us, taking part in the croquet game which was now the Doctor's way of exercising. The circulation in his legs was beginning to give him serious trouble (the price of having operated so long standing on that little stool). I saved up stories about Boston and Harvard and the Tavern Club to tell him, and I never ceased to tease him. Generally he enjoyed it, although once I over-stepped the mark. He had been the shortstop on the Yale var-sity, and if I remember rightly, captain of the team. In the final game with Harvard, which was played at Cambridge, he went back under a towering fly, caught his cleats on the wooden rim of the cinder track which encircled Soldiers Field, and fell flat on his back, missing the ball to his eternal mortification. I kidded him about it one day, and suddenly realized that even after all these years, I should never have brought it up. The Harvard-Yale football game, as it happened, was only ten days away and to change the subject and because I was feeling cocky about Harvard's chances, I bet him a hat on the outcome. Thanks to the Frank-Kelley combination, he won it.

There were times when, as his health worsened, he reached out in an affectionate way to cuff and tease me. In September of 1936 he had been invited to Harvard for the Tercentenary and I had been urging him to come. He wrote:

. . . In a moment of feeling, for me, moderately lively, I wrote Fitz [Dr. Reginald Fitz] to ask if I might motor from here direct to Memorial Hall and get a seat with the Faculty as an Emeritus Prof.

for the exercises on the afternoon of the 16th at which I proposed to wear a red gown and a John Knox bonnet. But the very next day I was back more or less on crutches and have now abandoned the idea.

Glad to learn that the Journal still sells though it is steadily falling off, I note, in the N. Y. Herald-Tribune's list of non-fiction. Expecting some day to have a windfall from you, I find to my horror that I spent $7000 last month on old books. So when you have a royalty check ready for me, you'd better send it, attention of Mr. Hobart W. Spring, direct to the Merchants National Bank for deposit on my Investment Account where I shall have less temptation to blow it in.

I am working on another book — fiction list this time — entitled "Experiences with the Meningiomas." Is that what you want to see me about?

> Always yours,
> HARVEY CUSHING

And when Warner Brothers wrote him to ask if they could consider the film rights of *A Surgeon's Journal*, Harvey was vastly amused:

. . . In the same mail comes the enclosed from Warner Brothers. So far as I can see, they missed their only chance for a good talking picture and that was one afternoon on our screened porch when we were persuading you to do another galley proof and the score was about 40-30 in the last game of the set. I shall write Mr. Deakin of the Story Department that I have forwarded his letter for you to answer.

> Always yours,
> HARVEY CUSHING

On one of our last meetings Harvey had been sorting through the records of some of his more difficult cases, and I remember in particular the humbleness with which he spoke of his operations on Leonard Wood. The Colonel had come to him straight from the Philippines in the early 1900s, lopsided, unable to disengage his left hand from his trouser pocket, the victim of a brain tumor and a big one, which Harvey removed. He had not been too sure of the operation at the time, Harvey told me. "If I'd known then what I know now, I could have gone deeper," he said, "and there would have been no need for the second operation at the height of his career in 1922." He spoke in an accusing way, and I sought to divert him. The second volume of his Osler was at hand, and I turned to the passage in the summary which seems to me one of the finest pieces of Cushing prose:

Osler had the God-given quality of being a friend with all, children or grownup, professor or pupil, and what is more of holding such friendships with an unforgettable tenacity — a scribbled line of remembrance with a playful twist to it, a note of congratulation to some delighted youngster on his first publication, a telegram to bring cheer or consolation, an unsolicited donation for a worthy cause, an article to help a struggling journal get a footing. He was sought far and wide not only because of his wide knowledge of medicine and great wisdom, but because of his generosity, his sympathy, and great personal charm.

"Never believe what a patient may tell you to the detriment of another physician," was one of Osler's sayings to his students, and then he would add with a characteristic twist, "even though you may fear it is true."

I read it aloud and added, "The guy who wrote that knew his business."

Harvey looked at me quizzically and then picked up a book

by Stephen Paget, *Confessio Medici,* which I knew to be his favorite. "Listen to this," he said, and he began to read:

Every year, young men enter the medical profession who neither are born doctors, nor have any great love of science, nor are helped by name or influence. Without a welcome, without money, without prospects, they fight their way into practice, they find it hard work, ill-thanked, ill-paid. But they stick to it, and Heaven, sooner or later, lets them know what it thinks of them. They hesitate to give the name of divine vocation to work paid by the job, and shamefully underpaid at that. Surely a diploma, obtained by hard examination and hard cash, and signed and sealed by earthly examiners, cannot be a summons from Heaven. But it may be. For, if a doctor's life may not be a divine vocation, then no life is a vocation, and nothing is divine.

Cape Codders

THOREAU, who used to love to walk its dunes and beaches, called Cape Cod "the bare and bended arm of Massachusetts." When he was alive, this arm was a peninsula, an arm curving sixty-five miles out into the Atlantic with Provincetown like a clenched fist at its extremity. But as a result of some land surgery the Cape Cod Canal was cut across the arm, and now Cape Cod is really an island with a pair of bridges spanning the rushing water of the Canal to connect it with the rest of the Commonwealth.

The clenched fingers at the tip are Provincetown, whose character no tourism can dim. It was here, on November 11, 1620, that the *Mayflower* dropped anchor in one of the finest natural harbors on this continent; and it was here that the Pilgrim Fathers first landed on American soil. They stayed here for five weeks, then they moved up the coast to Plymouth; and to the authentic Cape Codder, the fact that they refused to remain longer on its bleak flats means nothing at all. They came here *first,* and when he is asked about Plymouth Rock his reply is brief and contemptuous. "Plymouth Rock," he says, "is the name of a chicken!"

Provincetown on the Cape has had its great days. It was from here, and from Truro, six miles to the east, that the deepwater whaling men set out. And it was here that the Cape's great fishing industry was born and flourished in the mid-1800s. So important did the Provincetown fishermen become that a Western reporter was assigned to write the story of this strange community where the Fish was King.

"Fish," wrote the reporter, "is bartered at the grocery stores, shoe shops and bread stores for all commodities of life. The main business street is paved with rock cod. The women use the hind fin of the great halibut for brooms. Awnings shading the store fronts are made from the skin of the sportive porpoise. The bellrope in the church is made of eels, cunningly knotted by an old sailor. Provincetown ladies trim their hats with the red gills of the mackerel, and dog-fish lie around the shore at low tide and bark and howl in a frightful manner." A Western view of the Cape.

Leaving Provincetown, as you drive up the outer curve of Cape Cod, heading north, you see the great sweep of an exposed coast which stands out to sea like no other stretch of our continental shelf. The Cape at this point is a high cliff about three or four miles wide, and at its foot is a great beach on which the Atlantic thunders, a beach running north and south unbroken, mile upon mile, solitary, unsullied, remote. Truro, Wellfleet, Orleans, the wild, wind-swept island Monomoy, Eastham, the Nauset beach and marsh — this is the unspoiled shore which will compose the Cape Cod seashore park if the contemplated plans are carried out.

An elemental place; on the one side the Atlantic, the breakers foaming and pounding in as far as the eye can reach, then the wall of dunes, and behind them the tidal creeks and inlets. The barricade of sand narrows to a few hundred yards at Eastham, and at high winter tides the ocean breaks through to create narrow temporary inlets to the Nauset Marsh.

Cape Codders

The natives who live near this outermost beach have a fierce protective pride and a characteristic way of talking. Their fishing villages having English names but the pronunciation is pure Cape Cod. These people live in East-ham; or Ware-ham, or Chat-ham; they would never think of saying "Chatham" as an Englishman does.

The old story goes that one dark night two ships off Eastham came within hailing distance. The lookout on the little craft who first saw the riding-lights of the towering clipper shouted: "Ship, ahoy! Who be you?"

And the answer came back over the water: "The *Flying Mercury*. Out of Shanghai. Bound for Boston. Out eighty-eight days. What ship are you?"

And the reply came back: "Schooner, *Mary B.* Out of Eastham. Bound for Chat-ham. Out all night!"

A real Cape Codder never refers to a "thunderstorm": he calls it a "tem-pest." He has reason to know that the great gales roaring out of the north and east can do strange and terrible things. In the old days before there were lighthouses on Cape Cod some of the natives were known as "mooncussers" — men who made their living from the salvage of wrecked ships — "mooncussers" being those who cussed the moon, for if there was moonlight, the lookout could see the line of breakers, the shoals and the shore. The "mooncussers" were gifted with an extra sense that enabled them to smell a wreck as they lay abed, listening to the wind howl down the Wellfleet valley and across the plains of Nauset. As the storm rose they would put on their boots and make for the beach.

There they would divide into groups, one tramping the beach in one direction and one in the other. They would hold up a shingle to protect the eyes from the flying sand, and under the shingle they would strain to pierce the darkness for a rocket from a ship in distress. Whatever was washed ashore from the wreck became their instant property. During the days of the sailing ships this business of wrecking was profitable, and Emerson tells us there was considerable opposition in the town of Eastham before the people voted to erect a lighthouse on that beach. These are some of the details I imbibed from *Mooncussers of Cape Cod,* a quaint and quite fascinating book by Henry C. Kittredge.

The wrecks are fewer today, the ships stay farther off shore, and there aren't nearly so many in the coastal trade. But the Eastham beach in winter is still an exposed and lonely spot where a man can live in dramatic solitude watching the ocean's changing mood from hour to hour. And that is what one American writer named Henry Beston elected to do. Henry Beston had served as an ambulance driver in France and then aboard submarines in the First World War. On his demobilization, he wrote for the *Atlantic* and worked for a time as an associate editor on our staff. But he pulled out before I joined in 1924 and what pulled him was the magnetism of the Cape: he wanted to live the year round by himself on Nauset Beach.

At Eastham on this outermost beach he built the outermost house, a small box just big enough for one man. It measured sixteen feet by twenty, and he built it on top of one of the biggest sand dunes. He called his house the Fo'castle, and it had a tiny bedroom and a kitchen-living-room with a brick fireplace and an oil stove. To get his drinking water he sank a well pipe into the dune. Though the sea and the beach were alongside there was fresh sweet water there under the salty sand. On bitter cold days he would simply pump his few pails full, stand them in the sink, and then drain the pump immediately so that it wouldn't freeze. He tells us that he had one oil lamp and candles to read by at night, and for his fireplace he had all the driftwood he could use. To buy milk and eggs and butter meant a long walk down the beach. Rarely in calm weather he'd coax a neighbor to bring in supplies with a horse and cart.

His house was twenty feet above the high-water mark, and only thirty feet away from the great limitless beach and the ever-pounding surf. His nearest neighbors were the Coast Guards at Nauset two miles away. Beston kept a chronicle of what he saw and what he best remembered, and this as he fitted it together became a book such as Thoreau would have admired. Its title is *The Outermost House* and for those who love the sea in calm and angry temper this is a book to stir the mind. Here is how Mr. Beston's day began:

From the moment that I rose in the morning and threw open my door looking toward the sea to the moment when the spurt of a match sounded in the evening quiet of my solitary house, there was always something to do, something to observe, something to record, something to study, something to put aside in a corner of the mind. There was the ocean in all weathers and at all times, now grey and lonely and veiled in winter rain, now sun-bright, coldly green, and marbled with dissolving foam; there was the marsh with its great congresses, its little companies, its wandering groups, and little family gatherings of winter birds; there was the glory of the winter sky rolling out of the ocean over and across the dunes, constellation by constellation, lonely star by star.

In his world the sea birds became his companions. He got to know the sandpipers and the yellowlegs; the talkative seagulls and the little bobwhites. He never tired watching what he calls a "raft" of coots, a whole congregation of birds sitting in the ocean just seaward of the surf with the raft rising and falling unconcernedly as the swells swept under it.

"In Thoreau's time," says Mr. Beston, "these rafts of coots formed a flock which was practically continuous the whole length of the outer Cape." In short a raft of birds miles long. And of course he kept track of the ducks, the blue-billed widgeons, the dipper ducks, the king eiders, and those other visitors from the Arctic, the auks. He noticed how many of these birds fell victim to the crude oil which was dumped into the water by the tankers. He noticed that as soon as the bird swam into that gummy mass it was as good as dead.

Mr. Beston's little house, "being low and strongly built, stood solid as a rock, but its walls thrummed in the winter gales, and the dune beneath the house trembled incessantly with the on-slaught of the surf."

"Wonder what my friends at Nauset Station are worrying about," he would think to himself on a furious, pouring night, and sometimes he would go down to the beach to join one of the Coast Guards on his patrol. So it was that on a Monday morning in March shortly after 5 o'clock, he saw "the big three-masted schooner *Montclair* stranded at Orleans and go-ing to pieces in an hour. It had been blowing hard all that weekend and the *Montclair* bound from Halifax to New York with her rigging iced up and her crew dog-weary became help-less and unmanageable. She swung inshore, struck far out and then began to break up. Her foremast and her mainmast worked free, and scissoring grotesquely back and forth across each other they 'levered the ship open,' as one of the Coast Guards said. The vessel burst, the cargo poured into the seas from the broken belly of the hold and the crew of seven men clung to the rocking, drifting mass that was once the stern.

"One great sea drowned five of them. Men on the beach saw it coming and shouted. The men on the deckhouse shouted back and were heard, and then the wave broke hiding the tragic scene in a sluice of foam and wreckage. When this had poured away, the men on the afterhouse were gone. A head was visible for a minute, and then a second drifting southward, and then there was nothing but the sea. . . .

"Two men still clung to the stern rail, one a seventeen-year-old boy, the other a stocky, husky-built sailor. The wave tore the boy from the rail, but the stocky man reached out, caught him and held on . . . Somehow those two hung on and at last were rescued. The whole primitive tragedy was over in a moment of time.

"As the vessel was breaking up, men came to the beach and helped themselves to the cargo and what wreckage they fancied. Later that day there was a kind of auction of the salvaged material." (The "mooncussers" were still going about their business.)

"Some have asked me," he wrote, "what understanding of Nature one shapes from so strange a year? I would answer that one's first appreciation is a sense that the creation is still going on, that the creative forces are as great and as active today as they have ever been, and that tomorrow's morning will be as heroic as any of the world. *Creation is here and now.*"

Editing is the most companionable form of education, and the next friend who added to my understanding of the Cape was a Boston physician. Dr. Wyman Richardson was a big man with a directness and a simplicity most endearing. He stood six feet one-and-a-half and in his prime weighed upwards of 220 pounds, but his bigness was not boisterous; he had a light touch with the fly rod, was soft-spoken, and could watch birds as silently as any. I marked him first, years ago, at the luncheon table at the Harvard Club, where his long back elevated him above the other doctors from the Medical School. Later our kindred interest in the striped bass led us to compare notes at the Tavern Club. Then in the spring of 1947 he admitted shyly that he had been doing some writing about the Cape and would I like to see it. This was the first of a dozen essays we were to publish in the *Atlantic* — essays which are the quintessence of Cape Cod: the winds and the stars, the moods of the sea, the pounding beauty of Nauset Beach by night or dawn, the sound and smell of the fish feeding in the marsh, the land birds and the shore birds of which he had such expert knowledge. These were his heart's desire which he dreamed of in the winter and reveled in during the summer and autumn when, away from his practice, he entered his native element at the Farm House.

The Farm House is a rudimentary shingled cottage at Eastham which looks as if it had grown up out of the earth. The walls of the living room are covered with murals of the Canada goose by Wyman's uncle, the late Frank W. Benson, and in one or two spots the paint has cracked and flaked, but the great birds are still marvelously in motion, and one of them seems to have been shot in the neck — as indeed it was by a younger Richardson, who, home and warm after an icy day in the marsh, had taken aim with the remark, "Want to see me hit that old gander?" not realizing that his shotgun was still loaded. The shot luckily missed the elders who were mounting the stairs on the way to bed, but it must have raised an enormous commotion in that snug room, and the spot was left bare thereafter as a warning to other casuals.

Opening off the living room with its kerosene lamps, the arrowheads, the reels, and the gunrack, the fireplace with its deep bed of ash and on the mantle the little square clock which only Wy could make go, was the kitchen with its coal stove on which Wyman and Charlotte, his wife, prepared dishes which still make my mouth water. Wy was an exquisite cook, and I can see him stooping so as not to decapitate himself on the old oak beam as he entered the door to serve us. With our martinis we might have whitebait fried in deep fat, crispy and so flaky hot that it would burn your tongue, or crabmeat served in quahog shells. The striper chowder was a meal in itself, made from the big majestic head with just the proper accompaniment of onions, potatoes, and butter. Pilot crackers went with it of course. The striper itself Wyman might boil and serve with an egg sauce, new potatoes in their skins, and fresh peas; or you might have it cold for supper with mayonnaise in a salad. Either way, you ate to immobility.

When the tide had flooded in the marsh and was at the turn we would set forth in the long white canoe; Wy paddling stern, big as a Viking with his binoculars hanging on his great torso, one of his sons in the bow, and the guests — young Ted and I — in the thwarts, facing stern and armed with fly rods. We trolled a white feathered fly with a red head; Wy, who knew the pools and the holding grounds where the school stripers would be feeding, maneuvered the boat so as to swing the streamers into the window of the fish and when a three-pounder struck you could hear the reel scream. Paddling home at sunset, he would pause to spot for us the terns, the plover and the different gulls. The canoe would be lifted out and stowed in the boathouse. We would wash the salt water off the gear — then a nightcap before the embers until yawns sent us upstairs to seek the trundle bed under the eaves. Happiness is a quiet thing.

Wyman Richardson did not begin to write until he had had an intimation that his enjoyment of this blessed place might be limited. He had done the work of five men on the home front during the war, and the arthritis which began to afflict him after V. J. Day was a warning that he would have to watch himself. It made him sleepless at first; and in the black hours, he began writing in his mind descriptions and recollections of this Nauset life he loved. When day came he put them down longhand on paper.

He wrote in two ways: mystery stories about the Cape which he hoped would be popular and which were, alas, as stiff as cardboard; and when the spirit moved him he wrote essays that are as natural and comfortable as an old shoe. What he did, what he saw, what he felt, he has preserved for us simply, with a vivid sense of participation, in his book *The House on Nauset Marsh,* an account of his golden days, which will be lived vicariously by those who read of them. Wyman's writing celebrates the beauty of the casual, the serene and the observant. To savor this, one has only to look at the table of contents: "Time Sense," "Blue Crabbing," "Do-Nothing Day," "Eelgrass and Depressions," "Beach and Sea," "Around the Horn," "Tide," "The March Doldrums," "Bird Flight," "Bird Language" — the very titles suggest the range and sensitivity of a wise and devoted man. If I had to pick one to indicate the flavor of his writing, I should choose Chapter 9, "Do-Nothing Day," and for these particulars:

It is September. A before-breakfast weather observation has revealed a sparklingly clear day. A deep blue sky already is beginning to be spotted with fluffy white cumulus clouds, carried before a fresh

northwest breeze. Just the day for energy and activity, you say? No!
It soon becomes apparent that this is a do-nothing day . . .

Then comes a period of sitting on the edge of the low platform on
the south side of the house, with bird glasses near at hand. A gray
marsh hawk, looking almost blue in the bright light, follows his
customary beat between the hills and down across the little meadow
by the Salt Pond Creek. He sails along close to the grass with very
little effort, and sometimes hangs almost motionless on an updraft
as he scans the grass for sign of mouse or other succulent morsel.
Suddenly, over toward the Cedar Bank, the crows begin a great
racket. From all directions more crows can be seen, flying fast and
true to the scene of the disturbance. Shortly, the cause of all this
commotion becomes thoroughly annoyed. A very large red fox, pursued by fifty chattering crows, comes out of the cedars, lopes down
through the hollow and up back of the barn, and disappears through
Mrs. Doane's orchard. Undoubtedly, he will cross the road and make
for the thicket the other side of Robbins' Pond.

Now butterflies claim our attention. The stunning black swallowtail comes floating gracefully by and obligingly lights on the short
grass not far away. She seems not a bit skittish and will allow a
quiet approach to within a few feet, as she spreads her lovely irides-
cent wings to catch the warmth of the sun and to show off the brilliant coral spot in her lower wing. Her mate is never very far away.
He is perhaps not so beautiful as his colorful spouse, but he carries
a fine yellow band near the margin of his wings that contrasts
sharply with his otherwise dark coloring. He is a great fighter, too,
as any black swallowtail who makes the mistake of wandering too
close will soon find out. We see occasionally the tiger swallowtail,
and the powerful monarch is not uncommon, but the black swallowtail belongs particularly to the Farm House . . .

We take to watching the antics of a very large orange and black
wasp with a long, narrow waist — one of the sphecid wasps. We
have previously noted a slanting, half-inch hole in front of which
the sand is piled up in a little mound. This wasp has succeeded in

killing (or drugging?) one of those big flying grasshoppers which are so common down here, and is obviously trying to drag the monster, which is twice her length and three times her weight, to the hole. The distance is six feet, and what to the wasp must seem like a jungle of grass and weeds separates her from the hole. Her method is to grasp the grasshopper near his head with her front legs, and back up towards her destination. Unfortunately, this largely deprives her of the use of her best eyes, her delicate antennae, and she frequently goes astray. Then she lets go her prey and makes a reconnaissance, after which she hurries back. In fact, the most striking thing about her is her panic of haste.

Nothing else can be done until we have seen the feat accomplished. After a long time, the hole is reached and the wasp backs down, dragging the grasshopper after her. For a while nothing happens. Then the wasp comes out minus the grasshopper. How she managed to by-pass him in the tunnel remains a mystery. Feverishly, she starts plugging up the hole, using the mound in front, until it is completely plugged. Then she circles around a few times, comes back once and again to tamp down the plug, and finally flies away — where, we do not know. I suppose she has laid her eggs in the tunnel, and having supplied her future offspring with food, has gone off with the feeling that she has accomplished her mission.

The day ends with Wyman and Charlotte preparing the big meal of broiled striped bass and creamed potatoes, with Orleans cookies and coffee to top it off, a plain and bountiful delight.

Wyman died before his eloquent, observant book appeared, but not before he had heard from *Atlantic* readers who rejoiced in it a piece at a time. I only wish that in his shy way he might have known how many thousands of Americans have found, and would continue to find, pleasure in his heritage.

Hans Zinsser

ON THE wall of my workroom among my prized photographs is one of a man in white ducks and white shirt sitting on the top of a paddock fence grinning down at a fat mare grazing placidly below him. The man is Dr. Hans Zinsser, the bacteriologist, and the mare was the healthy container of the typhus serum which he had devised as an antidote to typhus; the picture was taken by Hans's and my friend Charles P. Curtis, and because the photograph was snapped in the spring sunlight when the fruit trees of Dover were in bloom, one can almost catch the glint of Hans's blue eyes and the color of his crisp, sandy hair.

The country place in Dover, Massachusetts, the mare from which he could drain off the serum needed to combat the plague in Rumania, or Mexico, or China, the hunters which he also stabled here for his rides with the Groton Hunt were the rewards of thirty years' campaigning against infectious diseases. He carried the fight to the vulnerable fronts in the First World War, and thereafter to those points of outbreak where his foreign students were most in need of his aid. The finest portrayal of Hans's spirit was written by his good friend, Dr. John F. Enders, when he said: "Always loving and even often seeking out a struggle where benevolent causes were at stake, this lifelong conflict with the agents of syphilis, tuberculosis, typhus, and the rest — which he regarded perhaps only half humorously as sentient malignities — satisfied in large part his need for dangerous experience in the pursuit of generous ends. Those who surrounded him were set alight and newly energized by this flaming idealism." In his exposure he had contracted typhus fever and it was characteristic of Hans that in his greatest book he employed the incident as an opening for his tribute to the nursing profession and in particular the nurse who prevented him from jumping out a fourth-story window.

He could never take himself too seriously; what he did he did with a smile. Across the front of his barn in Dover in letters a foot high were the words:

DÉFENSE DE JOUER PELOTE

OU

DÉPOSER DES ORDURES

(Since Hans refused to have his foreign quotations translated in his own books, I shall respect his wishes here.)

The grandson of one of the German revolutionaries of 1849, Hans was a cultivated blend of the liberal European tradition and the audacious American spirit. He had within him the resources of four men, and it was part of his greatness that he kept all four actively employed throughout his life.

Poetry was an early love, and he published his first volume of verse while still an undergraduate at Columbia. He wrote in the traditional forms, taking infinite pains in revision; he knew precisely what he wanted to say and if he had trouble it was in making his lines scan. When in doubt he let the sense override the meter. The German romanticist and the rebel in him both showed themselves in his poetry which we published, inciden-

tally, not under his own signature, but under the initials "R.S."
These two poems are, I think, characteristic of his best:

BROTHER

Not long ago when we were dragging hounds
An old hound left the youngsters far behind him,
And wandered off beyond the paneled grounds.
I rode ten miles in vain, that day, to find him.

I failed to track him; but on brittle nights,
When not a cloud obscures the northern lights
And frost holds other creatures snug and still,
I hear his lonely baying on the hill.

Weary of phantom game and aniseed
His brave old heart yearns for ancestral habits,
And hungry, lean and cold, as fits his breed,
He roams in frugal freedom, hunting rabbits.

THE GOAT

His conscience held his passion on a tether
As a wanton goat is fastened to a stake.
The fragile bond that held the two together
Was always taut — not quite enough to break.

Callow romanticism, in youth,
Disguised desires by which he was molested.
Much later he, confronted with the truth,
Could not forgo the virtue he detested.

And thus, forever tugging, yet restrained,
He chafes, the painful collar round his throat;
Takes pride in the convention he's maintained,
But still remains, at heart, a thwarted goat.

[131]

Hans was grounded in the classics, and since his family made annual sojourns on the Continent he came to speak French and German fluently. With this background and his love for poetry it would have been quite natural had he devoted himself to letters. But while still an undergraduate he saw service in the Spanish-American War, in the cavalry, and was shocked at the "unbelievable, miserable sanitary condition of the camps." Hans was a quick man to spark, and when his indignation was aroused it was not easily dampened. It was at this time, and I believe at the urging of his father, that his thoughts turned to medicine, and the relatively new field of immunology.

"I had luck with me," he once told me, "when I began studying the infections of the blood. It was like stepping into a new hotel on the coast: I could have any room for the asking and they all looked out to sea." But leaving the figure of speech aside, it was the laboratory which attracted him, and wherever he worked, whether at Columbia or Leland Stanford or Harvard, the pure flame of his research and enthusiasm, and the banter with which he tended it, fired those who were working close to him. Hans's dedication has been well described by Dr. Enders: "For more than three decades, and until the very last, he was in the laboratory every day and frequently at night. And he was there because he could not stay away. The problem of the moment absorbed him completely. It broke his sleep and dragged him willy-nilly to his experimental animals and his cultures. Its progress, as he has said, largely governed his mood, which was either *'himmelhoch jauchzend'* or *'zum Tode betrübt,'* depending on the success or failure of his experiments." From these experiments came one hundred and six scientific papers recording the research, many of them I suspect published at his own expense. From them too came conversation so pungent and of such breadth that those who formed the habit of lunching with him in the laboratory were never to forget his talk.

Then there was his love for music. He played the violin and the piano with considerable skill, and they were as necessary as his versification. Dr. Harvey Cushing used to tell the story of a visit he paid to the College of Physicians and Surgeons, the old building on 49th Street, in search of Zinsser. It was after 5 on a wintry afternoon and the visitor was told by those who were homeward bound that he would find Dr. Zinsser two flights up and at the end of the corridor. As he approached Cushing thought he heard the sounds of music, and there was no doubt about it as he opened the door. Before him were two men in their stained lab coats: the Professor of Bacteriology playing intently on his violin, and his laboratory assistant playing just as intently on his flute. Cushing was motioned to a seat until the piece was finished.

With this went his passion for horses and for riding (which was why he was in the cavalry). Barbara Danielson, who was Master of the Groton Hunt when Hans was a member, has told me that "he loved the excitement of it, loved a headstrong horse, and he rode well. No flinging at walls, etc. but he loved flying over them. When he was coming down with typhus he spent the night at the Club and had a chill. The next A.M. he rode. I can't remember if he finished or drew out but he went home and had a temperature of about 105°."

He took the tenderest care of that fat mare which was the reservoir for his serum. To keep her company he had procured, I don't know where, an ex-circus horse who was pure white and who would lie down and roll over at command. To the hay-loft he had brought one of the laboratory monkeys who happily adapted himself to the life in Dover. The monkey liked to tease the circus horse and would lie in wait in the loft until the broad white back was beneath him. Then he would drop down and go for a jog around the paddock. The mare lived on clover and unlike Hans she did not come down with typhus fever. In the last months of his life when he was no longer able to ride, he had his saddle brought up to his bedroom so that the smell of the leather could send his thoughts afield.

It was very good luck for me when we moved into an old house on Beacon Hill, one which was directly across the street from the Zinsser residence. This brought us into almost daily contact at a time when my fortunes were rising at the *Atlantic* and when I definitely needed the advice of an older man. Hans's library with bookshelves up to the ceiling and mounds of books stacked on the floor was in the front of the house. He did most of his writing at night and when his light was on I might saunter across for a beer break at 10, and if he didn't want to be interrupted he would throw me out. On Sunday evenings my wife and I would often be invited over for supper and sometimes we would bring with us the tasty leftovers from our icebox to add to the buffet, as there was never any telling how many might turn up. The Bernard DeVotos would come in from Cambridge, Charlie and Frances Curtis down from Joy Street, and likely as not ex-Chancellor Bruening or Lawrence Henderson, and former students from India or China or Paris, with the talk ranging from T. S. Eliot to Pareto, to Hitler and the Black Death.

Hans and I had been drawn closer by the editing of his book, *Rats, Lice and History*. He had accepted my habit of close scrutiny, indeed he had written to Ellery, although I did not know it at the time: "Ted Weeks is perhaps the most skillful pruner I have ever known. I think he could get a larger yield of apple jack from a barrel of hard cider than anybody I know." As for myself, I was enormously taken with the independent thinking, the history, and the racy skepticism which he brought to this book.

Hans says in his Preface that *Rats, Lice and History* was written in protest against "the American attitude which tends to insist that a specialist should have no interests beyond his chosen field — unless it be golf, fishing, or contract bridge. A specialist — in our national view — should stick to his job like 'a louse to a pig's back.' We risk — because of this performance — being thought less of as a bacteriologist. It is worth the risk. . . . We hold that one type of intelligent occupation should, in all but exceptional cases, increase the capacity for comprehension in general; that it is an error to segregate the minds of men into rigid guild classifications; and that art and sciences have much in common and both may profit by mutual appraisal. The Europeans have long appreciated this." The text is written in the vein of one of his favorite authors, Laurence Sterne, and it indulges in the discursions and the sudden pauses for reflections and appreciation and satire which one finds in *Tristram Shandy*. *Rats, Lice and History* purports to be the biography of a disease, typhus, and in passages of fascinating analysis he showed how that enemy of man by ravaging the armies of the Crusaders and those which Napoleon had led to Moscow had changed the fate of Europe. Hans's statistics were appalling and they came right down to our own time. I remember one in particular: "between 1917 and 1923 there were 30,000,000 cases of typhus with 3,000,000 deaths in European Russia alone."

In his digressions Hans spoke out as a scientist who dared challenge the arts. The cult of unintelligibility in poetry and criticism had aroused his ire, and now he had his fun with what was obscure and pretentious in contemporary literature. He satirized Gertrude Stein and T. S. Eliot (whose poetic gifts he did not question), he twitted Whitehead for being needlessly abstruse, and in his scrutiny he was unsparing and provocative as these samples indicate:

Freud is a great man. But it is dangerous when a great man is too easily half-understood. The Freudian high explosives have been worked into firecrackers for the simple to burn their fingers. It has become easy to make a noise and a bad smell with materials compounded by the great discoverer for the blasting of tunnels . . .

If an epidemiologist on a plague study talked and behaved in the manner of the hero of *Arrowsmith,* he would not only be useless, but he would be regarded as something of a yellow ass and a nuisance by his associates. And de Kruif is far too intelligent a man not to have known, when he wrote his thriller on *Men Against Death,* that raucous laughter would be its reception in the laboratories and in the field where the work he describes is being done.

The response to *Rats, Lice and History* was immediate. We went through four printings in the first month. Critics praised it for its erudition, and for the wit and penetration of the writing. Dr. Thomas Barbour, an old friend of Hans, reviewed it for the *Atlantic,* and I sent Hans advance galleys and received back this letter of protest:

"It was kind of you to send me Tom Barbour's review. It filled me with consternation, though I know how warmly it flowed out of a friendship for which I am very grateful. Can you tone down the personal stuff about my 'reckless courage' and getting myself injected, etc. a bit without hurting his feelings. Don't for anything let him know how it affected me. His heart is proportionate to the rest of him."

In an age which glorifies publicity, it is something of a surprise to find how rigorously opposed to it most professional men are. Hans was a martinet in this respect. He was opposed to our using photographs of him in our advertising, he went over the jacket blurb pruning out every reference which he thought excessive, and he kept an eagle eye on the advertising. I could not police what other editors did, though he thought I should have been able to, and when the *Saturday Review* reproduced a snapshot of him they had dug up from somewhere, I received a cable from the League of Nations Conference on Immunology reading: PLEASE PREVENT PUBLICATION MY PICTURE GIVES ME JITTERS. ZINSSER.

There was a lesson in this for me as for any editor, and Hans summed it up very fairly in a letter to me which deserves to be quoted:

It is quite natural that the points of view of publishers should be different from those of professional men, but since we work together we ought to explain ourselves clearly to each other. It is not merely my own personal opinion, but an almost accepted tenet among scientific men who do not wish to cheapen themselves and their profession, to avoid using any kind of scientific standing or reputation in advertising anything they may undertake in other directions. My writing is an entirely separate occupation, and while of course it is impossible to conceal the fact that I am also a bacteriologist and am writing to some extent about medical things, I would seriously object to any exploitation of whatever position I may hold in the scientific world or of scientific work I am doing for the sake of advertisement and efforts to increase the sales of any of my lay writings. It is not only a matter that is repugnant to me personally, but it would humiliate me as well in the eyes of my scientific peers.

The reception accorded to *Rats, Lice and History* was gratifying and the demand for the book continues to this day; the copy from which I have been quoting is from the twenty-fifth printing. Hans felt encouraged to go on, and he made some preliminary sketches about his parents in Westchester and some travelogues, etchings about Europe in the manner of the *Sentimental Journey*. As always this was done at night, for his program of research and teaching at the Medical School was a heavy one and the writing suffered from being spasmodic. "I stub my toe against the first person singular," he wrote in January 1937, "and know that I could write faster and better if, in some way, I could write more impersonally." What he was aiming for was, in his own words, "as much as possible, an optimistic *Education of Henry Adams,* somewhat disconnected, dealing with the educational career, medical development in America, episodes and occurrences in epidemic regions, war and hospital and university life, etc. . . . Of course, it sounds ambitious when I mention Henry Adams because I think he was a great artist, but I give you my model only because it was through a rereading of the *Education* that I conceived this plan."

The project came into focus when he decided to write, in the third person, the life of a bacteriologist who would be known as R.S., a medical man known intimately to Dr. Zinsser and whose career touched his at many points. This device freed Hans from the feeling of personal mortification; it gave him the opportunity to open or close doors as he pleased; it also gave him the opportunity of being very discursive. The writing was broken into by many interruptions, and when at last the first draft entitled "More Truth Than Poetry" was submitted, I had to tell him that we were disappointed. It was a work of great promise but it rambled, and there was too little live connective tissue to bind the parts together. I wrote out a chapter-by-chapter analysis indicating those pages and those passages that I was sure he could strengthen, and my notations read like this:

Chapter III Though I sympathize with everything you say through here, I do feel that this chapter is rather slow motion, especially if it is to be read so early in the book. It needs more narrative and locomotive power to carry your reflections on anti-Semitism. Couldn't you work into it one telling example of racial intolerance that has come within your experience? Were this inserted at the outset, it would give more movement to the whole.

Chapters IV and V Both of these need good chapter headings. Both of them have that static, essay quality which one expects of a philosophical discussion, but which is hardly appropriate to the robust years of adolescence, through which you are supposed to be passing at this time. Chapter IV seems to me the more vulnerable of the two, and although the episode about your mother is very moving, I think the chapter as a whole would be more effective were it moved back to serve as an interlude between the romantic reminiscences and the early medical life. Chapter V gives us an endearing picture of Woodberry, but here again I feel the need of spice, and the briskness of a little additional narrative. Would it be appropriate to mention your Spanish War experiences here by way of contrast, even though the episode be no longer than two pages?

Chapter XV, page 213 Your passing allusion to the New York cavalry and the Spanish War makes me wonder why this phase of R. S.'s experience did not receive its proper mention in his adolescent years. It would add spice to one of the early chapters, and chronologically it belongs there.

Chapter XVII, pages 235-8 This is the second time that you speak of the reaction against the Germans in America during the War. To avoid the repetition, might it not be better to move these episodes forward to that early chapter where the subject first arises? The episodes themselves are good.

There was much more, several pages single-spaced, and Hans took it in good heart, although it was clear to us both that the book would have to be deferred for at least a year.

Early in 1938 Dr. Zinsser was in China helping pupils of his stave off an epidemic of typhus which came raging on the heels of the Japanese invasion. He returned to Boston late that spring feeling below par and went for a physical checkup to his physician and personal friend Bill Breed. Perhaps he had already guessed what the finding would be for he took it stoically: he was incurably ill with lymphatic leukemia. He told me in July; he thought at that time that he had twelve months left and the thing he wanted most to do was to revise and finish that book. It was the first time I had seen one I loved under the death sentence, and his courage was contagious and wonderful. He carried on his work at the Medical School and in the laboratory; he submitted himself as a guinea pig for the most exhausting X-ray treatment for leukemia, and in the evenings he devoted himself to the big manuscript. He was determined to finish it and "Damn you, don't you ever refer to it as an autobiography," he said jokingly, "for it isn't." I crossed Chestnut Street a number of times in those spring evenings, for under his relentless concentration the book came magnificently into the clear, a work in biography whose gaiety and laughter, whose tenderness, whose knowledge of men and of medicine make it unique.

The questions which it posed were fascinating. For instance, the text was sprinkled with foreign quotations, and the question was should they be translated. Hans said no. "I took a good deal of trouble with the style of this book, and it is my conviction that one must write naturally, as one thinks, and not cut up paragraphs with a lot of translations of minor phrases. . . . The kind of audience for whom the book is largely meant will not be troubled by the present arrangement."

The question of the title was resolved by Mr. Sedgwick on a postcard. It read:

Here's a go at it —
Reflections in the Glass
My Lifelong Friend
Myself and I
Said I to Myself
My Next Friend
A Friend of Mine
He and I
R. S. and I
In My Mirror
My Looking Glass
R.S., As I Remember Him

Mirror of Life
Living
Ladders of Life
R. S. and His Friend
My Other Self
A Part of Myself
Living It Over
These may set you thinking.

E. S.

Of self-pity there is none in *As I Remember Him*. The note of poignancy heard toward the close is that life is of necessity so brief. "Ted," he said to me one morning when the book was nearly done, "if I could only find a raft to step onto from this old hulk — there is so much more writing I would like to do." He did keep the "old hulk" afloat for a year longer than he expected and so lived to see the book published, selected by the Book-of-the-Month Club, and widely praised. I myself rank it on the very top shelf of American biography; for its warmth and clarity I think I should put it ahead of *The Education of Henry Adams* which was its prototype.

Hans had to answer all manner of embarrassing questions about the identity of R.S. Did the initials stand for his Romantic Self? No. Did they stand for Dr. Richard Strong, a contemporary of his at the School of Public Health? No. Did they speak for Lawrence Henderson in disguise? No. The simplest explanation perhaps is that they are the last letters in reverse of Hans's own name. The invasion of a doctor's privacy still troubled him. He objected to the tone of our advertising; he winced (and gave me hell) when Henry Seidel Canby, writing for the *Book-of-the-Month Club News,* constantly alluded to the volume as an autobiography; and he roared when a representative of *Life* telephoned him to say that they wanted to make a pictorial laboratory study for the magazine. "I told him that one of the strongest purposes of my life was to prevent that sort of thing from ever happening and I could promise him a flat refusal. I also indiscreetly said I would pay money not to have it done and would threaten him with murder if he did it. Nevertheless, perhaps thinking that he has the attributes of a snake charmer, he insisted on seeing me for five minutes tomorrow morning. I will try to make these five minutes interesting for him and will feel that I have done my duty to you thereby. The whole idea is dreadful, especially at a time like this."

Hans Zinsser

Hans Zinsser was sixty-two when he died. In the memorial exercises which were held at the Harvard Medical School his colleagues and his students paid their tribute, and the most eloquent of them all was Dr. Enders, who said at the close: "And so it would seem that all his life he was preparing himself for these last two years, when he came to know that the end could not be far away. We who were with him then will ever be the better for having seen him tranquilly continuing his researches, writing his books, and teaching his students as if no term had been set. But the attainment of this inward calm was not as easy as he would have us believe from what he has written. . . ."

At this point it seems appropriate to recall the words which Hans himself had written at the end of *As I Remember Him:* "As his disease caught up with him, R.S. felt increasingly grateful for the fact that death was coming to him with due warning, and gradually. So many times in his active life he had been near sudden death by accident, violence, or acute disease; and always he had thought that rapid and unexpected extinction would be most merciful. But now he was thankful that he had time to compose his spirit, and to spend a last year in affectionate and actually merry association with those dear to him."

"T. B."

DR. THOMAS BARBOUR, known to his friends as "T. B.," was a legend long before I ever knew him, a legend compounded in Florida, Cuba, Panama, the East Indies, Harvard, Boston, and Beverly Farms. The legend told me that he was big — six foot five, 255 pounds in his prime — with a curiosity and a generosity that went with his bigness; that he had a prodigious memory, and a hearty humor; was fearless; had a way with snakes, and a willow thumb for fossils. Rumor said that he had identified a vast number of reptiles and amphibians in North America and that his work on the birds of Cuba was unique. He did much of his work underground in caves, and when the going was dangerous he would unroll a ball of tough twine, the end of which he had secured to a tree at the cavern's mouth: this would serve as a guideline in case he had to back out.

"Why don't you get Tom Barbour to do you an article on snakes?" said my friend Theodora Codman. "He knows more about boa constrictors than any man living. Ask him about the one that escaped from his suitcase in the Pullman." But actually the first manuscript he wrote for us came uninvited in the summer of 1942, and it was a brief but very amusing account of some zoological atrocities which he had unearthed in the museums of Boston, Salem, and Cambridge. He spoke of horrors such as a cask containing the pickled heads of Chinese garnered many decades ago on the beach at San Francisco after a riot, and of absurdities such as the miscellaneous collection of gallstones which he ejected from the Peabody Museum in Salem — more than a pint, and all donated except for "MRS. CHASE'S GALL-STONES," which, according to the card, were the largest and on loan — and had been for a century. Dr. Barbour in his house-cleaning of the Glory Holes, as he called the museums, gave fresh emphasis to the objects worth preserving and the cata-loguing came alive. "Think what a story you can build about the giant tortoise of the Galapagos," he wrote. "The old whalers called them turpin. For generations all the ships that chanced to be near the Galapagos Islands, about six hundred miles south-westward of Panama, went ashore turtling. The crews carried the beasts down to the beach, boated them to the ships, and piled them up in their empty holds. Here, being the strange creatures that they are, they survived for months without food or water. When scurvy appeared the turtles were butchered. The flesh was savory even when poorly prepared. There was enough fat in each one to shorten a mess of duff, and the water in their bladders was cool and clear . . . Seventeen zoological species of turtles have been described. But this is not the point which we want the magnificent specimen at Salem to illustrate — rather, what turtles like this meant to seamen from the time of Dampier down to about 1867, when petroleum knocked out whale oil. Probably no fewer than half a million turpin were carried away, and now all the races of the creatures are rare or extinct."

When I accepted his article, it was natural to ask for more, and so our acquaintance began. I went out to Cambridge to lunch with him in his little private dining room, the "Eateria," a part of his spacious quarters in the Agassiz Museum, full of books, photographs, and curios. I remember that we had delicious chunks of fried eel with papaya for dessert. Dr. Barbour was gaunter than I had been led to suppose, but his head was massive with square-cut features, bushy brows, and a mass of thick white curls. His right hand had the habit of twisting and retwisting one of those curls, and I noticed that the hand itself trembled. Present were two of his good friends, Bill Claflin, then the Treasurer of Harvard, and Dr. Henry Bigelow, the famous oceanographer. The talk ranged widely; this was the closest I had ever come to biology and I tried to conceal my ignorance by listening, but I understood enough to realize that there were the makings of a remarkable book here.

Man's relation to the animals' world and theirs to their own peculiar environment, this had been Dr. Barbour's lifelong study; he strove to repopulate and to document the earth before spoliation, as his heroes Darwin and Wallace, Audubon and Bertram had done before him, and his travels had taken him everywhere, to remote islands like the Solomons, to deep-sea caves and tropical forests. On his honeymoon, which lasted two years, he and Mrs. Barbour had followed in Wallace's footsteps to India, Burma, and Malaya, along the Irrawaddy River to French Indo-China, and thence to China and Japan. He knew the interior of Brazil and had crossed the Andes; Panama was like the back of his hand; he had been twelve times to Cuba, twenty-two times to the West Indies. The editorial problem was how to segregate such rich but diverse material; how to shape the continuity so that the pungent anecdotes would build the interest instead of being self-contained, and *how to get it all on paper.*

Dr. Barbour suffered from a heart condition which had left him agitated and apprehensive; it was clear that any writing he did longhand would have to be sustained by relaxed periods of dictation. His health was much on his mind. "I can't sleep," he complained to me early in our friendship. "I wake up every morning at five."

"What time do you go to bed?" I asked, being an insomniac myself.

"Oh, about ten."

"Well, that's not too bad," I said. "Seven hours. What do you do when you wake up?"

"I just lie there," he said pitifully, "and listen to the soughing of the pines." (This was at his summer place in Beverly Farms.)

"Well, instead of suffering," I suggested, "why don't you begin to think of the new episodes you're going to dictate, and when they are clear in mind, have breakfast and be driven up to Cambridge?" Miss Helene Anderson, his infallible secretary, did not thank me for this, for it resulted in his appearance in the Museum at sunup — and hers, too — but it explains why the first draft came so quickly into being. It was at this point that we became "Tom" and "Ted" to each other.

Reminiscences when they are dictated tend to move in circles. Tom's chapters as he first thought them out took off, again and again, with his grandmother as a focal point — for reasons I shall come to — or they began with his fabulous honeymoon; they would then follow out a line of thought or an expedition with its glorious, unpredictable sidelights, zoom through the years and come back to Cambridge and the present. His text sounded like his talk; it was charged with affection and gusto, it avoided self-dramatization, laughed at himself and his exploits in the field, and was agreeably random as it moved from the great botanists to memorable meals to butterflies to pygmy lemurs to whales. Repetitions crop out much more frequently in dictation than they do in handwriting, where the eye can catch them, and I soon came to know Tom's pet phrases. "It was my great good fortune" was one of them, and my fortune would be greater if I had a dollar for every time that I removed that tag from the beginning of one of his paragraphs. "Which has hitherto eluded notice" was another frequent customer, and I could tell that T. B. was getting tired when I met the cliché "Well, to make a long story short." But these were minor irritants; much of this was high-grade ore, and when we had a large chunk of it in type my enthusiasm prompted me to show it to my associates at Little, Brown.

Their reaction was not as expected. Roger Scaife's report began: "Thomas Barbour is a great man, a greater individualist, and the world's worst writer. I can't conceive of Weeks' sending it over in its present condition . . ." Ray Everett expressed the hope that we could divert it to a university press and Alfred McIntyre, who was the referee in such matters, wrote: "On the basis of the enclosed reports, it looks to us as if the Barbour manuscript needed the old Weeks touch and a great deal of work by said Mr. Weeks. I recall that some of our comments on the first draft of Zinsser's last book were a little discouraging but that you were able to pull it together . . ." I can explain some of this by saying that at the time William Beebe was the popular naturalist in print and that Beebe's prose was bland and silk-smooth. Compared to Will Beebe, T. B. was a diamond in the rough. But it might be quite a diamond!

For uncounted hours in the next seven months my assistant Dudley Cloud and I worked on the revision of Tom's manuscript. We removed the repetitions; we aerated the paragraphs which were too tight-packed; we questioned Tom about those areas where our curiosity had been aroused but not satisfied.

And we helped him rewrite — or ourselves rewrote — every second sentence. All scientists talk and write in a jargon which becomes the shorthand of their calling but which when reduced to print can be a very punishing, cryptic English for the layman. (The social scientists and the pyschologists are the worst offenders in this.) Tom responded to our probing; his memory was sunlit and like an IBM machine; he knew the Latin name and physical properties of every specimen he had ever identified and with a smile he would recall the particular hazards he had encountered in the more difficult quests. So the text took an additional color and depth.

This would be an impulsive book, not a step-by-step autobiography. We regrouped the contents under three headings: the first, the experiences of the young T. B. in the field, we called "The Making of a Naturalist." The next section described his life as a museum director and gave informal, affectionate portraits of his heroes and friends — Louis and Alexander Agassiz, March Cope and Shaler; David Fairchild, John Phillips, Alfred Kidder and Henry Bigelow. The final third, under the subtitle "The Leisurely Approach," showed the more reflective naturalist; here we put the agreeable voyages to Central America aboard his friend Allison Armour's yacht; his vivid speculation on whales; his account of the sanctuaries in Panama, Cuba and Florida which he had fought to preserve; his chapter on evolution which, in a very few pages, went to the heart of the question, and the philosophical walks and talks which he used to have with his summer neighbor, Mr. Justice Oliver Wendell Holmes. The tributes which he bestowed on all those who had served him loyally at Harvard we placed in an appendix.

The manuscript was resubmitted for judgment, and was accepted with the comment from Scaife that it was "vastly improved." Under my title *Naturalist at Large* it appeared in the fall of 1943, went through three printings before Christmas, and five more were called for thereafter. Not a spectacular sale but a steady one for a book which is truly an American landmark, a book which I believe the suburban-bound Americans of the future will resurrect because of what it tells, as David Fairchild puts it, "of this vanishing world of forests and prairies, watercourses and bubbling springs — the world of wild animals and untouched wilderness."

While the revision was still in progress Tom was literally pouring out, like a magnum from which the cork has been drawn, the contents of his second book, about the state which was dearest to him, Florida. He was dictating more skillfully now, but my friendly questioning sessions continued and that I must occasionally have kept him waiting I see from the inscription of the photograph he then gave me: "To the Timeless Weeks from the poor, punctual, old cuss, T. B." He was in a hurry.

What diverts a unique mind from the habitual pursuits, the practice of law or of medicine, or, as in Tom's case, from the manufacture of linen thread, the family's mainstay since 1784? T. B. was blest with sharp eyesight and a photographic memory, but it was his grandmother who put him on his way. She must have been a remarkable and perceptive woman, Sarah Elizabeth Barbour: small, fine-featured and alert as she looks out at us from the picture taken on her veranda in Eau Gallie in 1898. That was the year when Tom, recuperating from typhoid, made his first visit to her in Florida. Walden Cottage was what she called her spacious, white-frame house on the

Indian River, and the name speaks for the impetus she was to give the boy. In a fishing launch with an engine made of solid bronze — "Grandmother hated the idea of sitting near a rusty engine" — she and her fourteen-year-old grandson went fishing, trolling for sea trout. The channel deepened opposite Merritt's Island where the Indian and the Banana Rivers join and here they passed back and forth across the front of a great shell mound, thirty feet high from the river shore to its top. As the hand line throbbed in their fingers they speculated about this great mound, and she fired his imagination. "We often talked about how smelly the top of the mound must have been," he wrote, "as a dwelling place, for of course the whole great accumulation was formed by Indians sitting around their campfires and for years unnumbered throwing the shells of the mollusks they ate over their shoulders, so to speak." Her desire to unlock the past gave him confidence; it imbued him with a single purpose. A year later in 1899 Tom visited Cambridge, and on his first trip to the Agassiz Museum, officially known as the Museum of Comparative Zoology, he spotted some specimens which he believed to be mislabeled — as indeed they were — and there and then he resolved that one day he should become its director.

Florida played a formative, indeed incisive, part in his career. He came to it first when Miami was a settlement of a few hundred, and as David Fairchild has said, he was "the last of the great naturalists to have set foot in Florida when its charm as a naturalist's paradise was still unchanged by fires and canals and roadways" — the roadways that now bring to it eight million tourists a year. There has been nothing quite like this rise of a great tropical peninsula from its days of wilderness and beauty to one of cities and civilization. Tom saw it all. For half a century he dug and collected, hunted and fished his way through the 67 counties. He had a Model T station wagon rebuilt for his expeditions: little cupboards for the onions, sweet potatoes and other staples; slings overhead for the guns, and a rear compartment for a tent, folding chairs, camp cots, and a dog. With Rosamond, his wife, and their inseparable friend, John Phillips the naturalist, and Frank Carlisle for their man Friday, they explored the waterways, the forests and scrub, and Tom's findings as he dictated them for his second book, *That Vanishing Eden,* made it an invigorating and poignant classic. Poignant, because so much of the wildness that he saw is gone.

There is an old saying that "he who fishes most catches most." One day when Frank Carlisle was rowing the boat and Tom, in the stern, trolling for big-mouth black bass, as Tom tells it, "I looked up — and there, sticking out of the canal bank just above the water level, was a little black patch of something, a couple of square inches in area. I said, without feeling much of the spirit of surprise: 'There's an elephant's tooth.' Frank was utterly bewildered and began to argue that there had been no circus about." They put ashore and Tom dug the tooth free with his fingers, for the sand was soft. He marked the spot, and on his return sometime later he unearthed the great shoulder blade and other fragments of a gigantic elephant, a beast which he estimated was over thirteen feet tall.

It was Tom's passion to preserve, and when the Barbour fortune permitted, he bought what would otherwise be destroyed. So it was with the old Raeford Thomas Farm, 45 miles from Gainesville and long abandoned, which Tom bought and deeded to the University of Florida. Fossils of the Lower Miocene Age were found here, and when Tom took control the "dig" deepened to an excavation from which came the skull of a rhinoceros, the remains of small camels, and other ancient beasts which seemed so far removed from our continent. When Rosamond visited the excavation in 1944 she too began to dig, and before the afternoon was over she had accumulated quite a number of bones, including the molar tooth of a giant rodent, an earlier, angrier forefather of the North American porcupine. "Here," said Tom, "in a short space of time spent scratching about she had found evidence of the presence of a whole category of animals, no vestige of which had ever appeared before." When such things happened to the Barbours, it wasn't just luck.

Tom's home place in Florida after the death of his grandmother was the Kampong, the eight-acre estate which David and Marion Fairchild had converted into a tropical garden. Tom loved everything about it: the old original house of silverygray pine; David's office in the ancient potting shed with the workroom on the second floor nested right in the heart of a live oak. Tom admired what David had done with the oriental trees and flowering shrubs which flourished in this rich tropical earth as if they had been planted here for centuries; he doted on the exotic food which David delighted to serve: the Chinese jujubes and persimmons, the dasheen which David tried to persuade me was richer than any potato, the mangoes, alligator pears and always the delicious fish. The Fairchilds had built a little bungalow of native stone for Tom and it became his sanctuary. He was always up at dawn, would cook his own breakfast, and then go down to watch the sunrise across the bay and to enjoy the flight of the pelicans, the gulls and grebes and egrets. The bungalow was his hideaway, and in it he planned and wrote most of his book on Florida.

The Kampong preserved the Florida that might have been.

The instinct to safeguard for perpetuity small areas of virgin natural beauty prompted T. B. as it prompted Thoreau. It prompted him to take a leading part with his friends Robert and Nell Montgomery in the creation of the Fairchild Tropical Garden; it prompted him to join with John Phillips in setting aside a small forest of virgin pine in New Hampshire; it prompted him to establish the Barro Colorado Island Laboratory on a tropical hilltop, filled with wildlife, which had suddenly become an island with the flooding of Gatun Lake in Panama; it prompted his gifts and his devotion to the Garden at Soledad in Cuba.

I have said enough to indicate that what Grandmother Barbour began, Rosamond carried through to completion. It was indeed Tom's "extreme good fortune," to use his words, that he found Rosamond. Her humor equaled his, and was saucier; her resourcefulness, her courage, her adaptability — which could hardly have been pre-tested in the Back Bay — were equal to any occasion.

They were married in 1906 when she was twenty-three, and then set forth on that honeymoon which was to take her to the most improbable spots. In her Gibson girl trousseau, the long skirt, blouse with high whalebone collar, straw boater with a wide brim, white gloves and a gay parasol — a parasol to match each dress — she suddenly found herself transported to New Guinea and so photographed in the center of an admiring tribe of pygmies who were as naked as Adam. When they came to Lucknow in India, she and Tom were taken to a village which had been terrified by a giant cobra. The cobra lived in a burrow near the path leading to the village; only a few days before the Barbours arrived a child had been bitten and had died. No native was going to take a chance with that cobra, but Tom decided to go after it. Here is how he describes it in *Naturalist at Large:*

We trudged out across the dusty plain and came at last to the little hole where the villagers said the cobra lived. I had an old entrenching tool which I used to dig insects out of rotten logs, and with this I commenced to enlarge the hole cutting down in the hard-baked earth. I got down about a foot before I saw what was obviously the skin of either a lizard or a snake. I gave it a poke with my digger and out came the most magnificent cobra you ever saw.

It came out, reared up, its beady eyes peering from side to side as it moved its head inquiringly, its tongue flashing. I had to have a picture of it. [Tom's camera was one of those large old-fashioned boxlike contraptions in which you insert a whole plate.] I got the picture by lying down on the ground and edging up until I was right in front of the snake. My wife stood by with an open parasol and when the cobra saw fit to make a nip at the camera, which meant coming pretty close to my face and hands, she would lower the parasol in front of him and he would sway back and straighten up again. I took a number of excellent photographs and then carefully shot the snake with a charge of dust-shot in a .38 cartridge so as to damage him as little as possible.

Ros never lost her composure, not even on that afternoon in India when she and Tom had been collecting butterflies. There were clumps of flowering shrubs, waist high, and in they waded, making passes with the net until, happening to look up, they saw before them in a small clearing "a perfectly magnificent tiger —" the phrase is Tom's — "his tail straight in the air, its tip flicking." Since there was no place for them to run to, they simply stood there side by side with that absurd butterfly net — and watched the tiger walk majestically out of sight.

To think of Tom is to remember some of the stories which created his legend and to which he added fresh luster every day he lived. He is a sophomore at Harvard and instead of worrying about clubs he is striving to win the approval of Alexander Agassiz. Agassiz, who has been exploring the sea, is deep in a study of coral reefs, so, come summer vacation, T. B. charters a schooner to dredge for sponges in the Bahamas. The reward is in Tom's words: "He was obviously interested in what we found, and I remember one sponge over which he was really excited."

There is a postscript to this: he found that regularly at 10 o'clock each evening Agassiz was in Cambridge "he would go to the Holly Tree at Harvard Square, famous for its beautifully poached eggs. He would eat two of these, drink a glass of beer and then walk back to his house on Quincy Street. I made bold to meet him there quite casually and after a while often walked home with him." This singleness of purpose is endearing; how else could an undergraduate get close enough to question Agassiz informally.

Whatever he did was in his style. He was showing Theodora Codman the collection of pickled snakes in the Museum, and she remarked that one of them which had its head stuck out of the jar must be disintegrating. Tom reached it down, thrust his nose deep, inhaled and came up with a grin. "Sweet as a nut," he said.

David Fairchild, the plant explorer, was, as I have said, Tom's mentor, and David's famous book *The World Is My Garden* a model never to be attained. But when David read an advance copy of *Naturalist at Large,* he wrote to T. B. in Boston:

"T. B."

To say that the tears came to my eyes when I gazed at you and Jimmie standing before the cave [in the frontispiece] would not be an exaggeration for the mixture of memories that it brought up out of the depths was something amazing. I saw you seated on a rock with your feet in the surf and your trousers wet through when you said, "This is the kind of thing I could no longer do if that high position which some of my friends are boosting me for, should be offered to me and I should take it." I saw Jimmie with his gun trembling in his hands when he missed the "Sea Pie" on Great Inagua. I saw you with a crowd of eager collectors about you selling you bags full of snails. I heard you say as we climbed over those needle-sharp rocks on East Plana Key, trying to get near the Osprey's nest, "If you stumble here you would be so messed up that the only thing to do would be to fill you with shot and bury you on the shore."

Tom's voice was hoarse and low and he said things like that with a brusqueness to cover his emotion.

On a walk through the Harvard Yard with President Lowell, Tom expressed his dismay at the disappearance of all the great characters in the college: Shaler gone, Professor Sophocles, William James, and Kittredge about to retire, the whole place had lost the zest, there were no characters left.

"Tom," said the President, "how long since you've looked in the mirror?"

Agnes Newton Keith

THE *Atlantic* is more receptive to unknown writers than any other magazine I can think of in America. The truth is that we need young writers quite as much as they need us. Their unsolicited manuscripts come to us "over the transom," tossed in and uninvited, and always one — sometimes as many as six — will be found in any issue.

In the autumn of 1937 a manila envelope with bizarre stamps reached my desk. The letter accompanying the manuscript began: "I enclose the account of Saudin, a young Murut of North Borneo, who visited America. I was recently engaged in the struggle with home mail when Saudin arrived back at our home in Sandakan after his visit to the United States. Saudin and our 'boy,' Arusap, are brother Muruts from the same village and Saudin has always been accustomed to weekend in our back-quarters when in the vicinity of Sandakan. When Arusap interrupted my mail to tell me that Saudin had returned from my country with news of its strange doings we called him in, and my husband and I spent all morning listening to his naive but not un-wise comments about what he had seen." And it ended, "I am an American woman married to an Englishman in Civil Service, the Conservator of Forests for British North Borneo." The author signed herself Agnes Newton Keith.

Saudin, it appeared, had taken care of the wild animals the Martin Johnsons had captured in Borneo and were shipping back to the States; at the end of the voyage he had passed several months in New York City, wandering about with an "IF LOST RETURN TO ———" tag on his collar and marveling at the behavior of American women who in the dead of winter "did not wear many clothes except around their necks, where they wore the skin of animals."

When he was asked what he liked best of all in New York, he said "the red electric signs that run like streams of fire," and he added, "Mr. Johnson took me to eat at a place where you put money in a hole and take out a plate of food. I think this place was very cunning indeed, because the hole to receive a ten-cent piece was so small that you could not put in a five-cent piece, and the hole for a five-cent piece did not answer if you put in a one-cent piece." Saudin's experiences, so shrewd and innocent, were related in Malay to Mrs. Keith and her husband, and her translation was a happy discovery for the *Atlantic*.

It took six weeks for my letter of acceptance to reach Sandakan and by return post came a second manuscript accompanied by this message: "Saudin visits us occasionally, and I give him news of America. His natural niceness has not been spoiled by his travels. He does not work energetically, but why should he? His bank account will last him a lifetime, as a Murut spends money. His store clothes have been much admired. A few years ago the popular picture postal card in Borneo was Mensaring, the Murut Chief, in loin cloth. Now it is Any Murut in Saudin's borrowed New York suit." The letter went on: "The natives of this country are a saddening, maddening, lovable, heartbreaking lot. They are a gentle and courteous people, yet one from whom the zest of life seems to have been taken since the ancient rite of Headhunting has been banned by Government . . ."

I held up the publication of this second paper, since it gave me the definite hope that we had the makings of a book here and I knew that the serial would be more effective when the volume was finished. Instead of acceptance, I sent her the announcement of an *Atlantic* $5000 Award which we were offering for the best book of nonfiction to reach us by February 1939, and I added this encouragement:

. . . What I want you to do is to tell the story of your daily life in North Borneo so that any stay-at-home here or in England might read it with an active sense of participation. Sandakan, you say, is "ultra-conventional English." Well, so it may be to your experienced eye, but from the evidence I have seen thus far in your narratives, there are trimmings which would set your headquarters apart from most other outposts of England. The book should begin, then, with a friendly account of your headquarters, how long you have been in Sandakan, the scope of your husband's activity, the nature of your compound and its staff, and once having defined your daily orbit, you will be free to take up the strangers who interrupt your routine — Usip and Abanawas — and equally free to write about those excursions to Sulu Sea or that longer jaunt up the Kinabatangan River . . . I want you — "Agnes Newton Keith" as you sign yourself — to be the connecting link, and thus your presence in every chapter is required, whether as referee, partisan, or merely an observer.

"To journey together is happiness," she had once written — indeed, this was to be the theme of the book — and she gave me fascinating itineraries of the journeys she made with her husband: "We plan to leave here in three weeks for a trip into

Agnes Newton Keith

Interior North Borneo. From the border of Dutch Borneo we will go in native canoes up the Kalabakang River to its head-waters, then cross the watershed on foot, and come down the rapids of the Kinabatangan River in small native boats. This country is the last stronghold of the headhunters, and has not been visited by white men since about 1880, at which time a punitive expedition was directed against the headhunters for their activities. We will see natives who have had no contact with civilization, living their own way of life. I can see material for stories which should come from the trip in time. Might a more direct journal form of the trip also be acceptable? No white woman has been in the part of the country I mention. I do not mention this from the Adventuring White Woman point of view, because all the initiative in these trips is my husband's and I just go along. But I do find in comparing notes with men that I see different things in the native villages from what the men see."

Of course I wanted the journal of that trip for the book, and I wanted other more homely details too. Where did she go for a hair-do in Sandakan? (To the Chinese, she replied.) How did Harry protect his rare books on botany from the damp heat? (They had built an inner room, she said, which could seal off the effect of the rains.) How many Europeans were there in Sandakan and what was the attitude toward the Eurasians and the other racial groups on this, the third largest island in the world? This was deliberate needling, but I was eager to have her finish the book for the contest, and I was not sure she could make it in the intervening year for she seemed to be laboring under difficulties, whether from the heat or illness I could not determine.

Her manuscript arrived in the closing days, and as the outer wrapping with the gay, even more exotic stamps was removed, here was a mound of white paper bound up in a sarong of striking brown and blue design. (We were to reproduce that lovely pattern later for the binding.) The top page bore the title *Land Below the Wind* and beneath the last page, separated by tissue, were pencil sketches of Sandakan, the houseboys, the affectionate apes who were the family pets, a tent in a dripping jungle and the author propped up in a cot, writing underneath an open umbrella — casual drawings which conveyed so surely, often humorously, what Agnes wanted the reader to see.

The title was beautifully euphonious, but whatever did it mean? *Land Below the Wind,* we were told, was the translation of the Malay name for Borneo. The use of the southwest monsoon for trading led the ancient navigators to divide Southern Asia into lands "to its windward" and others "to its leeward." Borneo, in the latter group, was thus the "land below the wind." This point being clarified, the judges went on to read.

As I have indicated, this was a book of episodes, some of them laid in Sandakan, which was the capital of North Borneo, others deep in the forests or in remote native villages. When Harry went on his official expeditions, Agnes went with him, eager, protesting and usually vulnerable. The trip to Timbun Mata Island held moments of "immoderate joy." "On the other hand," as she says, "there were also the leeches, pig-ticks, mosquitoes, sand flies, and red ants, and the night when our palm leaf hut blew away in a changing monsoon, and had to be reassembled leaf by leaf from the jungle." Some of the episodes were better than others, and the time sequence was not always clear; what bound the book together was Agnes's ability to make do under any conditions, her extraordinary sympathy for the common lot of mankind, no matter what color the skin, and the trust and fidelity which the Keiths reposed in each other. Of the three finalists, *Land Below the Wind* was the most absorbing and refreshing; it was different from any other book we had ever published, and I was elated when it won the Award by a vote of 6 to 1.

All this time I had envisioned Mrs. Keith as a short sturdy little woman in a felt cloche and heavy tweeds, an image derived from my concept of those who dwelt in the periphery of the Empire. The Keiths flew to America for a six months' leave in June of 1939; Harry stopped off at Victoria, British Columbia, to see his ninety-year-old mother, and Agnes after a family reunion came East for the *Atlantic* reception, the press interviews, and the Prize. When she stepped off the plane at the Boston airport I had my first sight of that slender, long-legged Californian whose high cheekbones and dark almond eyes reminded me instantly of Queen Nefertiti, and I could tell from the admiring glances of the reporters and from the way people turned to look at her in the restaurant that we had here one of a kind.

On this first visit to Boston she spent the mornings working with me on the manuscript as we fitted it together chronologically, and the afternoons in her room inking in her drawings. She bought a trousseau of new clothes, for she and Harry were planning to spend the late summer and early autumn at Oxford where he was to take a refresher course. Bit by bit she pieced together for me the mosaic of their background. They had met at the University of California where Agnes was majoring in English and where Harry Keith in his thorough English way was soaking up everything he could learn about the tropical rain forests and the agriculture of the Pacific. After her graduation

Agnes went to work as a cub reporter for the San Francisco *Examiner*. Here she did well until one bright Saturday noon, as she left the building, she was attacked by a dope addict with a two-foot iron pipe who had made up his mind to kill the first person to emerge from the *Examiner* doors. He very nearly succeeded. The concussion with its aftermath of blinding head-aches (these were what interrupted her writing) invalided her for nearly three years. When she was at last well enough to travel, she went abroad with her brother Alfred, an engineer who had just graduated from the California Institute of Tech-nology, and it was on this trip that she again encountered Harry Keith, once of Berkeley, now a young forester, home on his first leave after four years in North Borneo. Their attraction for each other, which was irresistible, and their determination to marry hastened her recovery. Her family was dubious that she could stand up to the demands of the life in the tropics, but Agnes seemed to thrive on the prospect. She went out to Borneo as a bride with the eagerness of an American, uninhibited by the traditions of colonial civil service. The headaches had lost their hold, she told me, and as she was caught up in the adventure of her new life her writing became obligatory.

The exhilaration of the Atlantic Award was the high point, for the Keiths never did get to Oxford. The outbreak of the war cut short their holiday; they were recalled to Sandakan and Agnes took back with her in her trunk the *Atlantic* trous-seau, much of which she was never to wear.

The success of *Land Below the Wind,* which we first serial-ized in the *Atlantic* and which was then chosen by the Book-of-the-Month Club, I reported to her long distance. The royal-ties we arranged to pay her over a series of years, for she had serious misgivings about the future, but the first check assisted in the arrival of Henry George Keith II, who was born in Sandakan on April 5, 1940. "The producing of young George," she wrote me, "who spent his pre-natal days travelling by plane, by bus and motor, by train and by ship, through war zones and blackouts, in a violently unorthodox manner much disapproved of by consulting obstetricians, has about monopolised my creative energies for this last year. However I have literary hopes for the future now that young George has his toes dug firmly into life on his own account."

From the first Agnes had no illusions about the Japanese invasion, and after the fall of Singapore she was under pressure to return to America with her baby. Instead she built up a life-saving kit of drugs for George, Harry and herself, and in an article which reached me shortly before Pearl Harbor she foretold how the three of them might retreat by canoe into the interior to hide away with friendly natives in the jungle until the Japanese had been driven off. We published the paper, "Before Invasion: A Letter from North Borneo," in the *Atlantic* for February 1942, and the week after it appeared Agnes and Harry and George were prisoners of the Japanese; when the Japs landed, the Keiths like the other officials were at their posts.

For three and a half years they survived in separate prison camps, Agnes and baby George with the other white women and children, Harry with the other males from Sarawak and Dutch Borneo. What happened to them during their long ordeal we were not to know until later: the humiliation and the filth, the bodily depletion due to malnutrition, the spirit-cracking degradation of captivity, and the torture (at one time the Japanese questioned her for several days, and during this episode they broke her collarbone, dislocated and strained her left arm, and broke a rib) could hardly be imagined by us who were free. Three times the curtain was lifted by prisoner-of-war postcards from the Imperial Japanese Army, the first to her mother, the other two to me:

Xmas Day, 1944

Dear Ted:

Quote Sherman reference war. What about Red Cross? Resources this country limited. Our one hope peace soon. All three ragged, tired, homesick, but surviving. Love,

AGNES & HARRY & GEORGE KEITH

Internment Camp, Borneo

May 18, 1945

Meet husband occasionally. Health moderate. George fine, energetic. My new professions: truck gardening, white wing, privy engineering.

Fed up with war. "Hope deferred . . ." etc. Love,

AGNES, HARRY, GEORGE KEITH

Internment Camp, Borneo

On the eleventh of that September they were liberated by the 9th Australian Army Division after Sandakan had been burned by the Japs and reduced to rubble. This is what Agnes wrote me as they waited for the prison gates to open.

Kuching, Internment Camp
Sept. 11, 1945

Dear Ted:

At last! Peace & freedom! We hope to be completely free in a few hours time, as the Nipponese are expected to evacuate Kuching at 12 noon today. There are no words to express our feelings. War is Hell — Peace is Heaven. Thank God, Thank God, the end has come. We have been fed by parachute from Australian Red Cross for 2 weeks now. I have put on almost a pound a day. Harry is also improving in strength. George is fine. Ate his first piece of bread & butter with terrific excitement. First parachute dropped bread. We showed it to children with wonder. "That's BREAD!" Children had all forgotten what it was.

There is a GOOD story here. I long for time & paper to finish it. I have much material & notes, etc. Of course much difficulty in hiding everything while under Nip. rule. When I arrive U. S. shall CONCENTRATE. Home soon as possible. Nobody knows yet. Love to you —

AGNES & GEORGE KEITH

The Japanese commandant of their camp, for whom at the close Agnes had pity, committed hara-kiri; the prisoners — Agnes was down to 87 pounds — were fed and doctored; Agnes eventually wangled them a passage by plane to Manila and thence by Army transport to Seattle.

So the Keiths came home. Six years had elapsed since they had last seen California. Agnes's mother had died while they were captive; Jean their daughter had grown up into a life of her own; she and Agnes's beloved brother Alfred were there to greet them; and there was a second happy reunion with Harry's mother, whose age was now edging up to the century mark but who had been holding on indomitably until her son's return. It was a small family circle contracted even further by Alfred's tragic death from a heart attack within the month of their return. Grief-stricken, the Keiths went to the hospital for the treatment and surgery they had so long needed.

In October with her strength building up Agnes again flew into Boston bringing with her the notes for a new book written on tissue and other scraps of paper which she had hidden in George's stuffed panda and in the tins which she buried. She was much thinner and the strain she had lived through had left its mark, but the eyes still held the same eagerness and luster and her spirit was intact. Her fingernails which she had lost through malnutrition were only beginning to grow in and her fingertips were so sensitive that she could not type for more than an hour each day. She stayed with my associates Dudley and Jeannette Cloud, and her cogitating was done in a quiet room they put at her disposal. At the office we had plenty to talk about, for the manuscript pages she had brought with her, occasionally and very naturally, went into excessive detail. There were passages that read like overstatements and the fact that they had actually happened as she said did not lessen my criticism that they lacked the power to convince. Agnes was quite aware of this herself and of something deeper: she was writing against war, not against individual cruelty, and she summed this up when she said, "All I want is to forget talk of revenge, and get down to the basic fact that as long as we countenance the great atrocity of war, it is ridiculous to protest at personal atrocity." So we sifted and read aloud and tried by the eye, now modifying, now letting the stark realities stand until the pages spoke for her as she intended, and with magnanimity.

Three Came Home as it emerged that autumn is a unique book. No other woman in any country has so perfectly preserved the undaunted will and the compassion of the spirit in defeat. The last page of the book is the most eloquent, and it should be quoted for those who have not read it:

I know now the value of freedom. In all of my life before I had existed as a free woman, and didn't know it.

This is what freedom means to me. The right to live with, to touch and to love, my husband and my children. The right to look about me without fear of seeing people beaten. The capacity to work for ourselves and our children.

The possession of a door, and a key with which to lock it. Moments of silence. A place in which to weep, with no one to see me doing so.

The freedom of my eyes to scan the face of the earth, the mountains, trees, fields, and sea, without barbed wire across my vision. The freedom of my body to walk with the wind, and no sentry to stop me. Opportunity to earn the food to keep me strong. The ability to look each month at a new moon without asking, How many more times must this beauty shine on my captivity?

I will never give up these rights again. There may be more to life than these things. But there is no life without them.

I must also quote the beginning and the end of a letter which she wrote me on her return to Victoria in November 1946.

Dear Ted,

I am wanting to thank you for all that you and the *Atlantic* family did for me in Boston — but I find that I just can't do it. Unless you know what *I* was before you can't possibly know what you did for me.

My secretary, who had typed out my original almost illegible diaries for me, has been reading the typescript sent from Boston of the finished manuscript. She is pleased with me — and disappointed with the book; she says the starkness and terror are gone from both of us. That's what Boston did; took the starkness and terror out of me, and made of the facts a readable book. I hope I haven't sacrificed too many principles by the way. And if I have — well, it's something to be a human being again . . .

My dear Ted, again thank you for my pleasure in Boston. To come home to the *Atlantic,* the only home and family in my own country that I now have, was everything that a homecoming should be — and something to remember dearly when I am again in exile.

[169]

And for your help on my book I also am at a loss to thank you sufficiently. But if I didn't know you were so damn good, I would never forgive you for cutting out some of my favorite vulgar phrases!

As it proved Harry Keith was actually back in Sandakan and hard at work less than six months after his release from the Kuching prison. The compulsion which took him there Agnes explained in a letter written shortly before his departure. The book could not go to press until we had received her final additions, and the last of the illustrations, and here is her accounting for the delay:

Harry may go at any moment. Just waiting for the High Commissioner at Ottawa to get him a seat on the next push-bike to the orient. Fortunately, there do not seem to be many boats, planes, submarines going to Borneo just now. How wonderful if there was never another one!

As soon as Harry goes I will get down to work. But at the moment — well, one must live sometimes. It will appear ridiculous to anybody else that two middle-aged persons can be madly in love, but there you are. There is nothing like prison life to make married life seem good. After 3½ years with 280 females I center all my affections on your sex.

I guess the reason Harry is going back is because he is English. If you see his face when somebody remarks philosophically that England is finished, and the British Empire a thing of the past, then you know.

Also in Borneo we had many Asiatic friends who risked their lives, sometimes gave their lives, to help us. We can get no news of these people now. Harry wants to ascertain their fates, and help those whom he can help. Those are his reasons for going — But as for me, I couldn't possibly go for any reason yet. I just become ill at the thought.

Agnes Newton Keith

Agnes followed Harry out to the East in July of 1947 after the publication of *Three Came Home,* and after she had spoken at Irita Van Doren's Book and Author Luncheon with an intensity which moved and stilled that vast audience. She went with dread. Harry had flown up to Hong Kong to meet her, and when she went ashore with him, her nerve came back.

I arrived at Sandakan on September 2, having left Victoria on June 26. Coming back here with Harry, after a month of happiness together, subdued the ghosts of my past, and it wasn't as bad as I feared. We have a glorious location for our shack, surrounded by sky and Sulu Sea on the very top of a hill, and I like it.

To my surprise I find that the tropical beauty, the wildness, and the primitive people of Borneo enthrall me again. So much so that I want to write another book . . .

In 1950, after four years of reconstruction, the three Keiths came home on leave. Agnes brought with her the manuscript of her new book, *White Man Returns,* and after perusing it in Boston I flew out to Seattle where we spent one forty-hour day in a bedroom of a Seattle hotel with Harry stretched out and drowsing beside us while at the desk Agnes and I went through it page by page.

There was need for haste and not only for the book. The Korean War had broken out and North Borneo had been calling for Harry to come back immediately. It was a wrenching decision, and most of all for Harry who had been considering the possibility of teaching in a school of forestry. This, of course, would hold the trio together. If they went, it would reopen scars which were just healing; it would force them to leave George at home alone in Canada for schooling; and it would expose them to the new hostility which was breaking out in

[171]

"Asia for the Asians," a hostility which had already resulted in the assassination of a British official known to them both.

At the day's end we dined on "New York T-bone steaks," which always seem such an absurd item for a Western restaurant, and afterwards they escorted me to the airport. As we waited for my flight to be announced Agnes drew me apart. We stood there looking at the Indian gewgaws and Alaskan souvenirs which were on display and suddenly I noticed that there were tears in her eyes. "Ted," she said, "we are going, and I am very afraid. If anything should happen to us, will you please look after George?" The eyes and the pressure of hands can only acknowledge a trust like that.

Two years later at the behest of the United Nations the Keiths moved on to the Philippines to take part there in the reconstruction and the revival led so magnificently by Magsaysay. Their extended tour of duty there opened up still another window on the Pacific, and it was here that Agnes wrote *Bare Feet in the Palace,* growing out of her living knowledge of the Philippines. Today, still under orders from the United Nations, the Keiths, with George as a young assistant, are in Libya, where for three years they have been devoting their skill and energies to the problems of that impecunious but hopeful and developing country.

This is a century when in America it has been fashionable to deride colonialism and those who bore any part of the white man's burden. The dedication of the Keiths and their heart-testing decision to go back when they could so understandably have retired from the field is unselfishness beyond the call of duty. The Keiths have been doing in the Southwest Pacific what Dr. Schweitzer has been doing in Lambaréné, and what Barbara Ward and her husband, Sir Robert Jackson, have been doing in Ghana — devoting their skill, their en - couragement, and their farsightedness to the faith that what men hold in common is so much more important than that which divides them.

Richard Ely Danielson

EVERY editor must have back of him a president and a partner who will give him the trust and the latitude which he needs. Trust and latitude are indispensable if an editor is to make the experiments and the changes which his times require, and I was very fortunate to have back of me Richard Ely Danielson, for a kinder, fairer man never lived. When Dick and his wife Barbara became the proprietors of the *Atlantic* in 1939, the publisher, Donald B. Snyder, and I were in the midst of renovations. The magazine had been losing ground all through the depression years. The newsstand sale had dropped to less than fourteen thousand copies a month. The contributors — too many of them — were in the higher age bracket and they were all of them underpaid. The format which had been designed in the '20s by the master hand of Dwiggins was out of date. We needed new blood in our own veins and we needed to find a sizable body of younger readers. Any periodical that has lived to a great age, and the *Atlantic* was then over eighty, must be subjected to a periodic checkup and the process can be hazardous.

The *Atlantic* had always been printed on a soft uncoated paper such as you would find in any good book, and on this paper we could not print fast enough for economical production. Now the Graphic Arts Unions in the Rumford Press, which does our printing, were asking for another raise (they have had five during my editorship) and the only way we could meet it was to get off the obsolete presses and change to a tougher, thinner paper which could be sped through a hot-ink rotary press at the rate of seven thousand copies an hour. The less time we were on the press the better. The *Atlantic* had always been hand-stitched. It was an expensive form of binding but it made the magazine pliable and easy to handle; now Don found a wire stapling device — it was just as secure, just as supple, and it saved us $2000 a month. The *Atlantic* had a table of contents cover, a listing of the contributors and the departments against a buff-brown background. Mr. Sedgwick had stepped up the color to a Chinese red but the magazine still had a sameness of appearance which was a handicap on the newsstand and in the home. People could never tell at a glance whether this was an issue they had read before, and it is fatal for a magazine to be taken for granted. But a magazine's cover is an index of its character and the problem before us was whether we could alter ours in a way to make it more attractive without impairing the quality which was our trade mark. We worked over this for years. Don Snyder set up a trial run in three Midwestern cities, Minneapolis, Indianapolis, and St. Louis. For ten months special photographic covers, the best picture we could get of our leading contributor, were transposed on the copies destined for these three cities. The comparative sales showed conclusively that the biographical cover had a much stronger drawing power than our traditional table of contents, for these special copies outsold the regular magazine at better than three to one.

These were only a few of the alterations which we believed would rejuvenate the *Atlantic*. The size of the page was enlarged so as to accommodate the advertising plates prepared for *Time* and *Newsweek* — when at last the agencies decided to place them with us. Dwiggins devised a new format with more attractive title pages and with decorations to break up the somber columns of type. Don took the initiative for most of the physical alterations and I for the change in the contents; I was bird-dogging hard for new contributors, I was paying more for our contributions (borrowing against the future readers), and by 1947 my annual expenditure for manuscripts was double what Mr. Sedgwick had spent ten years earlier (it is three times today). In all these changes we drew on the advice and the reassurance of Dick Danielson, who was wary of change, and we were talking to a professional, for in his editing first of the *Independent,* then of the *Sportsman,* he had lived with rising costs. He shuddered when some of our decorative covers did not pan out as we had hoped: "Shadrach, Meshach, and Abednego," he remarked when we showed him the engraver's proofs of Clarence Randall, the president of Inland Steel, painted against a fiery steel furnace, but when the cover with the profile of T. S. Eliot outsold any other we had placed on the newsstands, and when we featured a painting of Robert Frost leaning on his fence in Vermont, smiling quizzically at the onlooker, Dick knew and we knew that we were moving in the right direction.

Dick brought to our editorial roundtable a profound knowledge of American history; the Revolution and the Civil War were his favorite epochs, and Washington, especially the young Washington, appealed to him. The loneliness, the immense stamina, the iron self-discipline, the forethought about the developing West, and Washington's careful husbandry of Mount Vernon — these Dick appreciated far more closely than most of us. He knew the battles of the Civil War by heart, and when he talked about them, which he enjoyed doing, his hero worship of Lincoln and of Lee, of young daredevils like John Pelham and Will Cushing, touched the mainspring of his sentiment. Dick had served in France in Army Intelligence in the First World War and under Colonel Percy Black in G-2 in the Second; he had had a hand in the planning of the North African invasion and had gone to Dakar as an aide to Admiral Glassford. Out of this had grown his respect for the armed services and a veneration for our leaders in the high command. He was a patriot in the real, rare sense of that word and his patriotism had its roots in Connecticut where his forebears had founded the village of Danielson. The best of his short stories, "Corporal Hardy," "Laylocks," and "Grandma Robinson," have their origin in the memories which were implanted in him in his Connecticut boyhood.

He had the leanings of a scholar — he taught at Groton immediately after his graduation from Yale — and the classics were never to lose their luster for him. In the autobiographical "Grandma Robinson" he draws the character of his grandmother and tells how in her old age she made him learn the *Odes* of Horace as she herself had learned them from her father. She had no patience with Caesar's *Commentaries* with whose hateful, meticulous bridge Dick had been struggling in school. She said: "I suppose you want to spend the rest of your life building bridges?"

"I said, 'No, Grandma, no!' It was inconceivable to me, even then, that any human being or domestic animal would have trusted him — or itself to any bridge built by me. It would probably have been constructed of straw and some form of moss, and under the pressure of any creature weighing more

[177]

than five ounces would have collapsed in fearful ruin. I simply could not see myself as a bridge builder or construction engineer. Nothing in my unduly prolonged afterlife has led me to change this opinion so precociously adopted. But Grandma was not satisfied; 'Fools,' she said, 'can be hired to build bridges, but *you* must think for yourself; you must study and know and do." That passage catches them both, the firm old Puritan and Dick who even at twelve could regard himself with such whimsical self-deprecation.

He grew up to be a broad and muscular six-footer, powerful enough for the tackle slot, first at Penn Charter, and then on his freshman squad at Yale. He claimed that he was never good at games and I don't think he liked them. At New Haven, where he was a member of the Class of 1907, the lectures of William Graham Sumner the historian and the lectures and talks which he had with Chauncey Brewster Tinker were what he most prized. He was elected to the board of the *Yale Lit* as his classmate, Sinclair Lewis, was not, and those in college at the time, so I have been told, rated Dick the better writer. My informant, Charles Seymour, added, "We have never forgiven Dick for not writing more."

There are some in every generation who light up in action and in conversation the flame they might have kindled in their writing. Dick was the best of company whether at a hunt breakfast or cruising with his older friend, William Amory Gardner, or in a fishing camp with those master fly-fishermen, Drs. "Chubb" Newell and William Ladd, and Richmond Fearing. He loved life, he enjoyed the company of older men, as they enjoyed him, and he was much in demand. In his middle years and especially during his decade as the editor of the *Sportsman,* what he wrote was spurred on by the needs of his magazine — editorials, articles, accounts of race meetings, dog shows, and the Kentucky Derby. It was his gay, vigorous taste which made that periodical the beauty that it was until the depression drove it to the wall, and so often it was his gay humor which brightened the text. The National Amateur Championship was played on the famous links of the Country Club in Brookline in 1931, and six weeks before the event Dick arranged a match between Francis Ouimet, who had scored his greatest triumph on the course, and Powell Cabot, who was the business manager of the *Sportsman* and a pretty average hacker. Dick walked around with them, solemnly making note of Ouimet's affinity with par and of Cabot's aberrations. The paper which resulted was the perfect way of introducing distant readers to the test that was coming and the laughter in it made it all irresistible.

When the *Sportsman* had to be given up Dick, whose spirits were badly bruised, turned for solace to his own writing. This is the period in which he wrote his short stories, "Corporal Hardy" and "Laylocks," which were about the Civil War, and "Martha Doyle" and "Banbury Cross," which were dedicated to the horses he had ridden and loved in the hunting field. In each case the narrative springs from the well of sentiment, not sentimentality, which lay deep in Dick, and which he had allowed the years to grow over. These were reprinted at the time, and twenty years later when we placed "Corporal Hardy" in the *Atlantic* anthology it delighted me to find that readers immediately responded to its undiminished emotion and integrity. Had it not been for the war which called him to Washington and away from this creative period, we should certainly have had more of Dick's stories for he loved doing them. And this was almost the last season of his good health.

He was a tired man when he came back to us in 1945, thin,

war-weary, and he showed the effects of his months in the tropics. He had been laid up in a hospital in Dakar with malaria and a high fever, and I remember his telling me that among their rather scanty reading matter they had two copies of the *Atlantic,* both from 1938, which had been read from cover to cover until the covers had fallen off, and in each of which was a story of his. At Arlington Street he took hold where he had left off, resuming his administrative duties as our president, reading hard for the magazine and reviewing for us at essay length the war books which were then in spate. His comments were crisp and salty and to the point. When Hanson Baldwin sent us a longish manuscript dealing with "Our Worst Blunders in the War," Dick wrote:

Very strong for this. Baldwin assembles all the major mistakes as no one else has done. Besides, he speaks objectively, whereas most of the other commentators on strategic errors, etc., have been interested parties, Sherwood, Eisenhower, Stilwell, Churchill, etc.

I think all his strictures are sound, although I am too ignorant on the subject of General MacArthur to know if Baldwin's pretty severe criticism is justified or not.

The book needs editing. The text is lucid but has a good many minor mistakes. Second, I think the arrangement of his argument should be studied. For instance he outlines the four false premises and then proceeds to discuss False Premise No. 2. Some adequate marking should indicate in the text which premise is being discussed. Also would put "unconditional surrender" ahead of MacArthur.

If used as a book, a good foreword by some top Brass would be helpful.

Two long installments in the A.M. and the book to the Press. Pronto.

R. E. D.

Richard Ely Danielson

Commenting on a short paper by Raymond Swing on "Unconditional Surrender," he wrote:

"The phrase gave great anxiety — it was carelessly thrown off by F.D.R. — and maybe it worked a long time good. This is a classic example of F.D.R.'s frivolous and careless speech, seized upon as an expression of reasoned policy. Vote yes. R.E.D."

We found ourselves in a long-drawn-out argument with a Washington correspondent about an article threatening doom which the writer kept enlarging until it had lost most of its initial point and force. Each time it came back I asked for a new set of opinions which finally prompted Dick to write: "Haven't I written my little heart out on this goddam piece already yet? Have I got to read it again? R.E.D."

Our readers in the back room were much taken with a long, avant-garde literary essay involving the eccentric John Mytton. It told, among other things, how Mytton never hesitated to bite ferocious dogs when they snarled at him, and how, while driving in a two-wheeled gig, Mytton innocently asked his companion if he had ever been upset in one. No, said his friend. "What!" replied Mytton, *"never* upset in a gig? What a d —— d slow fellow you must have been all your life" — and up over the bank they went and wham! When the manuscript was shown to Dick, he would have none of it. "Mytton — Mytton," he said, "everybody knows about Mytton. Why, I *was* Mytton!" — the last phrase uttered with a plaintive reminiscent glow.

On another occasion at an editorial meeting Dick had been communing inwardly while the rest of us debated over the merits of an overly nice biographical portrait of John Ruskin. Dick woke up. "What Ruskin needed," he remarked quietly,

[181]

"was a good kick in the pants." And there was the time when we found ourselves caught up in a never-ending biography and while it was in progress Dick went off to the hospital for an operation. When he returned we were still at it. "Isn't this the last installment?" he asked. "I can't believe that *anyone* wants to know that much about anybody."

In the years that followed Dick was dragged down by internal suffering and by an illness which for a long time defied analysis. He underwent innumerable tests and continued to do his manuscript reading for us in a succession of hospitals, until at last the surgeons at the Hospital of the University of Pennsylvania made the correct diagnosis and, in a dangerous, prolonged operation, removed his pancreas. It was touch and go but we knew he was on the safe side when in answer to our anxious inquiries came this characteristic message in his own hand:

Dear friends:

. . . I won't "tell you about my operation" — a dreary story for all except the teller. But I file an objection against the assertion that I am an Iron Man. Charles Morton sent me a nice friendly letter congratulating me on my iron qualities. Nothing — and please forgive me — could be more ironic. I seem to share, along with horned pout and some of the more sluggish snakes, a physical disinclination to expire. In other words I am hard to kill. But there is nothing steel-like about my performance. I feel like an angleworm impaled by Mr. Weeks, drowning and gesturing in a feeble and unbeautiful way. This body is such a worn out, patched, re-relined and made over garment that I don't believe Morgan Memorial would accept it as a gift, but it's all I've got and I'll go on living in it as long as there's a spark left in the ashes. My metaphors are more mixed than usual, for which I beg your indulgence . . .

Richard Ely Danielson

He returned to us a semi-invalid living on a precarious diet and a bushel of pills each day (85 by actual count), susceptible to insulin shocks but undaunted. He was in constant pain. It is pitiful for friends to see one they love reduced. Dick was knocked out by an insulin shock one day as he was leaning over my secretary's desk. I happened to be standing by and I caught him and we slid slowly to the floor together just missing the formidable corner.

I felt then how gaunt and vulnerable he was. But watching Dick brave life, with crutches and his grin, brought us much closer to him.

In the ten-year reprieve which was granted him he did some of his best writing, his clearest thinking. He encouraged his friend John Hutton, the Englishman, a fellow invalid who had lost the power of his legs but who was an artist with the fly rod, to do a book for us on trout and salmon, and I quote the opening paragraph of Dick's introduction as a shining example of his humor:

During three successive seasons on the Miramichi River in New Brunswick it was my good fortune to see and to admire the author of this book as a salmon fisherman. During the first two seasons the river conditions were atrocious: what water there was fairly steamed. In fact I am not sure that it was not dry. In the third year the river looked very handsome indeed, but the September run of fish failed to materialize and the salmon which had summered in the river were dark and sullen, and paid no attention to the assortment of flies which I — and the other anglers — hurled at them from dawn to dusk. Except to Mr. Hutton's. These they continued to take — as had the low water fish of previous seasons — with a steady, persistent, monotonous regularity. This unjust preference of his lures might have caused in us a deep anger and hatred toward Mr. Hutton, if he had not been so modest, so generous with his flies and other equipment, and so frank — when questioned as to the methods he followed and the technique of his art. He did not volunteer advice to an unsuccessful angler, but when such an unhappy wretch desperately queried, "How do you do it?" he explained with patient good humor exactly how he fished in various pools and why.

Injustice always infuriated Dick and the more he considered the costly, headstrong, futile strikes, some of them engineered by tiny minorities, to which America was recurrently subjected, the more he believed that they were the Achilles heel of our democracy. For months he worked on an article which we finally published in 1947 under the title of "The Right to Strike." It was clearly thought and forcefully argued, the principles back of it were undeniable, and it brought him an enormous correspondence from readers the country over. Here is the heart of the argument in which he shows the depth of his concern:

. . . Our common purpose in living and working together is, I suppose, to achieve a kind of civilization which permits a maximum amount of fairness and equality of opportunity, a maximum of compassion toward the handicapped, and a hope of reasonable happiness for all. This is an immensely complex and intricate business; it involves all manner of concessions, of give-and-take; it involves injustices and their rectifications, advantages and disadvantages which must be equalized. It is almost a miracle that it succeeds, here and there, in existing at all. An orderly city street where robbers and murderers dare not tread, where lights shine and houses are heated, where children walk in safety to school, where milkmen deliver milk and postmen deliver mail — this phenomenon, which we take for granted, represents a coordination and cooperation of human effort so widespread, an integration of divergent interests so involved, as to stagger the imagination. *It is a condition possible only where private interests are subordinate to the public good.*

If certain members of society combine to dim and extinguish those lights; if, as a result of their action, houses are cold, children are at the mercy of the hoodlum and the thug, and enforced unemployment stalks the streets, those members of society have committed a crime against the civilization of which they are themselves a part. They have exercised a right which ceases to be a right and becomes an agent of anarchy.

Not only labor leaders and members of militant unions, not only the writers for *PM* and the *Daily Worker,* but all men everywhere, owners of property, white-collar workers, managers of businesses, all of us, must think more clearly before we invoke our particular rights or prate about human rights in general. Let us consider always what the unlimited applications of an individual right may involve before we push our argument to the brutal absurdity of an attack on society in general.

A better method of settling disputes between labor and management in the public services and public utilities and in the vital industries and services, a better solution, *must be found* than the paralysis of the strike, local or national. It must be found because that method is intolerable and contrary to the public good.

A paper he took particular pleasure in writing was his essay appraising the fifth volume of Douglas Southall Freeman's *George Washington.* It deals with the skillful and fortuitous concert of power at Yorktown; it gave Freeman's and his own estimate of Washington's leadership in the field, and it revived a scene which was surely one of the most affecting in American history. In these words:

. . . Peace had been declared, the treaty signed; the British were preparing to evacuate New York, taking with them the unhappy and embittered Loyalists. In due course, while the last of the British warships and transports were still in the outer harbor, Washington entered the city and, having completed his duty as a soldier, saw the civil authorities take over; it only remained for him to say farewell to the small group of officers who accompanied him before resigning his commission in person to Congress.

Mr. Freeman is at his best in describing the infinitely touching scene in Fraunces Tavern. Washington's composure and iron self-discipline for once broke down. Tears were blinding him. "I cannot come to each of you," he said in a faltering voice, "but shall feel obliged if each of you will come and take me by the hand." Chance fixed it that in the absence of Nathanael Greene, the soldier best entitled to be first among them was nearest at hand — Henry Knox, the man who had brought the cannon over the ice from Ticonderoga, youthful father of the artillery corps, the one senior officer of whom it could be said that in eight years of service he had not given his General an hour's needless concern. Knox stepped forward silently and held out his hand; Washington extended his own, but as he looked into those honest eyes and remembered what Knox had meant to him, he could not say farewell with a handshake. Impulsively he put his arms around Knox and, weeping, kissed his Chief of Artillery. Once done, this had of course to be done with all, from Steuben to the youngest officer. With streaming eyes, they came up to him, received the same embrace and passed on. Even the most talkative was awed. Not a man had the bad taste to attempt any expression of thanks or of admiration. "The simple thought," Tallmadge wrote long afterwards, "that we . . . should see his face no more in this world seemed to me utterly insupportable."

That scene in the Fraunces Tavern was one which Dick lived in vicariously; it was almost as if he knew the men in that line who came up to embrace the General. I have heard him characterize them and their achievements, and I believe that he treasured that farewell because of the fundamental loyalty it revealed. I used to lead him on to talk about such things in our evenings at Tihonet, the little trout club in the cranberry bogs at Wareham where he still fished when it was a miracle that he could fish at all. Even after both his hips had been broken he managed somehow to scrabble down the banks and endure for an hour the bow seat in the small aluminum canoe. It was his last touch with the out-of-doors and he loved it.

In the evenings we sat before the Franklin stove, bourbon in the glass and the lamplight falling on the water-colors of the bogs which Frank Benson and Ralph Gray and Bob Bellows had done in their day, and on the laughable mementos anglers always seem to collect, and Dick's mind would rove back to the night at the Tavern Club when coming in late he had almost assaulted Waddy Longfellow with a beer bottle, mistaking for a burglar the little figure crouched at the roundtable, sleeping it off after the lights had been extinguished; back to Dakar and to the Inauguration in Liberia when the flags of the United Nations, which fluttered above the reviewing stand and which had been painted by the schoolchildren, suddenly released their colors in a cloudburst and Dick in his dress uniform found himself inundated with vermilion; back to Marseilles in 1918 when he had requested and been refused permission to cross the Spanish border and kill the German agent who was directing the submarine tracking of our transports. "I knew where he was to be found, and I'd have killed him," Dick said simply, and I believe he would.

One morning at Tihonet I had driven the car to the upper reach of A.D.M. bog and was unstrapping the boat from the rack while Dick with his rod and crutch went limping down to the brook. I thought I heard a thud and when I turned he was on his knees propped up with his left hand, while with his right, tip up, he was playing a heavy fish. I came running. "Not a bad fish," he said, looking up with that beatific smile. "I wish you'd been here to see him take it."

The Quest

THE quest for new material is as arduous as it is unpredictable. The *Atlantic* has prospered under those editors who traveled far and hard and has been most precarious under those who stayed put in Boston. New York does not attract any such galaxy of writers as are found in London, and Hollywood for all the money lavished on visiting authors will never produce half as many good books as Concord. The creative minds in America today do their writing either at the universities which are our centers of patronage or in those regions which are most conducive to their work. And what is true of established writers is equally true of beginners: you find them in teaching or advertising or journalism, in any number of jobs that will pay their way and still keep them in touch with a typewriter. Usually they are far to seek, and for an editor like myself who is searching with one hand for new books and with the other for those ideas and issues which press upon the American conscience and which manifest themselves so differently in different parts of the country it is obligatory to travel. I average about thirty thousand miles a year; I have lectured in forty-six of the fifty states and shall never lose my zest for the all-season exposure to this country. I am simply thankful that I do not have to carry my blankets with me as did Emerson when he made his lecture circuit. During one of my absences Bennett

Cerf, on a visit to Boston, called at my office and learning that I was away said to our receptionist: "You tell Mr. Weeks that if he stayed home more often, he'd be a better editor." Bennett was teasing, for his peregrinations are only a little less than mine, and he knows as well as I that there is no substitute for hearing what the other fellow thinks — and laughs at — on his home grounds.

Sometimes I come on talent at the end of a long journey, sometimes it is unexpectedly close to home. Sometimes it is just a big idea — and my luck to be there when it sparks; sometimes it is the first third of a manuscript for which the writer needs reassurance and financial aid. In these initial encounters the editor's role is to appreciate the situation and to think quickly while he listens.

In the spring of 1933 I spoke at Worcester and at the end of the talk my friend Esther Forbes, the novelist, introduced me to the new Director of the Worcester Art Museum with whom we were going to have cocktails. Francis Henry Taylor, with his ample girth, merry brown eyes and fine hooked nose, looked like someone out of a Renaissance portrait, and his talk was captivating. He sat us before a tall glass funnel of martinis which he stirred and poured, and while his charming wife Pamela spread the cream cheese I found myself soaking up with my cocktails an account of J. P. Morgan the Magnificent as an art collector, the like of which I have never heard. Here were the Italian dealers who lay in wait believing they knew Mr. Morgan's whim; here was their skulduggery with which the work of art was extracted from its impoverished owners, and here finally was the boldness with which Mr. Morgan himself sized up the deal. A moment later we were in Mr. Morgan's dining room watching the effect his paintings had on his guests, other empire builders like Frick and Hill, who strove to emulate. This talk opened up a whole new world to me and I said, as any editor would, "But this is wonderful stuff; it ought to be in a book. Why not a History of Collecting in America, beginning with the earliest museum in Boston and coming straight down through the Empire Builders, the Armory Show and Mellon?" I overstayed, it was too much fun not to, but I had his promise when I left.

The Worcester Museum shone with a special incandescence under the direction of Francis Henry Taylor; the exhibitions attracted national attention, and it is no wonder that he was eventually called to New York to be the Director of the Metropolitan Museum of Art. There, the book which had begun as a gleam in the glass began to take form. Francis's research and reading notes were compiled through the dictaphone, and the related sections came into focus as they were revised by hand. It was a far vaster work than we had first contemplated, and there was cutting to be done if we were to fit the big text within a single volume; to his surprise Francis discovered that there was no authoritative history of collecting in Europe, no account of the great European collectors and of how their masterpieces had passed from hand to hand, from country to country, following the flow of gold, until they came at last, some of them, to the New World. So he had decided that his first volume, *The Taste of Angels,* would begin with the breakup of the Roman Empire and follow the great conquests, the court favorites, and the fluctuating fortune which made now Rome, now Florence, now London, now Paris the capital of art, down through the conquests of Napoleon. A huge undertaking for so busy a man, and a superlative and comprehensive book he made of it.

After fifteen strenuous years in Manhattan in which under his cultivation the Metropolitan flourished handsomely, Francis hankered for Worcester and the time for reflection. His gay spirit had turned somber, he was deeply troubled about the state of Europe and very evidently in need of refreshment. He asked me if I thought he could supplement his reduced income by steady writing and I was sure he could. The next book, covering the century from Napoleon through the Armory Show of 1913, beckoned and there were articles we wanted him to do for the magazine, chief among them his spirited and affectionate Letter to Bernard Berenson, for which he made a special trip to Florence, shortly before B.B.'s ninetieth birthday, and a second magnificent essay, "The Summons of Art," which I ordered for our Centennial.

When we lunched together in the summer of 1957 Francis told me that the lectures he had been giving at the Harvard Summer School were really a roadmap of the new book. "I've got the title for it," he added with his irreverent grin. " 'Mummies, Millionaires, and Masterpieces.' "

"You're having fun with it?" I asked. He said yes, and that he expected to have the opening chapters ready to show me by Thanksgiving. First he would have to go to the hospital for a small operation; it had been worrying him, no, it wasn't serious, but he had kept putting it off and now was the time. Perhaps not even Pamela suspected that time would cut him short.

Francis Taylor's writing was a spring which Esther Forbes led me to at precisely the right moment. The idea for Roland Hayes's book came from my life insurance agent, Herbert Sargent. Herbert as a young man had studied for the opera in

Germany. And he still sang for pleasure and, informally, with Mr. Hayes. "He's a remarkable person," Herb told me. "You know, his mother was a former slave, and at first she opposed his singing, thought it would land him in a saloon singing for quarters. He has made his way against all the old prejudices, building up his repertoire in Europe and through his study of African music — it is really a big story, and I think Roland is at the point where he'd be willing to talk."

Mr. Hayes, when I called on him at his home in Brookline, was only mildly interested. "But I've got so many other things to do first," he said with his modest laugh. "All my concerts, and then I've been making notes for a new opera, and this summer I'll have my teaching to do." We were seated in his dining room where we were being served a delicious meal in the midafternoon, for he had to sing that evening. From where I sat I could see over the living room mantel an oil portrait of an elderly Negro woman with a shawl over her shoulders. "That's my mother," said Roland. "We used to call her 'Angel Mo'.' She's the person to write about. Traveled with me on my tours, cooked for me, did my laundry, gave me courage when I was down. She was the greatest person I have known." From that and subsequent meetings it became clear that Roland's autobiography would have to wait for a fortuitous moment in his career, for a time when he would be in a relaxed and expansive humor, and even then he would almost certainly need an amanuensis. The problem for us both was eventually solved by MacKinley Helm, the art connoisseur and writer who was Roland's near neighbor and friend. Mac persuaded him to talk his book as they were summering together in Maine, and the text, spoken in the natural rhythm of a born musician with an individuality Roland might not have been able to impart with the pen, was fitted together chronologically and then opened up and amplified when Mac read it back to the author. As Roland promised, it was as much the story of Roland's mother as it was of the singer, and this we stressed in the title, *Angel Mo' and Her Son, Roland Hayes,* by Mac-Kinley Helm.

In the autumn of the book's publication, I received a request for Roland to appear at an autographing party. "Good gracious," he said, "I couldn't say anything before all those women."

"Of course you can," I said. "I'll ask you questions, and you'll sing your answers," and on that basis he agreed. I asked him three questions: What was his mother's favorite song on the program when she first heard him sing at Symphony Hall? And he sang it. Then I asked him what was the most important of the new songs which he added to his repertoire in mid-career after his original concert manager had said that he would book no more concerts for him. And he sang it. Finally I asked him to sing the German song with which he quieted the huge hostile audience in Hitler's Berlin after twenty minutes of hissing and catcalling. Roland had intended to open with a group of spirituals, but after being greeted by the hostile demonstration, he walked over to Mr. Boardman to change his program. And he sang *Du bist die Ruh.*

These books were surprisingly close to home. Ved Mehta's *Face to Face,* on the other hand, came to me at the end of a transcontinental trip which landed me on the campus of Pomona College in Claremont, California. Pomona, which is the Swarthmore of the West Coast, is one of my favorite small colleges, and its president, E. Wilson Lyon, a dear friend.

The Quest

Lunching with him and the faculty after my lecture on campus in the midwinter of 1953, I was told that they had a young Hindu student in their sophomore class who was quite an exciting boy. He had been blinded by meningitis at the age of three. He had been studying in this country since he was fifteen, and he had come to Pomona because of the state law in California which provides $1000 for blind college students. Ved used the money to pay his classmates to read aloud to him, and during the summer vacation of his freshman year he began dictating to a classmate the opening of his autobiography.

Ved's first chapters were typed, and I took them with me back to Boston. Reading them, I learned that Ved's family came from the Punjab and that during his boyhood and until they were driven out by the Partition they were well-to-do. Ved's mother was convinced that the Indian medicine men could restore the boy's sight; his father, who was a Western-trained doctor, knew otherwise. Ved himself was brought up in the big family compound with his brothers and sisters; he learned to ride a bicycle even though he could not see, and not until he was twelve did he begin to feel a sense of deprivation. Then he was left behind when the others went to school, for in India little provision is made for education of the blind.

At the time of the Partition, Ved and his family lived in terror of the Moslems, and eventually they were stripped of their property and driven into exile. Then Ved persuaded his father to let him study Braille at the rehabilitation center for the Gurkhas who had been wounded in the war. As he learned Braille, he also learned the addresses of the American institutions for the blind, and on his own initiative, and in fractured English, he wrote asking if they would accept him as a student. He received more than thirty turn-downs before at last the

Arkansas School for the Blind said yes, for $600 they would accept him. And so alone at the age of fifteen he flew to this country. He had never used a knife and fork before, and on the long flight, although he could smell the food the hostess was passing, he was too ashamed to ask for anything but orange juice.

I sent Ved an advance royalty and urged him to come on to Boston in the summer holidays to continue his work on the book, and so he did for the next two summers, thumbing his way without cane, or dog, or sign. In all I think he thumbed his way across our country seven times. Ved's boyhood in India, his struggle for self-mastery, the liberation that came to him in Little Rock, and the maturity which came to him in Pomona, he was to describe for us so eloquently in his book *Face to Face.* Every word of it was dictated and read back to him, with many sensitive suggestions from Nancy Reynolds, our managing editor. We tried to preserve as much as possible of the Indian imagery, and since the text was overlong we persuaded him to cut. But there was a reason for every sentence he spoke. He kept the meshwork of the book clear in his mind, and gave in very reluctantly and only when he agreed that it was for an improvement.

At Little Rock, where he called himself "a donkey in a world of horses," he learned "facial vision," and how to walk between spinning mobiles whose currents of air warned him to duck. At Pomona he learned self-assurance and the self-confidence that comes with knowledge, and he found such friendships that he was tempted to spend the rest of his life here. But Ved Mehta is as outgoing as Ralph Bunche. He believes that he has a job to do home in India, and when his graduate studies at Balliol and Harvard are at an end, I believe it will be a good job. His

capacity is incredible. The summer of his graduation from Pomona when he was living in Cambridge finishing the American section of his book, he also found time to take a course
on the modern novel at the Harvard Summer School which
required the reading of forty-two novels, only five of which
were in Braille.

All during that summer we had been searching for a title.
Across the Bridge or *Crossing the Bridge* were the titles in
Ved's mind, but I didn't think either one of them was quite
good enough; the problem must have been pressing on my
thoughts too, for I remember waking at two in the morning
with the words of Paul's First Epistle to the Corinthians echo-
ing as if they had actually been spoken: "For now we see
through a glass, darkly; but then face to face." And there it
was.

So the trail leads to Bective and County Meath for the short
stories and novels of Mary Lavin, to London and to Montegu-
foni for the big anthology of poetry by Dame Edith Sitwell,
and for that lustrous five-volume autobiography by her brother
Sir Osbert, a work which, as Evelyn Waugh says, is "surely a
monument of our time"; to Abingdon for my annual spring
visit with John Masefield, and to that other Abington under
the great beeches where I spent an unforgettable afternoon
with Sir Max Beerbohm; to Dorset, the Hardy country, to visit
Geoffrey Household; to Southwest Harbor, Maine, where
I have walked the bright September mornings with Walter
Lippmann, to Agnes de Mille's studio in Greenwich and
Agnes E. Meyer's library in Washington, and to Chicago, where
I had my first meeting with Richard Bissell and his beautiful
blonde wife Marian. By some freak of circumstance we were

seated at a table directly under the guns of Wayne King's forty-piece orchestra and only fragments of what we were saying drifted across the table over and under the trumpets. This, in brief, was coming my way from Dick: "Marian kept saying that if I didn't have a book published by the time I was thirty-five, I would have to . . . We have four kids and making [I couldn't tell whether he said shirts or pajamas] is at least a steady business . . . in Dubuque."

"How old are you now?" I shouted back at him.

"Thirty-six."

What keeps an editor young are the vibrations he receives from those who are younger. In 1956 we received a short story from an unknown, Jesse Hill Ford. We all read it, for it drew a most vivid picture of a Southern heel and the girl he was betraying. The ending did not seem quite right; we could not bring ourselves to accept the story — neither could we forget it.

Mr. Ford wrote from Chicago, and with my note of rejection, which kept the door open for revision, I made a mental note to look him up.

We had our first breakfast together sixteen months later in Memphis, Tennessee. Mr. Ford, who is thirty, had driven seventy miles to hear me the night before and had arisen at 5:30 that morning to catch me before I flew off to my next stop. We talked about writing, and to explain why he had moved back to the South he gave me a copy of an article he had prepared for his home-town paper, the Nashville *Tennessean.* These were the paragraphs that sank in:

I left the concrete canyons of Chicago a year ago to come to Humboldt, center of West Tennessee's strawberry industry.

The Quest

But I didn't come here to pick strawberries. I came to write my novel.

I am already famous. I have the biggest dog, the smallest car, the oldest house and the most scandalous children in town.

And I'm *still* writing my novel.

I left a good job with the American Medical Association's public relations staff to strike out on my own. When I decided to begin writing full time, my wife suggested we move to Humboldt. After all, it's her home town, and she could teach school while I worked on my novel. Meanwhile our children would be free to rove and roam as never they were in the Windy City.

Having been raised in Nashville, I was more than eager to return to Tennessee. We packed up our Volkswagen, and with our little girl, who is three, and our boys, who are four and six, we headed south.

On the way down we stopped at Omaha, Illinois, and ordered a Saint Bernard puppy at a kennel there.

Six months later I had made five dollars, averaging a little less than a dollar a month. The five dollars came from a sportsmen's magazine for a tip to fishermen on how to tape a fold-down fingernail snipper to a casting rod for clipping line. But the novel was going tolerably well and the St. Bernard had arrived, with a small but insatiable appetite.

I must explain that I am not an independently wealthy coupon clipper with oil wells in Texas. Would that I were! And unfortunately, no foundation has taken me to its bosom to nurture as I write.

I am here and writing because my wife was willing to leave her household duties and begin teaching in the sixth grade after seven years of marriage. I am here because we were able to save a little during the years I was in public relations, and I am here because my parents and her parents believe in me enough to bridge the gap between our income and our outgo.

We have swapped the latter-day American dream of two cars and a new house, complete with automatic dishwasher — a dream we had achieved incidentally — for one small car and an old, old house where you wash dishes by hand.

Naturally we cannot afford my role as a dollar-a-month writer indefinitely. Either I begin earning before the wolf breaks down the door or back I go into the salaried world of nine to five.

On January 21, I wrote accepting Mr. Ford's new story, "The Surest Thing in Show Business," and telling him we would print it as an *Atlantic* "First" in the April issue. Back came this reply:

26 January 1959

Dear Mr. Weeks:

There is jubilation here, and it is spreading like pond ripples after a stone; I am not going to say that I pinched myself, but I will say that I got a little giddy and almost waxed sentimental. I didn't open the letter until I was back outside the Post Office and on the way back up the sidewalk towards home. I'm always fearful when I open letters nowadays, especially those from Boston. So I held it a while and wondered. My dog, Captain, who is almost well after being hit by a car, was along with me, and his pal, the Labrador from next door, was along too. So finally, I opened it and there your letter was with the check.

I'm sorry now I just didn't go ahead and yell. It's all right in Humboldt to yell. They haven't quite forgotten David Crockett, a former resident of this country, and on occasions, and this would be one, you can just holler and nobody cares. In fact they are sympathetic. But I just kept on walking until I got home where the kids were shut in with chickenpox and their grandmother was reading to them. We kissed all around and they yelled and did an Indian dance and then I took off up to the schoolhouse and showed my wife, Sally, and she called several of the other teachers out in the hall and they read the letter and came very close to tears, but managed to hold them back.

I came back by home and the Cumberland Presbyterian preacher was there waiting for me. My father-in-law had told him down at the clinic and he was right there to shake my hand and read the letter. We talked about duck hunting a minute and he left and then the dogs had caught the excitement so they jumped the city trash collectors and I had to go out and separate them. Now I'm at the office writing you, and I want to say here and now that your letter couldn't have come at a better time.

I suppose the way to repay something like that is to write the very best I can, and you can be sure, Sir, that I will bend every energy in that direction. I'm too immersed just now in new emotions to write more.

I think it well that readers be occasionally reminded of the gamble, the dismay and sacrifice which young writers (and their families) make to be writers. There is a happy postscript to this: the story we originally rejected — in a letter which the author says "raised me literally out of the dust" — has been revised and accepted and now Mr. Ford is on his way.

III
An Editor's Holiday

Round Pond

EDITORS live by their eyes and mine go on the blink only after unremitting night work. In the spring at the conclusion of one of our prize contests I have occasionally developed a flick in my right eye and curiously this coincides with the opening of the fishing season. The tranquillity of water, the rest to the nervous system that comes from gazing at a shaded cove, the delight of watching an osprey or red-wing blackbird, the mystery of a pool where fish are feeding — these to me are precious, rejuvenating experiences.

There is a great pond not far from our summer cottage, whose changing moods it is a pleasure to explore. The body of water is thickly surrounded by conifers and beech out of which towers one huge landmark pine, and it can only be enjoyed by those who bring their own boat. No house, dock, or open road mars its shut-in tranquillity. Because it is little used, it is well used. Here are no eggshells, broken bottles, and stray papers to remind you of those casual travelers who love to litter. One deeply wooded point (known to us as Pulpit Corner because of the angler who still-fishes there for hours in his little high-seated skiff like a pulpit) has a rock-laid fireplace, and chunks of birch neatly cut and stacked for the newcomer. The few who use this pond do so with care and the apprehension that it cannot remain forever inviolate from the metropolis which lies only twenty-eight miles away.

With canoe lashed on the top of our car or in a borrowed truck, here we have come for innumerable family picnics. Noon is a good time to start, but even so, the hours are not long enough to satisfy the anticipation which has been building up since the night before. We lower the canoe gently into the little path through the reeds; we mount the fly rod; Ted takes his place in the bow; Fritzy or Sara in the thwart, with the lunch basket and Mickey, the spaniel — shivering with excitement for all his sixteen years; the fish box is placed under my seat; and then we pole and battle our way through the water-path and out into the lake. Mickey, hindquarters trembling, peers intently over the gunwale as the water slides back. When he lets out an irrepressible yelp he speaks for us all; whereupon Ted, who is just as eager as he is, pokes him with the paddle.

With three years' familiarity we have pictured for ourselves the ground plan of this hidden water. Along this left bank the white perch have their habitat (or had — have they moved?); Pulpit Corner is the private hunting ground of some big bass (we have seen and hefted a 4½-pounder landed by the Pulpit Corner fisherman); directly opposite among those rocks are the bass beds, now deserted; the yellow perch are thick in the marsh water by the Outlet; the pickerel congregate in White Pine Cover; and there are one or two other dens — which I would rather not disclose — where my flies and lures have caused explosions.

Round Pond is an unpredictable place. I am never sure when we shall find the cardinal flower, that small scarlet high-stemmed face close to shore, and whose reflection is so lovely against the green. Nor the wild white azalea. I have learned not to pluck the water lilies but not why there is an occasional one more rose-tinted than the rest. I have yet to know with any certainty which fly is the best for this water in July: I have seen a big bass come clear out of water for my Gray Ghost, and again and again I have seen a bass arrow after that fly when I had found their lair, but too often it is the pickerel, not the bass, which finally takes. I have seen all fish put down by a thunderstorm and I have been caught — alone — in one of those magical sunset hours when what seemed like a million fish were feeding on the hatch which lay strewn on the calm water, and when no artificial fly I had to offer distracted them for an instant.

So we spend ourselves. The excitement of fishing, like that of lecturing, shrivels the stomach; sandwiches eaten in the canoe are tasteless, while if eaten ashore the fever to be out paddling makes two of them a meal.

When the sun sets, the water under the trees turns black and cool fingers rise from the pond. In sweaters we ferry our way toward the exit. The back muscles are weary from paddling and the bottom has had quite enough of this canoe. We do things just a little irritably: Fritzy complains that the bilge has soaked her hair-do as we empty the boat and then lift it staggeringly up to the top of the car. Well, someone has to hold the lower end if I'm to lift the high. Grumbling, we lash it tight and tie the painter to the radiator cap; I strip the rod, call Mickey out of the reeds, and stow the gear, thinking how good a drink will taste. Then as I ease behind the wheel, for just an instant before I switch on the headlights we give back our benediction for such a sanctuary.

Flood Tide

THE summer after V.E. Day, when gasoline no longer had to be hoarded, three of us bought a 16-foot skiff and an outboard motor powerful enough to buck the tides of the Ipswich Bay. This lovely tidal water, like a huge open left hand, with the little finger the largest, is the estuary of five rivers, the Ipswich, the Essex, the Parker, the Rowley and the Merrimac, and it takes knowing, for what was over your head when you shoved off downstream will be mud flats and a quaggy channel when you pole home after dark. As our boatman and guide we found Howard Wills, a paratrooper fresh out of the 101st Airborne; he had fished the Rowley as a boy, knew its every contour and was eager to regain his peace in the sun.

The Rowley, like most of our tidal streams, is wide and deep at the river mouth and for perhaps four miles thereafter; then it narrows and twists like a small creek to terminate in the headwaters not far from the Rowley Green; on highwater we rode between marsh grass and moor, on low we followed the narrow channel between muddy banks. A 9-foot difference. Howard would be waiting for us at the float, and when we were set he would cast off and wind the outboard. The motor, with Howard in his Tyrolean hat, his fish box, the bucket and the rods, sank the stern; while up in the bow, half out of water, his blond crew cut against the horizon, perched Ted. My picture is of a bright August morning, the sun points flicking the water, the bow thwacking down on the little waves, drops of spray flying and Ted eager to get the lines out, so sure that this time we'd get the big one. The wind in the face and the salt in the wind.

The sandy moors and marshes are a natural feeding ground for the migrants. On one afternoon's run from Rowley to the mouth of the Parker River, I saw purple martin pairing, dipping, and swooping together in that flight which resembles the grace of a ballet, and farther down I watched their counterpart, the swifts, darting in and out of their tenements in the sandy bank. I saw white crane, cold and immobile above the eelgrass; heard the protest of the shrike; heard the ponderous beat of the gray heron and was answered for an instant by the piercing whistle of Canadian plover.

For a time our little boat lay motionless against the marsh grass while we unkinked the trolling lines which had crossed; and as I gazed downstream, the water fifty yards distant was suddenly riffled as if young fish were feeding. A striped bass broke surface in a curving leap; and while he hung suspended in air, the pursuing force was revealed in the hungry ferocity of a seal's head. Fish and seal disappeared in the twinkling and were, I suspect, one. And the tide continued to run in. "Those seal," said Howard, "push 'em right out of water."

The five rivers in their confluence form an ever-refreshed feeding ground for the schools that in August turn north from Cape Cod. These incoming cycles of fish recall that cold-blooded but beautiful novel of the sea, *Salar the Salmon,* by Henry Williamson: first come the squid and herring, and feeding on them the striped bass that are in turn pursued by the tuna feeding farther out in the bay. The seal just play along the edges and take their choice, while overhead the terns, hovering close to the purple-shadowed water — sure sign of the school beneath — dive and dive again for the silver splinters driven to the surface by the tinker mackerel or the larger perennial hunger beneath.

In times past — no time as fish go, but more than half a century for us — the sturgeon and stripers were commuters to these streams. Then wood pulp and rubber goods, textiles, and ladies' girdles monopolized the power of white water and polluted the run. The fish went elsewhere to feed and to spawn. Cunners, flounders, cod, smelt, and haddock kept to the outer reach, venturing in on the fresh tides; the game fish made new rendezvous away from industry. Came the depression, mills closed down, and as streams ran clean again, the telegram went out underwater. The fish returned.

By day we calculated to fish the high tide and that precious hour at the turn when the stripers should be inshore; we carried our lunch with us in a bucket and we calculated to eat it two hours before high tide. Picnics, to which I have become an addict late in life, are the better for being cooked on the spot and eaten without sand. These took time, for the seaweed was far to seek and the beach, swept clean by last night's tide, had hidden its driftwood under the eelgrass at the foot of the dunes. We built our fire in the lee of a big rock with an old spar for the backlog and rocks to support the grill. The driftwood snapped with a heat as quick as charcoal.

There are almost as many ways of cooking lobster as there are appetites. Personally I like them small and I like them soft with the cream of their own still in the claws. On this occasion we had three inches of salt water in the bottom of our bucket, then a layer of seaweed, then a bundle of three lobsters tied in a cloth, then another layer of seaweed, until all nine lobsters were submerged. Then the bucket went over the hot fire, and was allowed to steam for fifteen minutes. With our backs against the rocks, crusty French bread in one hand, an ear of roasted corn on the paper plate, and a can of melted butter within reach, we feasted as you do when you use fingers, chin, nose, and teeth for the inhalation of good food. As we ate, our eyes kept wandering out to sea to catch the terns who might show up where the fish were feeding.

The wind had dropped; the nocturnal surf-casters waded in and now it was our turn. Fritzy burned the scraps in the embers, the fireplace was sanded, and sweaters went on as the eelskins were fitted over our hooks for our first run. To have more room in the boat, the bucket and picnic basket were left in a trustful group ashore. We shoved off and then turned for a preliminary troll just beyond the breakers, as close to shore as we dared. It was Howard's skill to reduce the speed of the motor until we were barely idling along; at this low speed our lures would be trolling close to the ocean's floor, which was the natural lair of the sand eels.

A 16-foot skiff can be cramped quarters for four people, and there were times when nature called and it was a relief to be set ashore. I remember Fritzy's embarrassment when, early in our acquaintance with Howard, she felt that such a moment had come. We were downriver and fortunately not far from a little shooting box on the marsh with a plainly discerned single-seater behind it. Above the hum of the motor Fritzy made known her request. "Sure," said Howard, "we'll put you right in there by the landing."

"Do you think the place is occupied? What'll I do if there is somebody in there?"

"Well, if there is somebody in there already," said Howard, "just say 'Push over'."

The striped bass is a night feeder, and the best chance of taking him is at dusk or after dark has fallen. The sight of those salt-boxes on the marsh which give the duck hunters sanctuary in November suggested a new possibility: Why couldn't we borrow one for overnight and then fish the flood tide under the full moon and again in the hour before sunrise? Howard was agreeable, but because of the hazard of night fishing he made one stipulation — it would have to be a stag party and only one other rod beside myself, and he an adult. This just about broke Ted's heart.

In the midafternoon of our chosen day, Shaw McKean, Howard and I unlocked the borrowed salt-box, shook out the blankets in the soft southwesterly, tested the kerosene ring which would fry our eggs and bacon, and laid a fire in the little potbellied stove to warm us at midnight. The setting sun picked out the Coast Guard Station, the lighthouse and cottages on Plum Island in gold-edged detail. The wind dropped as we were eating our sandwiches and when night fell there was not a breath. We headed downstream timing ourselves to be at the very inlet of the estuary under the great cliff of Castle Hill as the tide turned at 10 o'clock. The moonlight was so bright you could read by it. As we approached the Hill we could see dark against the beach the surf-casters and hear the plop of their plugs. Keeping well beyond their range, we swung our lines over the deep side of the channel where the stripers would be entering with the tide. On our first run, I suddenly hit a cement wall, and the reel was spun out of my control. Howard cut the motor and got out the flash torch. Shaw said, "Well, I'm damned," and began to reel in. My fish took out line — 20 yards — 30 yards — 40 yards — in a run of great power. Suddenly there was a dead slack and I thought I'd lost him until reeling in at full speed I realized that he had turned toward the boat. Again the rod bent down as he made a further spurt, and now Howard, who had been battling to keep us well off shore, began to follow the line with the electric torch. The pencil beam picked out the joining of the line and the water, and as our eyes became accustomed it silhouetted the dark fierce turning shape against the clear bottom. Now we could all see him as he fought the reel, and now he was on the surface, the gaff went into action, and with a heave the silver-scaled 18-pounder thudded onto the floorboards. "Well, I'm damned," said Shaw.

"Quick," urged Howard as he started the motor, "get the lines out. We should pick up one more before they're upstream." And we did.

We had scrambled eggs and beer at midnight, and it seemed like only ten minutes later when the alarm went off at 3:30. It was a darker, grayer world for the moon had set and the tide was running out, surging and sweeping us downstream. I had always been curious about the big depressions in the marsh grass close to the water's edge, and now I saw what caused them. They were the nests of the sleeping seal. As we approached you could see the big fellow rouse himself, flip to the water's edge, and lower himself, his eyes as resentful as those of a clubman in a bay window. Then he disappeared. We aroused four seals on our way down the Rowley that morning before we reached the river's mouth, and there, still trolling the eelskin, Shaw took our final fish. Of course we didn't stop then, we never do. It wasn't until the sun was well up and boats with fresh expectant faces were coming downstream that we headed for home. Yawning and rather pleased with ourselves, we held up three fingers as we passed.

Riley Brook

FOR a few days each June I have the pleasure of exploring a brook in New Brunswick. The country is new to me, and the little stream seems quite inconspicuous judged by the open stretch which flows into the pond by the sawmill. I made my first entrance wading and splashing upstream against the current, and had gone hardly a quarter of a mile when I realized that this was a wilder, colder, deeper brook than I had imagined, and one that had not been soiled by visitors. I saw enough to invite another trip, and the next morning I followed the tote road into the woods, pausing now and then to eat the wild strawberries which lay in scarlet handfuls under the tall grass.

The right fork eventually led me into a clearing and on through thick alders and spruce into the calling water; now I started downstream, hugging the shore so as not to throw my shadow on the stream, and the journey which had taken me but half an hour by road unwound itself in three miles of twisting, tree-shadowed, rocky brook. I did not re-emerge at the mill until long past lunchtime.

What one first perceives in the brook world is the beauty of the light: in this sandy run the water is so clear, but down yonder as it coils under the shadow of the spruce it is blue-black, its depth a mystery. In each run one feels the cool of the shade, the fragrance of the conifers — this is the breath of the brook. One goes on to notice the innumerable prints of deer, fresh on the sand bars where they have paused to drink; as I rounded one bend, I saw in the dark pool below me the small-headed arrow of a swimming animal, ferret, muskrat, or otter — it was too far to tell; and all along I saw what nature's engineering will do to curl a brook.

It is always the biggest trees that fall; their great shapes athwart the stream form bridges, form islands, form pockets where the bigger brook trout lurk. These windfalls are sometimes powerful enough to break the brook in two. I spent some time at a fork where this had happened; a big hardwood provided the block for a dam of accumulated timber, mortised together by the spring run. The branch that curved off to the right was shallow, chattering, sunlit, but the one to the left ran deep under so many boles that my passage that way was out of the question. I probed the headwater with a stick and could not touch bottom; the fast current had eaten under the banks, forming the most desirable residences. "Lord," I thought, "what one could do here with worms and a hook!" I dropped in some scraps of bark and there was a swirl where the water sucked under the nearest log. "And how would you get him out if you got him on?" asked reason.

Eventually I wrenched myself away from that unfathomable run and went wading down the shallow branch. "What divides," I thought to myself, "must come together again in a really good pool. Perhaps a small Mickey Finn might do some business!" It did.

The dimensions of the brook world are ever-changing and this is part of its fascination. At one moment you are striding along like Paul Bunyan in a dwarfed river; then as you climb over the hurdle of a fallen tree, placing your boot carefully on the lower level, your balance teeters as the rotted wood gives way and you plunge forward into a pothole with a force that might have broken your rod or your leg. The conceit is jarred out of you and you right yourself with the feeling that this is a wild place.

The third day I went back as the afternoon shadows were falling. I knew where the pools were now, and I was intent on exploring with my fly rod every nook and cranny of the upper reaches, lovingly and minutely. For the more open water I had a little red fly with a yellow body, and for the deep pockets along the bank and under tree roots dry flies. Fishing is an act of privacy, and in a seclusion like this, one naturally talks to oneself. Rather irritably for the most part, for the woods are always conspiring against you. The kingfisher has flown ahead giving his warning, but your real antagonists are the trees at your back. You look behind you measuring the space for your backcast, and then facing front you concentrate on the square yard of water where you mean to place your dry fly, not in midstream but as close to the bank as you dare. You strip off line and cock your wrist for the first cast — and at that point one of two enemies may intervene: the spruce at your back reaches out its arms to enmesh your leader, or the bank at which you are aiming pushes out a few inches further than you thought and snags your fly tight. The printable portions of your monologue sound like this: "There, right there, under the root . . . let it drift down to him . . . now . . . damn it, you're in the trees again . . . you can't lose that fly . . . will it pull out? . . . easy, now, easy . . . thank the Lord . . . now, not so much line, you fool . . . that's no good . . . get it closer to his hole . . . closer, closer . . . oh, you ass, you've caught the bank . . . boy, you certainly have the touch today . . ."

But once in a while you do have it; the little fly floats down to the surface and the current edges it up to the door of the cavern; there is an explosion of water, the flash of a pink belly, and you are fast to a brookie, the most beautiful and certainly the sweetest-tasting of any small fish.

Then there is the pleasure of the return to the camp at Deer Point, the innocence with which you reply to Matt's skepticism, the moment when you spread the contents of the creel on the grass, and the aftermath when Helen has cooked that pink flesh just enough in the fry pan.

The Test

THE River Test as it flows through the village of Stockbridge is the most famous and exacting trout stream in the British Isles, and it was there that I went for my English initiation one spring. If ever there was a river made to order for anglers, this is it. It is a chalk stream and spring-fed, which means that there is a cold flow of water even on the hottest summer days. The banks had been freshly cut on the day of my arrival in early May, which meant that the fish — the brown trout and the rainbows — had an alarming view of anyone who stood erect at the water's edge. The stream itself is gin-clear, and the current moves at a perfect pace for a dry fly.

I was lucky to be there, for the Beats (approximately four hundred yards of the main river and its attending sluiceways) in the vicinity of Stockbridge are booked solid from the end of April to the first of July, so I was told by Miss Kay Potts when I telephoned to ask permission.

"Well, Miss Potts," I said, "I shall be praying that one of your members may come down with an unexpected attack of measles while I am still in London. If this happens, will you please be sure to telephone me? I shall be praying hard."

That was on Tuesday, and on Thursday morning there she was. "Your prayers have been answered," she said. "One of our proprietors has telephoned to say that he must go off to the hospital for a checkup and he has released four and a half days for the week of May 7."

Since those were days when I was supposed to be seeing authors and publishers in London, my conscience would not let me play hooky for them all, but I did reserve Beat No. 5 for the evening fishing Monday and Beat No. 8 for the whole of Tuesday.

There is nothing in America quite like a cultivated English chalk stream. The Test, which is seldom wider than forty yards, is here controlled by a system of weirs so that the depth of the stream is fairly constant; and breaking off from the main current are shallow, narrow canals forming small marshy islands before they rejoin. This means that there will be good pools at either end of the island and that the brown trout, who seldom move from their favorite lairs, will be dimpling the water at regular intervals when the time comes for them to feed on the new hatch of flies. They are late risers and are seldom hungry before 11 A.M. The evening hatch of flies will be the big one, and the finest fishing, when the water is really roiled, comes after sunset.

The evening before my initiation had been blustering and cold with no hatch whatever, but that blessed Tuesday was full of sun; the wind had shifted to the southwest with just enough of a ripple to help the upstream casts of the amateur. My wife and I took a packed lunch and left it and our extra sweaters in the shade of a big willow. I had Beat No. 8, which is a perfect beauty, with a big island with good pools at either end, and the fast water going under the bridge to Longstock and emptying into a wide, spacious pool with a narrow aisle runoff to the south of the bridge. This I decided to reserve until after sunset. Meantime I fished the island and by 11:30 it was a problem which rings to follow. For the fish were rising in number. They were bottom-feeding, showing their fins and tails, and they paid no attention whatever to Mr. Lunn's Particular. So I shifted to the Blue Upright and had three good strikes in the next fifteen minutes, each one of which I failed to hook.

I was striking too fast, and when Mr. Mott, the head keeper and a great gentleman, came by, he said, "Why, they really seem to have discovered the Blue Upright. Now let me show you."

And show me he did. He pulled up his boots and he got me down on my knees, and since my Wellingtons were short and the banks very wet, I was soon well soaked (I was to pay for this with three days of stiff rheumatism, but no matter). He showed me where to place the fly, and he also showed me how to hold my breath until I'd said to myself, "God save . . . the *Queen!*" — and then hit. Together we netted two good fish before lunch, the larger being two pounds two ounces, and the other one pound twelve ounces, and I took another brace of about the same size in the gloaming.

One good fish was feeding beside the gunwale of a boat moored to the bank. It was an impossible cast to bring the fly over him with the wind blowing into the boat, but when I suggested casting it downstream, "Oh, I wouldn't do that," said Mr. Mott. "You see, sir, the Test is for upstream dry-fly fishing only."

Of the fish I lost, I remember best a great green and silver cruiser who came out from under a bank and showed me his whole perpendicular beauty as he rose straight up to turn and close on the fly. I slept with that picture for months afterwards.

No fishing day is complete without at least one good bumble; I made several, and the best as dark was coming on. I had been fishing the lovely capacious pool under the bridge, fishing the shallows into which the trout had moved after sunset. One strong fish had been hooked and netted, and he was such a beauty that after applying the priest to him I left him lying there in my net on the grass while I drifted back to look at the water. A small disturbance was going on in the shallow canal to my left. I had been drying my fly with false casts, and now without much thinking about it I let it fall in the little runoff. There was an explosion and I realized that I was into a bigger fish with my net hopelessly beyond reach. The fish and I played each other up and down the bank; he showed no signs of exhaustion, and this might have gone on until dawn if the English angler and his wife who had the Beat below me had not suddenly made their appearance crossing the weir. "Would you, like a good guy, loan me your net?" I called.

He came running, and after a certain amount of sputter the trout came ashore. "But you really should carry your net with you," admonished the Brigadier, after he had weighed my prize. "Otherwise you may find it rather awkward."

"Yes, sir." I replied.

The following morning my wife and I drove across country to spend the weekend in Oxford. We were to dine with Sir Isaiah Berlin and his charming wife, and I had telephoned him from the lodge to see if he would care for a brace of our trout. "Do you like fish?" I asked.

"Yes, on principle," replied Isaiah.

"Never mind the principle," I said. "These are brown trout taken last night in the Test and they weigh just under three-and-a-half pounds. If you don't care for them, I shall give them to someone else."

"My wife will never forgive you or me if you don't bring them." So bring them I did.

The other brace were intended for John Masefield, and we took them with us when we went to Abingdon for tea Saturday afternoon.

I look forward to these annual visits with the Poet Laureate, for he has the gift of opening up unsuspected chapters in English history as if he had been present when they took place and were telling me what he had seen. So he has told me of Roman Britain, and of the building of Hadrian's Wall, and of what happened in Bath when Rome itself had fallen to the barbarians. He has told me of the White Horse and of the Cerne Giant and of how these monster figures were originally carved in the chalk beneath the Downs, and of the spring observance which still keeps them fresh for our generation. He has told me of the coming of the Armada, and of the sinking of the *Royal Oak* and of the disaster which overtook Sir Cloudesley Shovel when he led the Mediterranean fleet home from Gibraltar only to wreck it on the Gilstone Ledges almost within sight of Plymouth harbor. Each time the words are as vivid as if he had been present as a spectator.

At the end of this tea I asked John if he knew how to clean fish, and since he didn't I thought the least I could do was to roll up my sleeves and get it over with as quickly as possible in the kitchen sink. It is a messy operation at best, and these were sizable brown trout, and when I had finished, Mrs. Pitts, the housekeeper, was not to be contained. She turned to John, who had been watching the operation, and said, "Mr. Masefield, I don't know whether I can tolerate this in my kitchen, all this mess your friend has made when I could have done it myself in 'arf the time."

The Trail

THE river trails I follow in northern New Brunswick for ten happy days each summer are a complex of granite, moss, and the interlacing roots of spruce and fir, the path seldom wider than eighteen inches, where anglers and guides have been measuring their tread for nearly seven decades. Walking here is no straightforward business; the Northwest Miramichi has carved its winding way through a rocky gorge, and to keep pace with it the trail is alternately climbing or leaping down. There are only a few level stretches on the lip of the stream, and these are usually half under water; then a series of toeholds, rock and root, present themselves, and the mounting path takes one into the shade of the forest. One steps intently, eyes down, hearing the wash of the river, the four clear, plaintive notes of the whitethroat — why has no composer ever used them as a theme? — or the distant hammering of a woodpecker, and listening with expectation for the turbulence of white water which signals our approach to the salmon pool ahead.

The trail is most readable the second morning after rain, when the pockets between the roots will have dried and the moist earth will tell who has passed this way since sunset. One expects the print of deer and is always surprised by the larger evidence of moose: "Looks like somebody spilled a bag of prunes," remarks Henry, the more notional of our guides. A lacerated dead birch shows where the bear has been grubbing for ants, and once this summer I had the luck to intercept a doe between the path and the river's edge. Up she came, in steeple-chase jumps, her white tail flying, so beautifully unerring as she placed her springs between the boulders and the deadfall.

The mornings are the best, the trail then so fragrant and the green so moist. Head down, one takes in the little things. On either side of the path with its cover of spruce needles are masses of bunchberry, its square white blossom set off glossily by the six-pointed leaf. One looks for the white lady's-slipper, the clusters of lavender catnip, or the tiny pink colonies of twin-flower; shinleaf, the forest lily of the valley, and in rare openings, lady's-tresses and the purple-fringed wild orchid. The trail to Stony Brook dips through some rich river soil where for twenty yards the growth is outlandish: masses of Queen Anne's lace standing shoulder high ("stinkin' elders," Henry calls them), and topping them the fronds of the fiddlehead fern, from which we get a salad as delectable as cold asparagus. The logs which carry us across this mucky ground are guarded by a regiment of blue flags.

My feet are grateful for the moss which cushions the ledges. If it weren't for the thought of fish, I should study the mosses more closely, the plushy emerald green, the darker blue on the fallen logs, the needle moss like some tiny conifer. This green inlay is most vividly to be seen on the clearstone, the glistening white granite; here is a footstool for an Indian prince — or a Boston editor, if I could find a way of keeping the moss on it alive and the stone forever moist in my library!

Howard, the camp philosopher, who has been working on the river for half a century, tells me that the forest floor is now much clearer than it used to be; the slash and dense under-brush are gone, and through the corridor of the trees one can sometimes see a spruce partridge. I try to tell him what the woods give me: the feeling of privacy which has become so rare in our urban life; the absence of litter — not an empty beer can along the entire way — and the reassurance I find in the unchanging beauty of the forest and the river.

It is two miles and a half from Camp Adams to Sam's Pool, and four pools to fish on the way. Walking that trail in waders in the early day, one feels like Mercury; the ten-foot rod is sim-ply a longer finger; the musette swung from the shoulder, with its fly boxes and rain jacket, is no heavier than the bug dope on one's skin. Anticipation urges us, and if the heel skids on a slippery root it takes only an extra jump to restore one's bal-ance. But it's a different story five hours later when with wet and heavy feet we turn back to camp. The arches have fallen, the toes cry out, the roots and the stubbing granite become per-sonally belligerent; now a step wrenches the whole frame, and a mutter of protest ("Don't do that, you ape — watch where you are going — damn it, not that way") breaks out. At such times I remember an angler who was hit by polio in midlife and crippled from the waist down. But with that strength of arm and spirit which comes as compensation to such sufferers, he would literally haul his way along the trail, toiling half the morning for the joy of returning. I think how he must have studied every root, even the tiniest of the moss flowers; temper subsides and I go in humbleness.

Plum Island

We were on our way to Plum Island for what was the boy's last until he returns from the Army. The sunlight had that hazy, suspended beauty of mid-October prompting you to take a good look while it lasts, and as we drove we noted as one does the new things that are always changing the familiar: here on Heartbreak Road is the new wayside stand where we found the best sweet corn in the summer; we passed the famous blueberry moors that have been so barren this year because of the spring frost; we noticed the dying elms on the Rowley Green and wondered if maples would be planted in their stead, and as we crossed over the span of the Rowley River, we saw that the tide was almost high and, judging from the pull on the buoys, coming in strong. Now our gaze was to the east, to the tawny marshes with the white-topped sand dunes marking the far barrier against the Atlantic. That is where we would be in another fifteen minutes, but first we paused at the Sportsmen's Rest, not for a beer, but to hear if they had had any word about the stripers.

The bartender referred us to two customers in long-billed caps. "It's a sheer gamble now," they said. "Last we heard of were taken early Sunday morning out of the surf by the old Coast Guard station. Small ones, school fish." That's where we intended to go anyway, and the native skepticism was usual.

An Editor's Holiday

The white road which leads into the Parker River Refuge took us six miles down the sandy thumb. We met the warden driving out and hailed him. "Anybody doing business at Big Sandy, or the Station?" we asked. "Haven't seen a fish or a fisherman. You'll have it all to yourselves." So in time we parked, and with the long glass rod and our bag of plugs climbed through our favorite gap in the dunes.

At the high point you pause to take it all in: the nine-mile crescent of immaculate beach, the sandy parapet built up by the last flood tide, and below that the wet brown ocean floor and the breakers. We looked for feeding gulls and found them, a small cluster inshore but far down toward the point, and closer, to the north of us but half a mile out, a rowdy colony of others. They were settling on the water when we arrived, but a minute later they were dispersed and in flight, and now we saw why, for they were hunting over a mile-long reef of feeding fish. Here, far, far beyond our reach, were the stripers we had come for, an enormous school of them whose presence darkened the water with a slight riffle and whose pursuit drove to the surface the little fish the gulls were swooping for. The gannets plummeted straight down from fifty or sixty feet, the sunset on their wings, and they hit the water like a shellburst. We began laying out a tinclad as far as we could cast on the chance that a truant from the school might have wandered inshore. But reason told us they were hopelessly out of reach. Meantime, we watched the geysers of water that flashed again and again in the far sunlight over the incredible reef.

In this hour it was our luck to be spectators. We saw cormorants riding the water as stolidly as tugs, and in another instant gone from view. We saw four white-winged scoters evenly spaced jetting their way south in their low undeviating flight; a scurry of sanderlings landed beside us for their twin-kling, inquisitive business at the water's edge. I whistled, and the flock rose, took protective shape, veered away, and then settled right back again. The shellbursts continued far out in the fading light, and then as I lifted my gaze I saw coming toward us the ever-changing, unmistakable V of the Canada goose and heard at the same instant the creak and honking of their intercom. The first flight numbered twenty-five and was so low that we could mark and listen to the leader. Necks out-thrust, white cheeks showing, the wingbeat so powerful, so regular, they came in right over us and then broke formation to mingle and form up with a much larger flight that had been following. Then, still in a V, they angled away from the ocean to the security of the bay, where — did they know it? — no shooting is permitted. Now the light and the flood tide were gone, and it was time for us to head for home. Fishing is not always for fish, as we have cause to know, and there is a retentive beauty about these last hours of the open months. On the way out the boy picked up a giant clamshell as white and unblemished as if it had come from the carver's hand. It will remind us.

Last Time

THERE is always a feeling of ruefulness in putting a summer house to sleep for the winter. We cling to the woods of our three-acre moraine till the last possible moment, savoring the golden hours of Indian summer, reprieves which sometimes stretch into November, but conscious that we are doing things for the last time. This was my last fish on Beaver Pond, I think to myself, as I strip my rod in the dusk of a Saturday afternoon: the little lake is a cool black mirror enclosed with every scarlet variation of swamp maple, but not a single bass have I seen for three hours. In the shallows by the blackened lily pads the pickerel would occasionally arrow the surface; they have taken over the lairs of their large-mouth neighbors, where they were not privileged to venture in July. The bass have gone where all good bass go for the winter — to the depths.

On this last weekend I go alone for my last trudge along the sands of Plum Island: the honking of the Canada goose had pierced my early morning sleep, and now I was listening to it again as another long V glided down against the later afternoon sun. No guns spoke, for this is sanctuary. The marsh is a cold brown, and as I turn at the top of the dune for a last look at the breakers, the wind from the north makes me shiver. Last time, last time. On the road home the closed cottages seem desolate; the roadside stand where we shopped for baby carrots and Country Gentleman is reduced to pumpkins and cider. Don't stop.

As the days become colder, it is only a matter of time before we must shut the water off. Meanwhile there are certain small urgencies to attend to: the family of gray squirrels who have taken up residence in the barn and whose youngsters enjoy chewing up my wife's leaves must somehow be induced out. The carpenter ants in the guesthouse must have the same steady, insatiable appetite for the living room beams, as their daily scattering of sawdust suggests, and one day we shall be stove in if they are not dislodged. Hay scented, the fast-spreading fern which would like to take over the whole of the rock garden needs thinning. No need to worry about the raccoons; they must miss the soft touch we are, but the hollow tree where they lodge has weathered every hurricane and they will keep warm and multiply. However, we *should* worry about our oaks: they are constantly underfed on the sour, meager soil of our ridge, and now we mark the dead limbs which ought to be cut before they crash down on the guesthouse. This is a job calling for ladders and tree surgeons, and I have a mental picture of the bill.

The leaves fall, the scenery is stripped away, and underneath we see what the pattern of tomorrow is doing to our countryside. As the city moves out, the contractors move in with their trucks and bulldozers. It is infuriating that a movement which portends a greater good for a great number should be spearpointed by an agent so ruthless. Contractors demand and receive political favors; with the tips they are given they acquire an interest in marginal land before the community knows what is coming. The wood lots come down fast as the throughways are built; contractors supply the sand and the gravel needed for the roads, and when the excavations have grown as big as a baseball diamond, they can be rented back to the politicos as a town dump. Brooks are diverted or simply left to flow into ranch house cellars after heavy rain.

I don't say that all contractors are corrupt; I say that there are too many among them who have so little respect for American values — other than that of the quick buck — that they need to be restrained. Neither private rights nor zoning laws are proof against their assault, nor does it reassure me to be told that this is all in the name of private enterprise. Just as we have a commissioner of motor vehicles to grant licenses and protect us against the hit-and-run driver, so there ought to be a commissioner of community development, an authority as invulnerable to bribery as Robert Moses, to protect us from the hit-and-run contractor.

Today, development and desecration go hand in hand from Bangor to Virginia Beach, and there is no authority local or federal to whom citizens can appeal when they see the locusts coming. If we really want to beat Egypt to the sand, okay; if we really want to duplicate on the East Coast the neon-lit, chromium-plated resorts which have made the coastline south of Los Angeles so hideous, just let the boys keep going.

This is what I brood over when I come back to the open fire. We are right in the midst of the perilous decade: Cape Cod as unexploited as Truro, beaches as breath-taking as Nauset, woods as cathedral as the Essex pines are ripe for the plucking unless there are citizens angry enough to stop it. (As I write this the residents of Concord have voted 603 to 38 to move the town dump to within one-third of a mile from Walden. Where else would you put the stuff!) This autumn, this week, we may be seeing some things for the last time.

IV

The Changing Country

Less and Less Reading

EDITORS, even an editor as iconoclastic as Henry L. Mencken, are at heart believers. Mencken, who never ceased to rage against ignorance, lived with the belief that in the American language our native writers, blending the heritage of many bloodstreams, would one day produce literature of surpassing freshness and vitality. He looked for signs that this was coming and found enough of them to keep him hopeful. Indeed an editor like a teacher must fix his eyes on a polestar of such magnitude if he is to maintain his sense of direction in the midst of all the fogs and crosscurrents which daily become more distracting in this atomic age. The star by which I steer is Literature, and what concerns me is whether enough of our young people have anything more than a flickering interest in the light which has sustained me. Is it true that English, whether written or spoken, by high school seniors and college freshmen, has been steadily deteriorating in this country since the end of the Second World War?

The evidence is contradictory. Since 1946 I have spoken on the campuses of over one hundred and fifty colleges and universities. On my visits I invariably hear from the Deans of Admission and from members of the English Departments the complaint that the entering freshmen are ill-prepared, that they come to college with less and less reading, and that as a result most of freshman year has to be spent getting them ready to study freshman English. Yet on these very same campuses, I frequently find small groups of upperclassmen who are wholly absorbed in the writing which they are doing under the direction of an inspired teacher. Wallace Stegner at Leland Stanford, Hudson Strode at the University of Alabama, Edwin L. Peterson at the University of Pittsburgh, and Carroll Towle at the University of New Hampshire, the Avery Hopwood classes at Ann Arbor, English 77 at Yale, the personal direction which at Harvard Theodore Morrison provides in fiction and Archibald MacLeish in poetry — these are just a few of the electrically charged circles which, like Robert Hillyer's classes at Delaware, lift the student out and up into a different world.

Both things seem to be going on at the same time: among the many a slackening of interest and effort, a blindness toward poetry, a disdain for reading, a feeling that English of classic beauty is for the birds; among the few that blazing intensity of endeavor which a beginning writer must experience. My concern is lest the apathy be extended. To me the love for books is inseparable from that sense of wonder which we all know however briefly in our adolescence, and what I am seeking is some way to exhilarate the experience of learning, especially the learning of English when we are at the sunrise of our education.

All education is an awakening, and the teachers of English are the buglers who bring us to our feet. My friend George F. Kennan, our former ambassador to Russia, came to New England to address the school audiences at Exeter and Andover. He spoke to them much as he would have spoken to a college convocation — and his English is distinctive — about our relations with Russia; he gave his reasons for believing that we shall avoid war, and he was deeply impressed by the spirit of inquiry and the maturity which he found in both of those big audiences. "What responsive, open-minded boys they are," he said to me afterwards, and then after a moment's reflection he added, "They seem so different from the guarded, diffident, rather lonely undergraduates one sees on campus." We are all aware of that change and of the inner uncertainty, the dread of army life, the feeling of nervous insecurity which bring it about. Is there any prescription for opening minds and for keeping them open?

In the beginning was the word — and it was read aloud. Our very first memory of books is of the voice of a woman — mother, favorite aunt, or teacher — who gave us the unforgettable pictures we retain of Bob, Son of Battle, of Mowgli, and of Tom Sawyer and Huck Finn. My family were great ones for Mark Twain. I cut my teeth on *A Connecticut Yankee at King Arthur's Court,* and when I first heard Mark's description of the Yankee standing before all the court as naked as a pair of scissors, I literally rolled on the floor with laughter. I think Mark Twain is much better to begin with than Dickens; there is something too brutal and too bleak about Dickens. A book like *Life on the Mississippi* is an American adventure told so naturally that a boy can identify himself with the cub pilot who ran away from home. There is something very persuasive about being read to, and in these days when there is so little privacy in the home, and when television and recorded music fill every evening hour, perhaps the only remaining place where a child will hear a cultivated reading voice in quiet is in the schoolroom.

The Changing Country

The veneration for the beautiful but dumb athlete has long since passed its peak in the Eastern colleges, and on many a campus the boy of intellect, the boy in the top tenth, who can edit, act, or write, is as highly regarded as a halfback. This form of compensation has been slow to reach the state universities of the Midwest and slower still to reach down into the high schools, but it is coming and as it comes it will enlarge the opportunities for what Gilbert Murray and John Masefield so encouraged at Boar's Hill — the reading of plays, the reading of epic poetry aloud. The chance to act in a serious play — no one can possibly take part in Thornton Wilder's *Our Town* without yielding to the compassion of the lines — the incentive to appear in prize speaking and debating give students a memorization of clear forceful English some of which may stay in mind for life.

We live in a country which places too little value on the precise use of words. Partly this is the fault of those advertisers who commercialize cheap, bad English; partly it is the fault of the ghost writers who prepare the speeches for public men; mostly it is the fault of parents who are too careless to correct their children. America is the home of the ten-cent cigar and the nickel phrase, the cheap cliché endlessly repeated; the home of bastard words like "contacted" and "winterized"; of barbarisms like "think for real" and "tastes good like a cigarette should"; of glibness like "as of now" and "but definitely"; of sheer nonsense like "irregardless" and "rather unique" (*unique* is one of a kind; it is either *unique* or it is not — there can be no qualifier!).

I am not inveighing against American slang or American idiom, for they are, both of them, a muscular part of our new writing. What I am inveighing against is the American habit of using popular clichés without thinking.

How is one aroused to an awareness of words? I know it can be done, for it was done to me. At Harvard when I was trying to build up my vocabulary, it was Dean Briggs who encouraged me to carry slips of paper in my pocket. On one side I would write down a word that was new to me and that I was eager to acquire, and on the reverse I would write down its meaning and a sample phrase in which it was used. Harvard undergraduates spend a good deal of time shuttling back and forth between the austerities of Cambridge and the amenities of Boston, and on those subway rides between Harvard Square and Park Street I shuffled the slips and let the meaning sink in; so I became familiar with new words, words as fancy as "dichotomy" which happened to be a professor's cliché at the moment.

It is stimulating to watch Conrad's choice of the adverbs which give color and verve to his paragraphs. (Henry James said the adverb was always a controlling word in a sentence.) Students should be proud of using new words in their themes; they should be permitted to use slang, and to look for whatever dialect is still characteristic in their part of the country. When I joined the *Atlantic* staff in 1924, about one short story in every four was written in dialect. They came to us in Pennsylvania Dutch, in the dialect of the Kentucky mountaineers, and from the Cajun country in Louisiana. They were written in Swedish, Jewish, Irish dialect, and in the accents of the Negro. Today dialect is fading from the scene and the reason is clear enough; writers want to be thought of as essentially American, not as part of a minority, and what is more they remember that those old stories in dialect were too often an excuse for farce or for sentiment rather than the heartfelt truth.

But local color is irrepressible in this country and always will be; it crops out everywhere, and students should be encouraged to listen for it and use it to good effect.

The economy of the war years is to blame for the watering down of instruction in English. Reading is not as well taught as it used to be. I agree that the flash-card system is swifter, yet it has enormously increased the difficulty of those who are inclined to be left readers, and although there is no way of proving it, I believe it has produced some of the worst spellers the country has ever seen. As for writing, the only way to learn to write is to write, and I deplore the doing away of the daily theme and of the essay type of question on examinations. I realize that during the war there simply was not enough manpower available to correct these themes, and so it seemed economical to place the emphasis on questions of identification which could be corrected by machines. But there is no doubt that the writing, the writing of the vast majority, has suffered.

Finally, and most important, how can we induce in the eighteen-year-old a curiosity and then a desire for books? Teachers and their allies the librarians are, I sometimes think, our last resort in the impressionable years. The libraries today are a sanctuary for the quiet reflective child. Some children, a few, are still fond of quiet, and here in their part of the library with the low shelves, the comfortable chairs and the story hour, their minds can begin to feed and to imagine. If the zest for reading is aroused by ten, it won't stop. As we grow older, we begin to take tips from those we respect. I remember in my freshman year a Sunday afternoon walk I had with Geoffrey Parsons, then the editor of the *New York Tribune*. Parsons was an omnivorous reader, and in that walk by the sea he fired my imagination by what he said about three books I had never heard of: *Winesburg, Ohio,* by Sherwood Anderson, *The Brass Check* by Upton Sinclair, and *The Life of Oscar Wilde* by Frank Harris. One way or another I managed to borrow all three of them in the course of the next week.

These were impressive experiences, and I embarked on another which went deeper and lasted longer when as an undergraduate I heard Christopher Morley tell of the excitement of reading Keats's poems against the background of Keats's letters. One has to be a little bit in love to get the best out of that experience, and I was. Today if I found myself walking with an inquiring freshman I would surely tell him about *As I Remember Him,* by Dr. Hans Zinsser; I would speak of Virginia Woolf's luminous essays in *The Common Reader,* which seem to me the quintessence of biography and criticism; I would talk to him about Archibald MacLeish's play, "*J.B.,*" and about the courage, the unshakable values, and magnificent descriptive writing in *Dr. Zhivago.*

First and last it is the teacher of English who must arouse us. She — in four cases out of five it is a woman — knows us with an almost medical intimacy, and she has it in her power to aim us in a way which will change our lives. If she notices that we have a strange attraction for frogs, mud turtles, and garter snakes, she will see that a book about animals, a mature book like Tom Barbour's *Naturalist at Large,* comes into our ken. If our eyes light up at the mention of the Knights of the Round Table, she will know how to make Malory and Tennyson approachable. If we talk of a grandfather who came across the country in a covered wagon, she will remember *The Oregon Trail,* A. B. Guthrie's *The Big Sky,* and that other fine book,

The Forty-niners by Archer B. Hulbert. Lincoln's Birthday may prompt her to read aloud some chapters from *Marching On,* that brave novel by James Boyd, and the day before Washington's Birthday — always the day before a holiday — she might read to us Samuel Eliot Morison's superb essay on "Washington as a Young Man." And even if we resist books with all our might, even if the sports page is all that we hanker for, she may still leave with us, deep in the subconscious, echoes of a beauty we can never quite forget.

In the fall of 1920 a hulking young Southerner, Thomas Clayton Wolfe, of Asheville, North Carolina, then in his twenty-first year, came to Harvard to study for his master's degree. I remember seeing him in the Harvard Yard with his huge shoulders and his striking dark features. He was a rather lonely student, and in his moments of self-doubt his thoughts turned back to the woman who had taught him in Asheville, Mrs. J. M. Roberts. What she meant to him shines out in this letter which he wrote from Cambridge to Mr. Frank Wells, then Superintendent of Schools in Asheville:

My friend and former teacher, Mrs. J. M. Roberts, has lately written me, explaining that some testimonial is desired as to her quality as a teacher, and asking me if I would care to record any opinion I have on that subject. I esteem it an honor and a privilege to do this, although I find myself in constant difficulties when I try to keep my pen from leaping away with a red-hot panegyric.

But — with all the moderation and temperance and earnestness at my command I can do no less than consider Mrs. Roberts as one of the three great teachers who have ever taught me, — this with all honor to Harvard, who has not yet succeeded in adding a fourth name to my own Hall of Fame.

More than anyone else I have ever known, Mrs. Roberts succeeded in getting under my skull with an appreciation of what is fine and altogether worth while in literature. That, in my opinion, is the vital quality. That is the essential thing — the mark of a real teacher.

I didn't know, until Mrs. Roberts wrote me, that she had no University degree, but that is a matter of not the slightest consequence to me. So far does she surpass certain college graduates I know, who are teaching, in respect to actual knowledge, appreciation, and the ability to stimulate and inspire, that any difficulty as to a degree would be negligible, I think.

I have spoken of Mrs. Roberts merely as a teacher. This is perhaps the only testimonial you want. But I cannot stop before I speak of another matter that has been of the highest importance to me. During the years Mrs. Roberts taught me she exercised an influence that is inestimable on almost every particular of my life and thought.

With the other boys of my age I know she did the same. We turned instinctively to this lady for her advice and direction and we trusted to it unfalteringly.

I think that kind of relation is one of the profoundest experiences of anyone's life, — I put the relation of a fine teacher to a student just below the relation of a mother to her son and I don't think I could say more than this.

You can readily understand that the intimacy of such a relation is much more important in those formative years at grammar school or high school than afterwards at college. At college you don't get it but you don't need it so much. The point is that I did get it at a time when it was supremely important that I get it. It is, therefore, impossible that I ever forget the influence of Mrs. Roberts. She is one of my great people, and happy are those who can claim her as their teacher!

In those words so charged with affection, Thomas Wolfe speaks for all of us who can never forget what we owe to those who taught us English.

What Happens to Walden

WHAT happens to Walden Pond happens to us all. This small, green oasis, sacred to the memory of Henry Thoreau, is a symbol of the privacy which we are in the act of surrendering straight across the country. Water and privacy are today the two natural resources in short supply throughout the United States. Have any people on earth ever changed the face of their country as fast as we Americans? The Egyptians who made up in slave labor what we possess in bulldozers and power saws had nothing like our speed, and it took them more than a millennium to arrive at the desert which is theirs today. The English and Canadians seem to lack our rapacity for tearing down, for "modernizing" what is old.

We do our engulfing in the name of progress; nothing must impede "the wheels of progress," and nothing does. Today those wheels which have the light touch of a tank are being accelerated by the pressure of numbers, by our current mania for bigger and faster roads, and by the incredible growth of a hard-top, ranch-house suburbia. Like lava from Etna, this pressure of numbers overflows the countryside, filling in meadows and marshes, felling the woodlands, forcing the brooks underground. Nothing is impregnable. If old avenues of oaks or maples stand in the way of a new road, down they come; if the new Colby College campus is an obstruction to the plans of a throughway, surely the campus can give; if larger bathing facilities are needed in Middlesex County, why not Walden Pond?

Next to Boston, the village of Concord is the most visited, most revered shrine in New England. Concord is a self-respecting community, conscious that it has a dual responsibility in tending to the past and planning for the future. It is proud of its schools; it takes care of its trees (grieving as we all do about the ravage of the elms); and through private guardianship and public interest, it has preserved as much as it could of its famous heritage — such landmarks as Wright's Tavern, the Old Manse, the Emerson, Alcott, and Hawthorne houses, and "the battlefield." But a pond is harder to preserve.

Walden Pond is a little cup of blue water set in the woods within easy walking distance of Concord center; it is spring-fed and has no outlet, so that the level of the lake rises unpredictably. It is not large, half a mile long by three eighths of a mile wide; and it is very deep, 107 feet by Thoreau's measurement in certain places. The Emersons owned a large part of the shore, and Ralph Waldo in 1845 gave Thoreau permission to build a hut of the native white pine and to cultivate a two-acre bean plot. Henry Thoreau was then twenty-eight, rebellious, a nonconformist, with no job; the job he set himself was to live for two years beside this "forest mirror" until he knew its every mood. The record of Walden and himself which he left in his great book has made the spot a shrine for all Americans and has brought back to it year after year pilgrims who take the shore path thinking to see what Thoreau saw a hundred and ten years ago.

Thoreau was never to know what his sense of privacy had done to this sylvan spot. Walden has its vulnerable points, being bounded at one end by the railroad and at the other by a highway. For a time the railroad ran regular excursions even in Thoreau's day, but these ceased when Ford made it easier to go by car. In 1922 Emerson's grandsons gave the pond and land into the protection of the Commonwealth with the sole purpose of "preserving the Walden of Emerson and Thoreau, its shores and woodlands, for the public who wish to enjoy the pond, the woods and nature, including bathing, boating, fishing and picnicking." It is significant that the word "preserving" comes ahead of "enjoy."

But in the decades since the gift, the town and the state have treated Walden as a recreation area. The accommodations were gradual, but they added up to a casualness for which both are to blame. A dock and refreshment stand were natural enough for the modest bathing beach. But it didn't stay modest long. A trailer colony moved in, with the town fathers' acquiescence — not, of course, on the shore line, but across the road. And after that came hot-dog stands and filling stations. Throngs from the west of Boston come to swim in Walden and to picnic on the shore — ten thousand or more on a summer Sunday — and they leave behind them what Edwin Way Teale, the naturalist, calls "fearful and wonderful evidence of America's high standard of living." In his book *North with the Spring*, Mr. Teale describes a walk which he and his wife took at Deep Cove one July morning in 1949, and as they walked the shore line close to the sight of Thoreau's cabin, this is a list of what they found: "116 beer cans, 21 milk bottles, 7 Coca-Cola bottles, the remains of 14 campfires, a shoe box, eggshells, soap, half-eaten sandwiches, Dixie cups, cracker boxes, soda straws, cigarette packages, comic books, tabloid newspapers, playing cards, broken glass, paper napkins, mustard bottles, firecrackers, banana peels, orange skins, a baby-food jar, a piece of pink ribbon, the thumb of a leather glove, a flashlight battery, and a dollar bill." Since 1950 conditions at Walden in this respect have changed for the better. Bathing is no longer permitted in the Cove, and such litter as survives, we hope, has gone underground. I mention the horror list to show what could so easily happen again if safeguards were relaxed.

In the spring of 1957 Walden once more was in jeopardy. The county decided to widen the bathing beach by another three hundred feet, and to make the shelving shore shallow enough for a livesaving course for children. And on May 14 the Massachusetts legislature voted $50,000 to "improve" Walden. Bulldozers moved in and an area of an acre and a half was denuded; eighty-six trees of varying ages came down, and the gravel thus exposed was bulldozed into the lake to fill in the potholes that might be dangerous to the children. This is perfectly reasonable, if all one thinks about is recreation.

The donors, W. Cameron Forbes, Edward W. Forbes, and Alexander Forbes, are still alive as I write this. They knew what they were doing in their deed of gift when they stressed the word "preserving," and they detest the present invasion, as their letter to the *New York Times* of August 27, 1957 made clear. The men in charge of the "improvement," who knew what they were doing but not what they were ruining, are the county commissioners of Middlesex, and their original plans called for a hard-top parking area and a hundred-foot concrete bathhouse.

It should be clear to anyone that there is now a deep conflict of interests between those who wish to enlarge Walden's facilities for recreation and those who wish to preserve the reservation as you would preserve a stand of giant redwoods or

Valley Forge. In this predicament there must be a moderator, and the historic site should be taken out of the hands of the county officials and placed either under the protection of the state park department or the nation. If recreation is the only aim, the next step will be outboard motors, water skis, and a Walden Sextet in bathing suits. Seriously, better precautions must be taken. There must be a limit to the number of bathers in a pond of this size with no outlet. (Several mothers I know will no longer permit their children to swim there in the crowded season.) Finally, people should be encouraged to visit Walden for the *privacy and secret beauty* which is so rare as to be almost nonexistent in suburbia.

This has been a battle between the short view and the long view, and when I vote for the long view, I do so remembering Thoreau's words: "Walden is a perfect forest mirror, set round with stones as precious to my eye as if fewer or rarer . . . Sky water. It needs no fence. Nations come and go without defiling it. It is a mirror which no stone can crack, whose quicksilver will never wear off, whose gilding Nature continually repairs." So keep it.

Yes, but who shall be the guardian? Walden, like the Vieux Carré in New Orleans, like Georgetown and the ancient portions of Charleston, South Carolina, like Beacon Hill, like Chestnut Street in Salem and Main Street, Nantucket — Walden is a living reminder of a treasured past. It must not be hedged in by hamburger heavens nor made odoriferous with the town dump; it must be protected, if not by voluntary action then by federal law, for just as truly as Mount Vernon it is a reminder of privacy, of beauty, and of the character which we look for in national monuments.

Trees

WHEN we are young we take all natural beauty for granted. But because memory has a way of treasuring certain special moments, these come back to us unsummoned across the years. The spring robin I heard calling above a wet lawn on West Jersey Street — a shower had just passed — in 1908, I have heard a hundred times since; the sweet peas, dew-fresh, on the Nimmicks' latticework which I used to pass on my way to the beach just as the July sun was warming their perfume; the moonlight which made pools of darkness under our maples on Clinton Place — I never meant to keep these, but there they are.

It is a sign of age that as our time becomes limited, so we become concerned about other objects as destructible as ourselves. It never occurred to me to worry about the elms, not in my senior year in the Harvard Yard when a blizzard turned to sleet, hung them with snow and crystal, and broke down their tops and limbs. The damage was dismissed with the thought that you can always plant new ones. I only realized later how indispensable those old trees in their sunlight and shade were in the Yard.

The American elm is a New England character. It dates the oldest house; its wineglass silhouette is a landmark in the meadow; its branches make a summer cloister of the old streets in Williamstown, Danversport, or Salem; with the lilac bush it is the living memorial guarding the deserted farm. Or it used to be. It has been called "the patriot tree" — under its boughs treaties were signed with the Indians, Washington took command of an army; George Whitefield, the evangelist, preached to thousands on Boston Common under the Great Tree; under the elm came the rushing fierce embrace of the homecomings after Appomattox. You measure trees with your eyes, and the sight of an old elm makes you feel younger, and surer that good things last.

A century ago, when the *Atlantic* was in its second year, the Autocrat of the Breakfast Table sent out this call for a biography of distinguished trees. "I wish," wrote Dr. Oliver Wendell Holmes, "somebody would get up the following work:

Sylva Novanglica

Photographs of New England Elms and other Trees taken upon the same Scale of Magnitude. With Letter Press Descriptions by a Distinguished Literary Gentleman . . ." Thirty-two years later the very book was produced, *Typical Elms and Other Trees of Massachusetts,* a handsome green and gold folio with superb plates by Henry Brooks, the text by Lorin L. Dame, and the introduction by Dr. Holmes.

A labor of love, long out of print, it leads one back to a time when men seemed to revere trees more than we do. The early settlers of New England inherited from their English ancestors a desire for shade trees. In front of the new house for the bride, the bridegroom planted the memorial elm. The elm was their first choice and the reasons, says Mr. Dame, are obvious: it is a rapid grower, requires little care, admits of the severest pruning where branches come dangerously close to the roof, and combines in a remarkable degree size and beauty and shade. The French botanist Michaux termed it "the most magnificent vegetable of the temperate zones."

There are twenty-four superb photographs of elms here, and often we are shown two of the same tree — the one in its copious foliage, the other of its magnificent bare architecture in winter. These pictures were taken in the day of the buggy, the dirt road and the stovepipe hat, and they give one the view of another century.

There is a story about every one of these famous trees. The Whittemore Elm in Arlington was set out in 1724 by Samuel Whittemore in front of his house. A Minuteman at the age of eighty, he was shot and left for dead at the roadside. But he recovered and lived on to enjoy the shade of that fine tree until he was a hundred and one. (Postscript: When they widened the road, the highway moved off to one side to preserve *that* landmark.) For three centuries the oldest tree on Boston Common was of course known as the Great Tree, and it was so designated on the maps. Planted about 1640, it suffered from its first major cavity a hundred years later; a tree dentist of the period cleaned out the rot, filled the aperture with "clay, and other substances," and then bandaged it with canvas. The big beauty lived on until February 1876, and when the winter gales finally destroyed it, citizens rushed to the spot and took home slabs and cuttings for table tops and chairs. The Washington Elm, which stood close to the Cambridge Common, is shown at two stages: in its full foliage in 1870, and in its spindly decrepitude in 1889 — top gone, big limbs sawed off, the stumps tarred, dying. Just worn out as most elms are that pass one hundred and fifty.

Today the whole Yankee species of elms is threatened by

the Dutch elm beetle. The Wethersfield Elm, the great tree of Connecticut, which stood up under the hurricane of '38, succumbed to the beetles; the big beauties in Williamstown are, many of them, in danger; and the same ravage can be seen in Concord, Salem, Deerfield, or on any old country road. People speak of the pin oak and of the Norway maple as a better substitute for replanting, but I say "Don't despair."

The blight of the elm is not as desperate as that which wiped out the chestnut. Some of the veterans have shown surprising immunity — as, for instance, the Big Elm in Framingham, not far from Route 9, said to have been planted in 1775; the Whipping Post Elm and the Signpost Elm in Litchfield, Connecticut, are both well into their second century and both immune; so are the three ancient elms in Greenwich which have withstood twenty years of the Dutch elm contagion. The tree warden of Greenwich deserves praise for this, for he has labored mightily to preserve his more than six thousand public elms. What we need are more exacting tree wardens in every community, who will demand that the deadwood so easily infested be removed. And more spraying. For the American elm is hardier than the European species and it is just as ideal for civilization as it once was for the country town. It stands any amount of tramping, its roots survive under pavements, its form and foliage are of a beauty that cannot be replaced. Plant on!

It is hard for us to believe that trees were regarded as an enemy by the western pioneer. Trees stood in the way of his planting and they shut out his sunlight. The virgin forests which once covered Kentucky, Indiana, and Ohio with their impenetrable gloom into which a child might disappear forever were an enemy to be burned, axed, and uprooted. So the settler won his clearing and the forests thinned out. The story is told with unforgettable fidelity in that fine short novel *The Trees,* by Conrad Richter. My partner Donald Snyder, whose pioneer ancestors fought their way into the clear in Indiana, has a copy of that book stored away for his grandchildren so that they can understand what the virgin forests were really like.

After the settler came the lumberman and the sawmill, cutting for the needed houses and furniture and, ever increasingly, for the wood pulp from which comes newsprint. A few of the early lumber firms such as Weyerhaeuser, Pope & Talbot, and the Simpson Logging Company, all of which had extensive holdings in the Pacific Northwest, operated with a conscience, but they were the exception, not the rule.

Among the early lumbermen were William C. Talbot who hailed from East Machias, Maine, and Andrew J. Pope from Boston; they came to the West with the Forty-niners; they were experienced in shipping, and the first in San Francisco to fill the need for "windows, doors, sashes, and knees"; they prospered in the Gold Rush; their fleet doubled in the Civil War; their lumber schooners held a commanding place in the intercoastal trade, and they shipped over 60 million feet of lumber for the rebuilding of San Francisco in 1906, the year of the earthquake. The record of Pope & Talbot — cutting and planting — has been graphically related in their centennial volume, *Time, Tide and Timber,* by Edwin T. Coman, Jr., and Helen M. Gibbs; but as I have said, an operation like this was the exception.

Prior to 1920, the practice was to cut all that was worth cutting, dump your sawdust into the nearest stream, and then move the sawmill to the next likeliest spot. In Nova Scotia I paddled down trout streams which once held good trout, and might still were it not for the immovable, poisonous beds of sawdust dumped there fifty years ago. Too often the slash was left scattered on the ground, an unregarded fire hazard. (By-products from this wood waste were unthought of then.)

Fires on such cutover land were to be expected, and when they came were regarded as acts of God, not of man. But the scars are there to remind us, the black spindly skeletons and the brown scorched earth on which no new growth can be expected for years. It is disagreeable to remember that in ten days of October 1947, in a period of great drought, Maine lost 210,000 acres of good forest land to fire at a cost of sixteen lives and 32 millions of dollars. Fire fighters were flown on from Washington and Oregon as there were not enough trained men available in the Northeast; destroyers were sent north to generate power for the burned-out villages. New England forest industries have increased their vigilance since then. They'd better.

The country has been slow to acknowledge what it owes to the early silviculturists, like Edward Olmstead, Charles Sargent and Gifford Pinchot. The first professional forester was not graduated from an American college until 1900. Today there are over 12,500 of them, but they had to have time and experience before they could break down the grandfather heritage ("What my grandfather did was good enough for me!") and really apply the brakes. Only when our virgin timber was depleted, only when the value of all forest products began to rise, did Americans realize that the *growing* of trees could be a profitable and continuous business.

We are not yet able to achieve the balance between the volume taken by cutting and fire, and the new growth. The imbalance was at its worst about 1909, and it has been aggravated by our desperate need for wood in both wars: in 1944, for instance, we consumed 53 billion board feet with a new growth of approximately 35 billion. There have been years since when the discrepancy has been as bad as that. Misguided cutting has been only partially controlled by standardization of size and length within the industry. Weyerhaeuser and Marathon have taken the lead in converting wood waste and sawdust into products molded and bound under heat and pressure. For the future we must depend on the new growths, and if we protect forests from fire, insects, and disease, if we utilize wood efficiently, and if we harvest timberlands wisely, we may in time come close to balancing the economy of lumbering. A big "if."

The old order passes. Legend has it that the Machias River in Maine was the first on which logs were driven, and there is a tombstone on its bank in memory of a lumberman who was crushed and drowned in the drive of 1790. Today the Machias is the last stream in the United States on which the long logs are still driven with the old-time skill and risk. Close to 8 million feet of long logs come down it a year, and the same may be true for another decade. Then the cycle will be complete.

At this moment of transition, when the trees close to home have become more precious, it is important to increase our control of fire and pest. See what fire has done to the magnificent slopes of upland Maine. Keep an eye out for those beauties of the woods, the white birches (there are two particularly magnificent stands, one in Gorham, New Hampshire, the other at Manchester, Vermont); the birch dieback has been killing these trees from the top throughout New England. Notice the rust in the white pine and the damage of the spruce bud worm, unquestionably the most destructive insect in the Northeast, if not the entire country. Remember the blight that swept away every vestige of the chestnut. (Can anyone tell me of chestnuts that have taken hold again in New England?) Bear in mind that over 3 million elms have been destroyed by the Dutch elm disease. New Haven is, perhaps, the worst sufferer from this invasion, with a loss of more than three thousand trees, most of them the great patriots of the past. Read what the oak wilt is doing in Indiana, Kentucky, and Wisconsin. Only one state, and that Pennsylvania, which was lightly hit, has made a complete extermination of this oak wilt.

Ruthless cutting, fire, and disease — these are the public enemies of our trees. To offset them there are two hopes: the increasing vigilance of Americans devoted to conservation, and the ever-spreading knowledge of tree farming. Tree farming as a popular movement began in the state of Washington ten years ago in the little town of Montesano, a community that has lived on and in the forests for ninety years. People who are going into the business of growing trees need time; they need protection from fire; they need graduated taxes on their wood lots so that the seedlings will not be taxed as heavily as the growing trees twenty years later. They need mechanical planters such as are now capable of planting a thousand seedlings in an hour. Four years ago there were twenty-five such machines in operation. Today there are several thousand.

Tree farming is now being developed in thirty states; a tree farm may be a 10-acre section on a New Hampshire farm, or it may be the 500,000-acre holding of Weyerhaeuser. Every one of us stands to gain from the increase in these farms. If our descendants are to have access to any green oases in the future, woods to picnic in such as I knew in my boyhood, this is how they will come.

Taste and Time

LABOR leaders have been talking about a four-and-a-half day week, and this leads me to wonder what people will do with the other two and a half days and so to speculate about American life and taste in the mid-1960s, when we may have this much leisure, if indeed our standard of living continues to rise. I begin by assuming that we shall avoid a major war in the foreseeable future, that our birth rate will continue high, and that old people will live longer. The countryside will continue to fill in at such an alarming speed that a federal authority will be needed to curb the destructiveness of the hit-and-run contractors. During the four-hundred-mile flight from Boston to Washington, the city, as Bill Zeckendorf says "is always below us; only the name changes." This inundation of fluid suburbia — extending from Bangor to the Virginia Capes — will spread at a time when the work week is being shortened; as a consequence we shall be rather more sensitive to claustrophobia in these new communities, and because Americans are at heart a mobile people, we will react against this pressure by traveling even more energetically than we do today. Meanwhile, at home, service will be limited to high school girls for sitters, nurses so high-priced we can only afford them for birth and death, and grandmothers to do the extra fixings at Christmas.

It has been axiomatic in our expansion thus far that today's luxury is tomorrow's necessity. This has been made plausible by our invention which keeps reducing the price for the larger market. Assuming that invention does not fail us and that calamity does not fall, I foresee this standard equipment for the average middle-class family in the 1960s. There will be an air-conditioned house, a swimming pool if the children or grandchildren want it, and an icebox with compartments for frozen foods and game and another for tray dinners, such as we are served on the plane, for unexpected guests. Barbecue or home-cooked meals on holidays. Every family that wants it will have television: two out of five, color TV; one in ten, pay TV. The housing units will be smaller and more maneuverable, many will be supplemented with a guest cabin with bunks for the married children home on reunion. Book shelf space will be at a premium; only the odd collector, the crank, will think of buying an entire set of an author; contemporary novels and paperbacks will be discarded as strenuously as cracked records and the Sunday papers. In many a garage there will be two cars; one, the economy car, perhaps foreign-make, for commuting service; the other, an adventurous station wagon sleeping two adults with adjustable side walls forming a screened compartment for the kids. So a family will live for a time in the Yosemite, under the giant redwoods, in the Smokies, in Alaska, or in the Great Beach National Park on Cape Cod. The local garage will still keep a couple of antediluvian Cadillacs for funerals or parades.

"What the American economy needs," said Sumner Slichter recently, "is a more sophisticated consumer." It is my conviction that we shall have these sophisticated consumers in increasing number in the '60s; that their purchasing power will be highly selective and that their taste will radically affect our advertising. The pro-labor legislation of the New Deal enormously augmented the purchasing power of labor; then the subsidies to agriculture gave the farmer his turn; but the technically trained, the scientist, the research worker, the teacher, and the young professional were all left far behind. Today we are paying for that neglect; we are faced with a shortage of scientists, a shortage of good teachers, and a watering down of our whole public educational system as the Conant Report has shown. Because of this deficit and because we need them so desperately, the people who *will* receive the financial bonus in the coming fifteen years will be what Conant calls "the academically gifted," the 15 per cent of every graduating class; no longer a negligible minority, they will be a determinant and yeasty element in our society and their taste will make a profound difference. These college and professionally trained people who are my bread and butter today will be ten times as numerous, ten times as influential in the 1960s.

I have noticed that the higher the educational level, the more suspicious people are of excessive statements. No Harvard man ever uses a superlative. Well, hardly ever! Higher education carries with it an independence of thinking, a sharpening of the senses and a positive disgust with the banal. Those who cater to the mass markets have ignored this factor of skepticism and disgust. When I see in a periodical a full-page display of Yummy Cake Mix, blown up into a sticky cake, in living color and twice life size, and when this is followed by a full-page display of Colonel Belcher's Tomato Sauce without which one cannot eat Colonel Belcher's Sausages, in living color and twice life size, and when this is followed by a four-color beefsteak twice as handsome as what they serve at "21," I have not only lost my appetite, I have lost my belief.

The Changing Country

Is American taste really as gullible as this? Consider for a moment the intimate probings of the cosmetics and patent medicine experts. Every night on TV we see women soaping, greasing, polishing and sandpapering themselves, hiding their false teeth in wonderful germ-killing solutions, putting their dandruff to rout, and fondling their toenails. There is one woman who gets all lathered up and then steps under the shower. What next?

I notice one strange circumstance about all these proprietary substances: each contains a unique, mysterious, absolutely new *"scientific"* ingredient that none of the competing companies has sense enough to imitate. It goes like this: "Blank is the only blank-blank to contain Blank!" It's true of everything from a scouring powder to a cough sirup. These ingredients (which are not to be found in the dictionary) are part of a synthetic new vocabulary for TV audiences, and those actors who talk like doctors never have any trouble pronouncing such chemical absurdities.

It would be my guess that the amount of advertising we are all exposed to today is at least double what it was ten years ago and probably five times what it was in the 1930s. This has built up a kind of immunity: people look but they do not see; they hear but they do not listen. They have learned to turn off their mental hearing aids and this definitely complicates the task of those who are trying to reach them.

An editor, like an advertising man, is always in search of new stimuli. With the antennae of his own senses he has to establish an identification, a kind of sensory intercom with his readers, and if he is an acute editor, he will expect that when a manuscript excites him it will have much the same effect on his readers. He is not infallible, but this intercom — what

I have called his antennae — works both ways, and he learns to recognize very quickly what his people reject as well as what they accept.

The readers I serve have a loathing for ghost writers and those windy, vacuous generalizations which ghost writers propound for people who can't express themselves. Since so many American speeches today are ghost-written, my people have become very leery of speeches in print — and I know it. *Atlantic* readers are nonconformist; they expect the magazine to be nonpartisan and they would walk out on me in a body if I tried to confine the magazine to one point of view. They wish to be surprised, and they look for the unpredictable.

My readers are highly conscientious about education, about race relations, most of all about the threat of nuclear weapons. A young graduate of the Harvard Medical School doing his UMT was sent out to the island of Bikini, to help protect the army-navy personnel from radiation. He did his work with a Geiger counter, but during the tropical nights when he could not sleep he filled an old college notebook with his impressions of what that bomb test really portended. When we published those pages under the title "No Place to Hide," we knew that Dr. David Bradley was talking to our people about nuclear warfare as they had never been talked to before.

Our readers are eager for American history, and I suspect that they find courage in reading about those earlier Americans who stood up to crucial decisions. Catherine Drinker Bowen performed a great service for this country when she brought readers into close touch with that "Yankee from Olympus," Mr. Justice Oliver Wendell Holmes, and later when she performed the same function for the crusty, rugged, right-minded young John Adams. We drew on both of those books for the *Atlantic*. Biography is read today with avidity and it can be serialized with less internal damage than a novel: *The Years With Ross,* which my associate, Charles W. Morton, induced James Thurber to write for us, was our most popular feature since the war.

My readers have small appetite for the inbred, introverted short stories published with such dreary monotony by some of my more stylish competitors. As a change of pace I induced Peter Ustinov, who had never written a short story in his life, to embark on an exclusive series for the *Atlantic*. Peter is one of the most entrancing and original performers on TV. I felt he would be just as original, just as refreshing in his fiction — and so he is. My people like what is poetic and genuine, and they dislike what is synthetic and tired.

"Things are in the saddle and ride mankind." So wrote Emerson to William H. Channing in 1847. How will they ride us ten years from now, in 1969? Let me try a projection here. By 1980 it is estimated that the population of Red China will be 1 billion; of Soviet Russia, 340 million; of the United States, 270 million. Long before that date we shall be caught up in an economic rivalry with what we are pleased to call "slave labor," forgetting that slaves — with or without fervor — can outperform feather-bedded machines.

History always runs ahead of schedule. When I was a boy the Prudential Life Insurance Company used a traditional advertisement; it centered a photograph of Gibraltar, with the words "As Safe as the Rock of Gibraltar." Although the picture was of the rock, the implication was that your investment was as safe as the British Empire. When I attended the World's Fair in Brussels in 1958, I asked my friends how long they thought Belgium could hold on to the Congo. "Five years surely, perhaps ten," was the answer. But the riots of 1959 in Brazzaville show that history is running ahead of schedule. In his shocking novel *1984* George Orwell told of how the state would take young children away from their mothers the way we take eggs away from a hen. That is precisely what the Chinese communes are doing in 1959.

In the *New York Times* for January 28, 1959 there was an article about Soviet scientific equipment to be used in the teaching of physics in the United States. A firm in Cambridge, Massachusetts, has imported six thousand pieces of this apparatus from the Soviet Union which it expects to sell to our colleges at prices one-half to two-thirds less than the comparable items made in the United States, and this in spite of a 40 per cent import duty. This was a case where the Soviet economy, by its decision to place this educational equipment in mass consumption, has startled our complacency.

A news film has given us a brief glimpse of the new diamond field coming into production in Russia, and it is ironic to speculate on what would happen if the Russians chose to flood the market with diamonds only a little more expensive than rhinestones. Think what a blow this would be to the mobster members of the Apalachin Club!

Seriously, I do not think we can assume that our economy will be unaffected by the economic competition with the Soviets. Stalin predicted and lived with the hope that the United States would suffer a disastrous collapse as we emerged from the Second World War. But by his repeated, belligerent pressure upon us he made it unlikely that any such thing would occur: the aid to Greece and Turkey, the Berlin lift, the aggression in Korea kept our heavy industries fully employed producing armament. Khrushchev could be more subtle: he could keep the heat on while tempting us with talk of disarmament and at the same time making strenuous efforts to undersell us in the world markets. We will never cut back our expenditure for weapons until the Russians have agreed to a trustworthy system of inspection. But if that day comes, it will be a happy time for their economy and ours. It would mean for us that national taxes could be cut, releasing for local use — for schools, hospitals and recreation — money which today simply is not available.

I have no doubt that by the mid-1960s the production of steel and steaks and cars, of milk and cosmetics and alcohol will have grown to meet the demands of our expanding population. But in view of the need for the minerals and oil beyond our borders, I foresee that we shall have to struggle to retain our share of the world trade in the developing nations of Asia and Africa, and of our friends in Europe; we shall have to forego the present arbitrary, costly, often futile contests between labor and management, and work with a strenuousness which we once knew but have forgotten in the process of growing fat. We shall be faced with a standard of competition as opposed to a standard of living quite different from what it is today. If this coming test results in a new austerity, or as we may prefer to call it a new "simplicity," this could be a healthy thing.

Taste is just as strongly evinced by the things people do as it is by the things they possess. Perhaps it is my long exposure to the New England climate and the New England character which makes me feel that the return to a more austere life, to a life which demands certain sacrifices for the public good, would be far healthier than the present mood of quick money and selfish indulgence. I have spoken of the inundation of our suburban areas and of the claustrophobia which comes from the ever-present pressure of neighbors. But there is another side to this and a good side. In these quick-forming communities there is a blinding and cohesive strength which comes to us all when we do things voluntarily with others. Parent-teacher associations; community theatricals; the support of a local half-amateur symphony orchestra; the singing of Negro and white choruses in a community center; the work which goes into the preservation of historical America, whether it be Sturbridge, Massachusetts, or Shelburne, Vermont, or Beacon Hill; the groups which meet to discuss the Great Books; the groups intent on foreign affairs; the parents, the doctors, and the judges who have been aroused by the alarming increase in criminality; the parents whose children have become emotionally disturbed; the missionaries who meet under the slogan "Alcoholics Anonymous"; the citizen's committees which are working to reduce racial tension; the bird watchers, the photographers, and those who are struggling to preserve our shade trees and our community gardens — surely these people in their responsible vigilant concerns are just as much the taste-makers of America as those who own the finest collections of the French impressionists. We used to think that poverty was responsible for our juvenile delinquency, but we now find to our amazement that during the past decade of our prosperity the crime wave, especially among the adolescents and twenty-year-olders, has broken all records. The American conscience is rising to meet this domestic emergency.

Taste is evinced by the things we do. And do I dare suggest that in the years to come the more responsible advertisers will try to reach and influence the more responsible Americans? Yes, I do. After years of puzzling out the meaning of Walter

Paepke's advertisements for Container Corporation I really think that something like this, but more compelling, might be possible. Those who served on the Advertising Council during the war years will never forget the thrill that came to them when they discovered that they were, gradually and visibly, persuading the American people to accept meatless days and war rationing. To guide people's thinking in the right direction is not only good taste, it is good leadership.

Back in 1910 there were 7 million common laborers in this country; in October 1958 they had dropped to 5 million, whereas the number of professional workers has risen from 1 3/4 million in 1910 to 7 million in 1958. In the years ahead the increase in these professionally trained Americans — the increase in their college children and the increase in their purchasing power — will be astronomical. It had better be, for they are our best hope.

In the tense and dangerous competition that lies ahead, let us never forget that what really stimulates the American economy are decent, educated people. This is something we are always in danger of forgetting.

How Big Is One

MY LATE friend, the French writer Raoul de Roussy de Sales, who knew America intimately, used to tease me about our infatuation with bigness. "It's in your blood," he would say. "When I listen to Americans talking on shipboard, or in a Paris restaurant, or here in New York, it is only a question of time before someone will come out with that favorite boast of yours — *'the biggest in the world!'* The New York skyline, or the Washington Monument, or the Chicago Merchandise Mart — the biggest in the world. You say it without thinking what it means." How right he was, yet until he prodded me about it, I had never realized that this was indeed our national boast. We take pride in being big, and in a youthful way we used to think that bigness was our own special prerogative. But now we know better; now we find ourselves confronted with nations or with groups of nations which are quite as big as we are and which have the potential of being considerably bigger. This calls for a new orientation; indeed, I think it might be timely if we examine this concept of bigness and try to determine how it has affected our private lives and our thinking.

We have been in love with bigness ever since the adolescence of our democracy. The courtship began on the frontier: the uncut virgin forests, so dense and terrifying; the untamed flooding rivers; the limitless prairies; the almost impassable Sierras —

[267]

to overcome obstacles like these, man, so puny in comparison, had to outdo himself. He had to be bigger than Hercules. The English live on a small, contained island, and English humor is naturally based on understatement; but an American when he is having fun always exaggerates.

Our first hero of the frontier was a superman, Davy Crockett, who could outshoot, outfight, and outwoo anyone. One day he sauntered into the forest for an airing but forgot to take his thunderbolt along. This made it embarrassing when he came face to face with a panther. The scene is described in the old almanac, as Howard Mumford Jones says, "in metaphoric language which has all the freshness of dawn." The panther growled and Crockett growled right back — "He grated thunder with his teeth" — and so the battle began. In the end, the panther, tamed, goes home with Davy, lights the fire on a dark night with flashes from his eyes, brushes the hearth every morning with his tail, and rakes the garden with his claws. Davy did the impossible, and listening to the legends of his prowess made it easier for the little guy on the frontier to do the possible.

Davy Crockett had a blood brother in Mike Fink, the giant of the river boatmen, and first cousins in Tony Beaver and Paul Bunyan of the North Woods and Pecos Bill of the Southwest. They were ringtailed roarers, and everything they did had an air of gigantic plausibility. Prunes are a necessary part of the lumberjack's diet, and Paul Bunyan's camp had such a zest for prunes that the prune trains which hauled the fruit came in with two engines, one before and one behind pushing. "Paul used to have twenty flunkies sweepin' the prunestones out from under the tables, but even then they'd get so thick we had to wade through 'em up over our shoes sometimes on our way in to dinner. They'd be all over the floor and in behind the stove

and piled up against the windows where they'd dumped 'em outside so the cook couldn't see out at all hardly. . . . In Paul's
camp back there in Wisconsin the prunestones used to get so
thick they had to have twenty ox-teams haulin' 'em away, and
they hauled 'em out in the woods, and the chipmunks ate 'em
and grew so big the people shot 'em for tigers." Only an American could have invented that buildup, and I am grateful to Esther Shephard for having recaptured the legend so accurately
in her *Paul Bunyan*.

Texas, with its fondness for bigness, preferred the living man
to the legend: it provided the space for men like Richard King,
the founder of the King Ranch. Richard King's story as told by
Tom Lea is Horatio Alger multiplied by a thousand. The son
of Irish immigrants, he ran off to sea at the age of eleven; a
riverboat captain in his twenties, he came ashore, married the
parson's daughter, bought 15,000 acres of prairie at two cents an
acre, and went into the cattle business. His close friend and adviser was Lieutenant Colonel Robert E. Lee of the Second
United States Cavalry, and it was Lee who gave King what has
come to be the family slogan: "Buy land; and never sell." The
King Ranch has grown to 700,000 acres in Texas with big off-
shoots in Kentucky, Pennsylvania, Australia, Cuba, and Brazil,
and those of us who dwell in cities and suburbia have developed
a kind of Mount Vernon reverence for this vast domain. It is
just about as big, we think, as a good ranch ought to be.

As I look back over the thirty-five years of my working life,
I recognize that a significant change has taken place in our business community. The motorcars which I used to covet as a young
bachelor, the Stutz Bearcat, the Mercer, the Simplex, the Loco-
mobile, the Pierce Arrow — all these beauties and hundreds of

the lesser breeds, like the Hupmobile, the Maxwell, the Franklin, the Stanley Steamer, and the Moon — are museum pieces today. The beauty and the originality which went into their design have been melted down and vulgarized in the models of the five major companies which survive.

In the days I am speaking of, Mr. Potts was our family grocer, and he knew the exact cuts of roast beef and lamb which would bring joy to my father's heart, just as he was prepared for my mother's remonstrance when there was too much gristle. There used to be a family grocer, like Mr. Potts, in every American community. Then some genius in Memphis, Tennessee, came up with the Piggly-Wiggly, the first gigantic cash and carry where the customer waited on himself, and in no time there were chains of these supermarkets stretching across the country. Such consolidation as this has been going on in every aspect of business, and at a faster and faster tempo.

When I was a book salesman, an American book publisher who sold a million dollars' worth of his books in one year was doing quite a prosperous business. Today a publisher who sells only a million dollars' worth of books a year cannot afford to remain in business; he has to join forces with another and larger publisher so that their combined production will carry them over the break-even point.

In the 1920s almost every American city had two newspapers, and the larger ones had four or five, and there is no doubt that this competition for ideas, for stories, for the truth was a healthy thing for the community. Today most American communities are being served by a single paper.

Of the daily papers that were being published in this country in 1929, 45 per cent have either perished or been consolidated. This consolidation, this process of making big ones out of little ones, is a remorseless thing and it may be a harmful thing if it tends to regiment our thinking.

We Americans have a remarkable capacity for ambivalence. On the one hand we like to enjoy the benefits of mass production, and on the other we like to assert our individual taste. Ever since the Civil War we have been exercising our genius to build larger and larger combines. Experience has taught us that when these consolidations grow to the size of a giant octopus, we have got to find someone to regulate them. When our railroads achieved almost insufferable power, we devised the Interstate Commerce Commission, and we eventually found in Joseph Eastman a regulator of impeccable integrity who knew as much as any railroad president. We have not had such good luck with our other regulatory agencies, as the recent ignoble record of the FCC makes clear. What troubles me even more than the pliancy of FCC commissioners to political pressure is their willingness to favor the pyramiding under a single ownership of television channels, radio stations, morning and evening newspapers. Isn't this the very monopoly they were supposed to prevent?

The empire builders, who were well on their way to a plutocracy, were brought within bounds by the first Roosevelt. Then under the second Roosevelt it was labor's turn, and in their bid for power they have confronted Washington with the challenge of *what regulations* can be devised which will bring them to a clearer recognition of their national responsibility. In the not far future we can see another huge decision looming up: When atomic energy is harnessed for industrial use, will it be in the hands of a few private corporations or in a consolidation which the government will control? My point is that in the daily exposure to such bigness the individual is made to feel smaller than he used to be, smaller and more helpless than his father and grandfather before him.

I realize, of course, that twice in this century our capacity to arm on an enormous scale has carried us to victory with a speed which neither the Kaiser nor Hitler believed possible. But it is my anxiety that, in a cold war which may last for decades, the maintenance of bigness which is necessary to cope with the U.S.S.R. may regiment the American spirit.

In his book *Reflections on America,* Jacques Maritain, the French philosopher, draws a sharp distinction "between the spirit of the American people and the logic of the superimposed structure of ritual of civilization." He speaks of "the state of tension, of hidden conflict, between this spirit of the people and this logic of the structure; the steady, latent rebellion of the spirit of the people against the logic of the structure." Maritain believes that the spirit of the American people is gradually over-coming and breaking the logic of their materialistic civilization. I should like to share his optimism, but first we have some questions to answer, questions about what the pressure of bigness is doing to American integrity and to American taste.

Henry Wallace called this the Century of the Common Man. Well, the longer I live in it the more I wonder whether we are producing the Uncommon Man in sufficient quantity. No such doubts were entertained a century ago. When Ralph Waldo Emerson delivered his famous address on "The American Scholar" to the Phi Beta Kappa Society of Harvard in 1837, he was in a mood of exhilaration, not doubt, and he heralded among other things a change which had taken place in American literature. It was a change in the choice of subject matter;

it was a change in approach, and it showed that we had thrown off the leading strings of Europe. Here is how he described it:

The elevation of what was called the lowest class in the state assumed in literature a very marked and as benign an aspect. Instead of the sublime and beautiful, the near, the low, the common, was explored and poetized. . . . The literature of the poor, the feelings of the child, the philosophy of the street, the meaning of household life, are the topics of the time. It is a great stride. It is a sign — is it not? — of new vigor when the extremities are made active, when currents of warm life run into the hands and the feet. . . .

This writing is blood-warm. Man is surprised to find that things near are not less beautiful and wondrous than things remote. The near explains the far. The drop is a small ocean. A man is related to all nature. This perception of the worth of the vulgar is fruitful in discoveries.

This change from the appreciation of the elite to the appreciation of the commonplace, or as Emerson called it, the vulgar, has been increasingly magnified under the pressure of numbers. But were Emerson able to return to us for a short visit, I am not sure that he would be altogether happy about what we have done to elevate the vulgar in literature or in television.

In contemporary literature, new books — the best we can produce — are still published in hard covers and sold to a discriminating body of readers. If I had to guess, I should say that there are about one million discriminating readers in this country today, and what disturbs me as an editor is that this number has not increased with the population; it has not increased appreciably since the year 1920. What has increased is the public for comic books, for murder mysteries, for sex and sadism. This debasement, especially in fiction, was most noticeable in the early stages of our paperbacks, when the racks in any drug-store were crowded with lurid, large-bosomed beauties who were being either tortured or pursued. Recently there has been an improvement, both in quantity and in seriousness, thanks to the editors of Anchor Books and the New American Library, thanks also to a feeling of outrage which was expressed in many communities. But it still seems to me regrettable that after a hundred years of public education we have produced such a demand for the lowest common denominator of emotionalism.

Am I, I sometimes wonder, a minority of one when I shudder at certain photographs in our pictorial magazines — the picture of a Negro being lynched; the picture of an airliner which has crashed and burned, with that naked body to the left identified as an opera singer whose voice we have all heard and loved; the picture of a grieving mother whose child has just been crushed in an automobile accident? Am I a minority of one in thinking that these are invasions of privacy, indecent and so shocking that we cringe from the sight?

Television, for which we once had such high hope, is constantly betrayed by the same temptation. It can rise magnificently to the occasion, as when it brought home to us the tragedy in Hungary, yet time and again its sponsored programs sink to a sodden level of brutality, shooting, and torture. And is there any other country in the world which would suffer through such incredible singing commercials as are flung at us? Does the language always have to be butchered for popular appeal? Am I a minority of one in thinking that the giveaway programs, by capitalizing on ignorance, poverty, and grief, are a disgrace? These are deliberate efforts to reduce a valuable medium to the level of the bobby-soxers.

There was a time when the American automobiles led the

world in their beauty, diversity, and power, but the gaudy gondolas of today are an insult to the intelligence. In an era of close crowding when parking is an insoluble problem, it was sheer arrogance on the part of the Detroit designers to produce a car which was longer than the normal garage, so wasteful of gasoline, so laden with useless chromium and fantails that it costs a small fortune to have a rear fender repaired. I saw in a little Volkswagen not long ago a sign in the windshield reading "HELP STAMP OUT CADILLACS!" There speaks the good-natured but stubborn resistance of the American spirit against the arrogance of Detroit.

Is it inevitable in mass production that when you cater to the many, something has to give, and what gives is quality? I wonder if this has to be. I wonder if the great majority of the American people do not have more taste than they are credited with. The phenomenal increase in the sale of classical music recordings the moment they became available at mass production prices tells me that Americans will support higher standards when they are given the chance. I stress the aberration of taste in our time because I think it is something that does not have to be. The republic deserves better standards, not only for the elect, but straight across the board.

I wish that our directors in Hollywood, the heads of our great networks, and those who, like the automobile designers in Detroit, are dependent upon American taste — I wish that such arbiters would remember what Alexis de Tocqueville wrote a hundred and twenty-five years ago in his great book, *Democracy in America*. "When the conditions of society are becoming more equal," said Tocqueville, "and each individual man becomes more like all the rest, more weak and more insignificant, a habit grows up of ceasing to notice the citizens to consider only the people, and of overlooking individuals to think only of their kind."

It seems to me that our taste-makers have been guilty of this fallacy ever since the close of World War II. They have ceased to notice the citizens and consider only the people, just as Tocqueville warned. They no longer plan for the differences in individual taste, but think only of people in the mass.

In the years that followed the crash of 1929, Americans began to transfer their trust from big business to big government; if big business and banking, so ran the reasoning, could not be depended on to keep us out of depressions, perhaps big government could. Gradually in this emergency we began to shape up our version of the welfare state, a concept which was evolving in many parts of the Western world and to which both Democrats and Republicans are now committed.

A welfare state requires a big government with many bureaus, just as big government in its turn requires big taxes. We embarked on big government with the idea of safeguarding those segments of American society which were most in jeopardy, and now after twenty-five years of experimentation we are beginning to learn that the effects of big government upon the individual are both good and bad. It is good to provide the individual with security, and to give him the chance to adjust his special claims; another and perhaps unsuspected asset has been dramatized by Edwin O'Connor in his novel *The Last Hurrah,* in which he showed us how President Roosevelt had diminished and destroyed the sovereignty of the city boss. It is Washington, not Ward 8, that has the big patronage to give today.

The maleffects of big government are more subtle. Consider, for instance, the debilitating effect of heavy taxation. I remember a revealing talk I had with Samuel Zemurray when he was president of the United Fruit Company. Born in Russia, Zemurray made his start here by pushing a fruit cart through the streets of Gadsden, Alabama. Then he set up his own business as a banana jobber by selling the bunches of bananas the fruit company didn't want. He sold out to United Fruit and continued to acquire shares until he controlled the majority of the stock. In the autumn of F.D.R.'s second term, when we were sitting in adjoining Pullman seats on the long run to Washington, Mr. Zemurray began talking about the President's promises to "the forgotten man." "He made three promises," Zemurray said, "and he has kept two of them: the promise to labor and that to the farmer. The promise he has not kept is to the little businessman. Under today's taxes it would be quite impossible for a young man to do as I did — he would never be able to accumulate enough capital."

Some years after this talk, in 1946 to be exact, I was on a plane flying West from Chicago. It was a Sunday morning and the man who sat beside me at the window seat had the big bulk of the *Chicago Tribune* spread open on his knees, but out of politeness's sake he gave me the proverbial greeting, "Well, where are you from?" And when I said, "From Boston," his face lit up. "Do they still have good food at the Automat?" he asked. "Boy, that's where I got my start and it certainly seems a lifetime ago." And then in a rush out poured his life story in one of those sudden confidences with which Americans turn to one another: how he had become a salesman of bedroom crockery, and how his Boston boss had refused to raise him to thirty dollars a week. In his anger he had switched to the rival company, and under their encouragement he had simply plastered Cape Cod with white washbowls, pitchers, soap dishes, and tooth mugs. "Seven carloads I sold in the first year," he told me. The company called him back to its head office in Chicago, and then came the crash. The company owned a bank and lake-shore real estate, and when the smoke had cleared away and recovery was possible, he found himself running the whole shebang. His wife hadn't been able to keep up with it all, he said, shaking his head sadly. He had had his first coronary, and what kept him alive today was his hope for his two sons, who had just come out of the Navy. "But, you know," he said to me, his eyes widening, "they neither of them want to come in with me. They don't seem to want to take the chances that I took. They want to tie up with a big corporation. I just don't get it."

Security for the greatest number is a modern shibboleth, but somebody still has to set the pace and take the risk. And if we gain security, but sacrifice first venture and then initiative, we may find, as the Labor Party in England did, that we end with all too little incentive. As I travel this country since the war, I have the repeated impression that fewer and fewer young men are venturing into business on their own. More and more of them seek the safety of the big corporations. There are compelling reasons for this, the ever-shrinking margin of operating profit being the most insistent. But if we keep on trading independence and initiative for security, I wonder what kind of American enterprise will be left fifty years from now.

A subtle conditioning of the voter has been taking place during the steady buildup of big government. During the depression and recovery we took our directives from Washington almost without question; so too during the war, when we were dedicated to a single purpose and when the leadership in Washington in every department was the best the nation could supply. And for almost twenty years local authority and the ability to test our political initiative in the home county and state has dwindled. About the only common rally which is left to us is the annual drive for the Community Fund. Too few of our ablest young men will stand for local office. Their jobs come first, and they console themselves with the thought that if they succeed they may be called to Washington in maturity. We used to have a spontaneous capacity for rallying; we could be inflamed, and our boiling point was low. Our present state of lethargy, our tendency to let George do it in Washington, is not only regrettable, it is bad for our system.

I remember one of the last talks I had with Wendell Willkie. He was still showing the exhaustion of defeat, and he spoke with concern as he said, "One of the weaknesses in our democracy is our tendency to delegate. During an election year we will work our hearts out, and then when the returns are in, we think we have done our part. For the next three years what happens to the party is the responsibility of the national committeemen. Have you ever *looked* at them?"

The decision having been made to drop the atomic bomb on Hiroshima, President Truman tells us that he retired and slept soundly. But those in authority in these days are less sure. The delegation of so much authority to those in Washington and the difficulties of dealing with an opponent so ruthless and enigmatic as Russia seem to have developed in our most responsible officials a secretiveness and an uncertainty which make it hard for the citizen to follow. The administration has practiced a policy of nondisclosure toward the press and the electorate which has left the average citizen in a state of constant doubt. It was inexcusable not to have warned the American people that the sputniks were coming and that greater exertions must be expected of us. This is no time for remoteness or for lulling slogans or for the avoidance of hard truths. The volume of material, the thousands of articles dealing with the great issues of today which are pouring into my office from unknown, unestablished writers, testify to the conscientiousness and the courage of American thinking. The pity of it is that our people have not been taken more fully into the confidence of their own government.

I have said that the concept of bigness has been an American ideal since our earliest times. I pointed to our propensity to build larger and larger combines ever since the Civil War, and how the process of consolidation has speeded up during the past thirty-five years. I have suggested that we cannot enjoy the fruits of mass production without suffering the effects of regimentation.

And I ask that we look closely at what the pressure of bigness has done to American taste and opinion. Is the individual beginning to lose self-confidence and his independence? In short, how big is one?

Surely, in an atomic age self-reliance and self-restraint are needed as they have never been before. See with what force Van Wyck Brooks expresses this truth in his *Writer's Notebook:*

Unless humanity is intrinsically decent, heaven help the world indeed, for more and more we are going to see man naked. There is no stopping the world's tendency to throw off imposed restraints, the *religious* authority that is based on the ignorance of the many, the *political* authority that is based on the knowledge of the few. The time is coming when there will be nothing to restrain men except what they find in their own bosoms; and what hope is there for us then unless it is true that, freed from fear, men are naturally predisposed to be upright and just?

How Big Is One

As we look about us, what evidence can we find that in an atmosphere overshadowed by Russia and made murky by the distrust of McCarthyism there are citizens who still stand forth, upright and ready to speak the hard truth for the public good? How big is one?

One is as big as George F. Kennan, who believes that we cannot continue to live in this state of frozen belligerency in Europe. We do not have to accept all of his proposals before applauding his thoughtful, audacious effort to break up the ice.

One is as big as Omer Carmichael, the superintendent of schools in Louisville, Kentucky, who led the movement for voluntary integration in his border state; as big as Harry Ashmore, the editor of the Little Rock *Gazette,* for his fearless and reasonable coverage of the Faubus scandal.

One is as big as Frank Laubach, who believes in teaching the underdeveloped nations how to read their own languages, and then in supplying them with reading matter which will aid them to develop their farming and health.

One is as big as Linus Pauling, Harold C. Urey, Robert Oppenheimer, and the other editors and sponsors of the *Bulletin of the Atomic Scientists,* who have never underestimated Russian scientific capacities, who have always believed in the peaceful value of scientific exchange and never ceased to struggle against fanaticism in secrecy and security.

One is as big as Edith Hamilton, the classicist, the lover of Greece and of moderation; and as Alice Hamilton, her younger sister, who pioneered in the dangerous field of industrial medicine.

One is as big as Sheldon and Eleanor Glueck, who for years have been guiding lights in the resistant field of juvenile delinquency.

One is as big as Ralph Bunche and Eleanor Roosevelt.

One is as big as Louis M. Lyons, whose interpretation of the news and whose judgment of the popular press have provided, in the words of the Lauterbach Award, "a conscience for a whole profession."

One is as big as I. I. Rabi, a brilliant scientist and a passionate humanist, who, on being asked how long it would take us to catch up to Russia and to safeguard our long-range future, replied: "A generation. You know how long it takes to change a cultural pattern. The growing general awareness of this need will help us, but nevertheless we will have to work hard to succeed in a generation."

One is as big as Frederick May Eliot, president for twenty-one years of the American Unitarian Association, who worked himself to the bone for the deepening of faith and for reconciliation.

One is as big as you yourself can make it.

Why We Do It

WHEN I became the ninth editor of the *Atlantic* in June of 1938, a dinner was given in my honor at the St. Botolph Club in Boston. Present were a number of our distinguished New England contributors, including Robert Frost (who was later to read aloud a new poem provided I'd accept it "sight unseen"), such dear rivals as Fred Allen of *Harper's*, and my two immediate predecessors, Bliss Perry and Ellery Sedgwick. As I entered the cocktail reception, I heard Bliss Perry remark: "Here comes the next victim," and I remember his saying to me during the dinner — he sat on my right — "There are really only two rules of editing I can give you. The first: pay your contributors on acceptance — the money will never look bigger. The second is more personal: remember how vulnerable we all are to fatigue and indigestion; when you feel bilious, try to postpone to the next day your troublesome decisions." Well, I was forty and full of cocktails at the time and the possibility that I should ever be a weary or dyspeptic editor seemed remote. I felt that the buoyancy of that evening would last me as long as I could see to read.

Early in my editorship I learned that editors work on a weekend to weekend basis. During the week they dictate letters; they talk on the telephone, and to those pregnant with manuscripts; and they attend what are called Conferences — the surest de-

[283   ]

vice for killing time known to industry. I learned that an editor's work week really begins on Friday afternoon when with his secretary's help he stuffs his briefcase with all the things he ought to have attended to during the week. Beginning Friday night and continuing through Sunday he reads his prizes and makes his discoveries, blueprints the next issue, and dreams up his big ideas for the future in that ancient Indian posture of sitting and contemplating his navel. No editor worth his salt can live without a minimum of contemplation and privacy.

By Monday morning he is at his peak: he has caught up with his reading; he feels confident of his decisions and eager to explore the new leads which came to him while he was not listening to the sermon Sunday morning. This will be one of those rare days when he has the world in his hand, when writers and agents say "Yes" and when the telephone is like a voice from Heaven. "Get me Senator X in Washington," he says to his secretary, "and after that I want to speak to Harold Ober, the literary agent." Then he begins leafing through the morning mail.

The Quill Club of Terre Haute will appreciate it if he will serve as one of three judges of its annual short story contest. Not more than seventy manuscripts are expected, and they hope he can complete his rating by October 1. The Harvard Dames would like him to speak on a literary subject any Thursday evening in November. Unfortunately their budget is a modest one and they can offer no fee greater than their appreciation. That nice, if persistent, couple he met at Breadloaf has a daughter, fresh from Smith, who wants an editorial job. She has typing but has purposely not learned shorthand since it might tie her down. A reader in Kentucky wishes to point out that the word "thoroughbred" can only be applied to a horse with a pedigree. The *Atlantic* contributor who wrote that his heroine "had the look of a high-spirited thoroughbred" was not paying the lady the compliment he intended — and never mind what Webster says about it. "Would you like to read my series on the Orient?" asks a hand-written card. "Seven articles averaging 9000 words. Will come in for an appointment." The query is not inscribed on a regular postcard, no, it is written in the white margins of the get-acquainted, cut-price subscription reply card which we so thoughtfully insert in our newsstand copies. No postage necessary.

You will see that I have discarded my disguise, and that the editor I am talking about is myself. No Monday mail is complete without a letter from a contributor who objects to the way we have edited his copy. The one before me comes from Raymond Chandler in Hollywood. I had asked Chandler to do a piece for us on Oscar night. He did it, and it was a beauty: full of the most penetrating little daggers. The trouble was, our Boston proofreaders were not familiar with Chandler's style, and when he described the crowd in the free seats "giving out" that awful moaning sound, they simply deleted the preposition. I had also changed the title to "Oscar Night in Hollywood." Mr. Chandler, having read his galleys, is now in a slow burn:

Dear Mr. Weeks:

I'm afraid you've thrown me for a loss. I thought Juju Worship in Hollywood was a perfectly good title. But you're the boss. I've thought of various other titles such as Bank Night in Hollywood, Sutter's Last Stand, The Golden Peepshow, All it Needs is Elephants, The Hot Shot Handicap, Where Vaudeville Went When it Died, and rot like that. But nothing that smacks you in the kisser.

By the way, would you convey my compliments to the purist who reads your proofs and tell him or her that I write in a sort of broken-down patois which is something like the way a Swiss waiter talks, and that when I split an infinitive, God damn it, I split it so it will stay split, and when I interrupt the velvety smoothness of my more or less literate syntax with a few sudden words of barroom vernacular, this is done with the eyes wide open and the mind relaxed but attentive. The method may not be perfect, but it is all I have. I think your proofreader is kindly attempting to steady me on my feet, but much as I appreciate the solicitude, I am really able to steer a fairly clear course, provided I got both sidewalks and the street between.

Kindest regards,
RAY CHANDLER

(To be tossed and gored by a contributor can be a good thing; individuality is the spice of life.)

Now I've about reached the end of my Monday mail. My secretary has a way of saving the letters of abuse till the last and here they are. There is an anonymous postcard reviling us for publishing a respectful article on Russian education and calling me "The Red Brahmin of Beacon Hill." And what are these, these multigraphed letters on paper of gray burlap? They are all identical and there must be more than a hundred. Slowly the meaning becomes clear. In our Washington Report we had referred to "the organized Polish minority" which might affect the elections in Michigan. Before me is a Polish demonstration. "Dear Sir: I the undersigned wish to deny indignantly the accusation in the September *Atlantic*, page 39, that there is an organized Polish minority in the United States . . ." One hundred and thirty-nine of them by actual count.

All this time of eager assimilation the phone has been ringing, a conference with the Advertising Department has been set for 11; it is now 10:30; Senator X in Washington has not returned my call, and how many pinpricks do you need to deflate a balloon?

I sometimes wonder why we do it, and of course the truth is we couldn't be paid to do anything else. Editing is in our blood and all this attrition I have been talking about is simply the gristle in our meat. We edit because, God help us, we think it is important. If we were committed to Bedlam we would edit a handwritten sheet for our fellow inmates, and if Russia took over this country, we would edit underground. We think we were born to do this and we believe that what we are doing is in the public good.

At rare intervals we are confirmed in this belief. There are turning points in the career of every magazine and those editors who made the turn will never forget it. Sometimes you see the high point a long way ahead, as we did in Boston when for eighteen months we built up the big issues which signalized our Centennial in the autumn of 1957. That November issue, on our birthday, was our dream book; it sold out on the Eastern seaboard in 36 hours, and for the only time in our history we went back on press. We are a spontaneous people and quick to recognize a warning. In 1934 De Witt Wallace had a fateful conversation with a garageman in Armonk Village, New York. The mechanic asked him if he had any idea of the murder that was being committed on our highways every day. Wallace went home and brooded; then got in touch with J. C. Furnas who was told to spare no detail in arousing Americans to the horror of wild driving. I don't know how many times the article was rewritten; I do know that "And Sudden Death" permanently changed the character of *The Reader's Digest* and that 4 million reprints were requested in the three months after publication.

The Changing Country

Think of the audacity of Harold Ross in sending John Hersey to Hiroshima and of then devoting an entire issue of the *New Yorker* to his findings with no space reserved even for the advertisements. McCarthy was at the height of his intimidation when Max Ascoli had the courage to attack the China Lobby in two resounding articles in the *Reporter*. Think of the urgency of Norman Cousins in flying over to Lambaréné to persuade Dr. Schweitzer to speak out against the insanity of nuclear warfare. Think of the foresight of the editors of *Look*, particularly Dan Mich, when in 1956 they correctly forecast the Southern resistance to integration and went out to meet it in their lead article, "The South vs. The Supreme Court." Fred Allen of *Harper's* twice led the whole field with his exposure of the infuriating corruption in labor relations: first in 1948 in the blazing article, "The Blast in Centralia, No. 5," and four years later with Mary Heaton Vorse's unsparing account of the longshoremen and how those pirates were holding up the Port of New York. Again when Dr. J. Robert Oppenheimer was being demoted as a security risk, I like to remember that within a month three magazines, mine among them, sprang to his defense. This is the courage, this is the vigilance which the country expects of magazine editors.

The danger for us all is that we think too exclusively in terms of leading articles, newsstand sales and advertising revenue and far too little about our allies. We have bet our lives on the currency of the printed word, yet it doesn't seem to trouble us that reading — the habit and delight of reading — could be steadily diminished under the pressure of new competition. We have a powerfully hypnotic rival in television and there is no question whatever that television has seriously cut into the time once given to reading. In every college community we have a heavy competition in the long-playing record; undergraduates today spend as much money collecting records as they do collecting books. In this rivalry for attention we badly need the help of English teachers and librarians. They, too, are dedicated to the printed word and they tap the enthusiasm of the young, yet we hardly give them the time of day. What can we do? What awards could we give to show our appreciation of librarians and teachers and of all they do to make books and magazines desirable?

Why have we neglected radio, and why has radio neglected us? Not since the death of Alec Woollcott have we heard a nationwide voice exciting people to read. "I have been going quietly mad," he would say, "over a new book called *Lost Horizon*" and the next day literally thousands went out to find that volume. Why not again? As for the booksellers and magazine distributors, not till the well-merited failure of the American News Company as a wholesaler did we ever worry our pretty heads about them. Evidently we are dangerously self-centered.

The summer of 1958 it occurred to me to thank the management of the American Telephone and Telegraph Company for their loyalty in advertising in the *Atlantic* uninterruptedly for fifty years. In his reply, Vice President Sanford B. Cousins wrote: "The *Atlantic* was one of the 52 magazines to carry our national advertising when it first appeared in 1908. Of them only 8 have survived the ravages of whatever diseases magazines suffer." Eight survivors out of fifty-two. The old *Life* must have been one of the casualties and the reason why the new *Life* is such a powerhouse is the decision, the turning point their editors took some years back, when they determined that pictures simply were not enough: they had to have prose too. Significant that they made their pitch in history — the history of art, of culture, a retelling with pictures of *The Outline of History* which appealed as nothing else could have done so surely to the American zeal for self-improvement. There is a clearly discernible trend here. The success of *American Heritage* is in direct response to the rising interest in history which has swept through the nation since the Second World War. Now that we have become the leader of the West, people want to catch up with the past; what can we learn from studying our earlier crises? No one but ourselves can pull us out of the next. So too in science. The transformation of *Scientific American* under the lead of Gerard Piel from a journal of technology to a magazine with a broad approach to physics, biology and scientific research paid off long before sputnik. And when those two bellwethers, the *Saturday Evening Post* and *Ladies' Home Journal,* discard fiction as their cover appeal and instead play up biography and adventures of the mind, you may be sure that a major change in American taste has occurred.

It is my guess that this swing to the serious will be accelerated and naturally I like this, for it means a greater opportunity for my magazine. So it does for others. The eager developing interest in the thoughtful, the scientific, the how-to-do-it material is traceable to what the census calls "professional and technical workers." In number they have been rapidly increasing; so has their purchasing power, so have their children in college. In the census age group of "65 and over" only 3 1/2 per cent have a college degree, whereas in the age group ready for college today, white and colored, 17 per cent or five times as many are taking degrees. In the next decade that number will increase astronomically.

All editors have had to do with the young graduate and his college wife; we know their desire to have four or five children

where we had two; their capability for doing things for themselves; the intentness they bring to their reading, their music,
their homes, their travel and their use of leisure. This is the
coming and dominant readership. Can you reach them and hold
their loyalty? Certainly: not by talking down but by editing up.

Index

Index

Index

[295]

Index

Index

Index

Index

[299]

Index

[300]

Index